T0331092

Hayek's Market Republicanism

Friedrich Hayek was the 20th century's most significant free market theorist and over the course of his long career he developed an analysis of the danger that state power can pose to individual liberty. In rejecting much of the liberal tradition's concern for social justice and democratic participation, Hayek would help clear away many intellectual obstacles to the emergence of neoliberalism in the last quarter of the 20th century.

At the core of this book is a new interpretation of Hayek, one that regards him as an exponent of a neo-Roman conception of liberty and interprets his work as a form of 'market republicanism'. It examines the contemporary context in which Hayek wrote, and places his writing in the long republican intellectual tradition.

Hayek's Market Republicanism will be of interest to advanced students and researchers across the history of economic thought, the history of political thought, political economy and political philosophy.

Sean Irving has a PhD in history from the University of Manchester, UK.

Routledge Frontiers of Political Economy

Political Economy for Human Rights
Manuel Couret Branco

Alternative Approaches to Economic Theory
Complexity, Post Keynesian and Ecological Economics
Edited by Victor A. Beker

The Dark Side of Nudges
Maria Alejandra Caporale Madi

Inequality and Governance
Andreas P. Kyriacou

A New Approach to the Economics of Public Goods
Thomas Laudal

Marx's Capital after 150 Years
Critique and Alternative to Capitalism
Edited by Marcello Musto

The Political Economy of Prosperity
Successful Societies and Productive Cultures
Peter Murphy

Macroeconomic Measurement Versus Macroeconomic Theory
Merijn Knibbe

Hayek's Market Republicanism
The Limits of Liberty
Sean Irving

For more information about this series, please visit: www.routledge.com/books/series/SE0345

Hayek's Market Republicanism

The Limits of Liberty

Sean Irving

Routledge
Taylor & Francis Group

LONDON AND NEW YORK

First published 2020
by Routledge
2 Park Square, Milton Park, Abingdon, Oxon OX14 4RN

and by Routledge
52 Vanderbilt Avenue, New York, NY 10017

Routledge is an imprint of the Taylor & Francis Group, an informa business

First issued in paperback 2021

British Library Cataloguing-in-Publication Data
A catalogue record for this book is available from the British Library

Library of Congress Cataloging-in-Publication Data
Names: Irving, Sean, author.
Title: Hayek's market republicanism : the limits of liberty / Sean Irving.
Description: Abingdon, Oxon ; New York, NY : Routledge, 2020. |
    Series: Routledge frontiers of political economy; 269 |
    Includes bibliographical references and index. |
Identifiers: LCCN 2019042124 (print) | LCCN 2019042125 (ebook) |
    ISBN 9781138390973 (hardback) | ISBN 9780429423024 (ebook)
Subjects: LCSH: Hayek, Friedrich A. von (Friedrich August), 1899–1992. |
    Liberty. | Liberalism. | Republicanism. | Economics—Political aspects.
Classification: LCC HB101.H39 I78 2020 (print) | LCC HB101.H39
    (ebook) | DDC 330.15/7—dc23
LC record available at https://lccn.loc.gov/2019042124
LC ebook record available at https://lccn.loc.gov/2019042125

ISBN: 978-1-138-39097-3 (hbk)
ISBN: 978-1-03-208342-1 (pbk)
ISBN: 978-0-429-42302-4 (ebk)

Typeset in Bembo
by Apex CoVantage, LLC

For Ruth, Rosie, Con, Amy, Anne and Seamus

Contents

Acknowledgements   ix

Introduction   1
Hayek's epistemic economics 2
Hayek and republicanism 4
The nature of the emergency 6
Intellectual emergency equipment and liberal authoritarianism 8
Methodology, context and parameters 11

1   Government and the business cycle   15
Hayek's early work 15
The gold standard and the central banks 19
The exchange with Keynes 23
Conclusion 26

2   The socialist calculation debates   31
From economics to political economy 32
Planning vs freedom 39
The limits of Hayek's epistemic economics 41
Conclusion 42

3   Liberalism true and false   46
The British/continental binary 47
Mill and rationalism 51
Questions of history 53
Conclusion 56

4   Hayek's market republicanism   61
Hayek and the republican tradition 61
Hayek and non-domination 68

The limits of Hayekian liberty 73
Conclusion 78

5   The danger of 'unlimited' democracy   83
Unlimited democracy and the total state 84
A self-limiting democracy 90
Arbitrary power and ungovernability 95
Conclusion 97

6   Inflation and social justice   102
Full employment and the new morality 103
The politics of deflation 107
Social justice and market republicanism 110
Conclusion 112

7   A market republican constitution   116
Origins of the model constitution 118
The model constitution 121
A constitution of oligarchy 124
Conclusion 128

8   Market republican money   131
The denationalisation of money 131
Reception and viability of the scheme 137
Cryptocurrencies 140
Conclusion 143

9   Liberal authoritarianism and market republicanism   146
Isonomia, demokratia *and* demarchy *146*
Endorsing dictatorship 148
Dictatorship and the oligarchic market republic 154
Conclusion 157

Conclusion   162

Index   165

Acknowledgements

I would like to thank Stuart Jones, Bertrand Taithe, John O' Neill, Andrew Gamble and Chris Godden for their advice and example. I am also very grateful for the support and patience of Lisa Lavelle and Natalie Tomlinson.

Introduction

Any book about freedom should also be one about power. Friedrich Hayek (1899–1992) was the 20th century's most significant free market theorist and over the course of his long career he developed an analysis of the danger that state power can pose to individual liberty.[1] In rejecting much of the liberal tradition's concern for social justice and democratic participation, Hayek would help clear away many of the intellectual obstacles to the emergence of neoliberalism in the last quarter of the 20th century. Before him, the political was accorded primacy over the economic. After him, the logic of the market came to permeate all aspects of social life, very frequently under the banner of promoting greater personal freedom. Power, however, cannot be abolished. At best, it can be countered, and it can be made accountable. In this book I hope to show how Hayek's focus on the hazards of state power led him to neglect the danger that private power also poses to freedom. In this way, I will illustrate the limits of his conception of liberty. Determining those limits does not, however, mean that what lies within them lacks value.

Hayek distanced himself from the term neoliberal, and I have no need to make further use of it here. Yet in the recent debates about the nature, indeed the veracity, of the term we can discern one of the core problematics that has characterised liberalism over its history: the multivalent and contested nature of liberal language and hence the capaciousness of the liberal tradition. Since its popularisation in the early 19th century, the word 'liberal' has been used in a range of ways. Not only has its meaning varied over time and place, being used to describe competing visions of political economy, it has also denoted a more nebulous set of attitudes regarding how to behave as a proper person in society, encompassing generousness, self-reliance and tolerance. Liberals, however, have not always been particularly tolerant of one another. Indeed, the very capaciousness of the tradition has proved a repeated source of intellectual conflict.

Hayek sought to restate what he regarded as the 'old truths' of liberalism. This involved nothing less than an attempt to reorganise the history of European political thought, placing free market individualism at its heart. To this end, he regarded his primary task as winning the battle for the soul of liberalism. He held that the tradition had been led astray by 'doctrinaire democrats' and those who supposed that the power of the state should be used to construct social institutions and enforce a certain pattern of distribution in the name of freedom. His liberalism, which regarded freedom as inhering in the market, was, he insisted, the 'true' liberalism.

Convinced that his own political tradition had been distorted by others who also claimed to be 'liberals', Hayek was acutely aware of the perils associated with the confusion of political language. As we proceed through this book, we must be too. Although he regarded himself as a 'classical liberal', Hayek rejected the intellectual legacy of the 19th century which we commonly associate with the term. Although the 19th century may have witnessed the high point of market freedom, the ideas that brought this about were older. In order to acquire intellectual sustenance and direction, those who wished to reverse the rise of social democracy should, he argued, turn to the concept of liberty set down in the Roman Law; to the writings of Marcus Tullius Cicero; to the example of English Civil War republicans and American revolutionaries; and to the classically informed work of 17th and 18th century Whigs. Indeed, it had been the intellectual alliances made between liberalism and other traditions during the 19th century that had resulted in its distortion by Hayek's own time.

The tradition on which Hayek drew in order to make the case for the free market was not in fact classical liberalism, but that which, in the language of today's political theory and intellectual history, is referred to as republicanism. I will demonstrate that Hayek's own work in these fields should be understood as an attempt to articulate a form of 'market republican' political economy and I will explore how he attempted to reconstruct this aspect of republican thought for his own liberal ends. It is important to note that not all those who have employed republican forms of thought have necessarily been engaged in anti-monarchical struggles. The primary concern has always been individual liberty (Skinner, 2008). It has often been the case that the struggle to defend freedom has been waged against monarchies, but it has also been true that at other times republicans have regarded a restrained monarchy as being entirely consonant with liberty. Hayek was certainly not calling for the abolition of the monarchy in Britain or anywhere else, although his opposition to state power did echo the ideas of earlier republicans who opposed the centralisation of power by the King. Recognising Hayek as perhaps the 20th century's first 'neo-republican' has profound consequences not only for our understanding of his own intellectual project, but also for our understanding of the republican tradition, its relationship with liberalism and its potential role in the creation of a radical, emancipatory form of political economy.

Hayek's epistemic economics

'If there were omniscient men', wrote Hayek (1960a, p. 29), 'there would be little case for liberty'. His concern for freedom emerged directly out of his work in economics during the 1920s and '30s. During this period, he came to the conclusion that freedom mattered because it facilitated economic coordination. In 1936, Hayek gave a lecture entitled 'Economics and Knowledge' in which he argued that the economy should be understood in terms of the division of knowledge and considered in terms of how to make that division work most effectively (Hayek, 1948b). This was a problem equally, if not more, important than the division of labour. He regarded the lecture's insistence that market actors are best placed to make use of their own personal knowledge as the one 'discovery' of his career (Hayek, 1983). Economic planning is bound to be economically irrational, he argued, because knowledge is both tacit and dispersed. Consequently, any attempt to communicate it to a central agency will inevitably be incomplete. Furthermore, a planned economy lacks the capacity to discover the scarcity and the value of certain goods, whereas under conditions of free competition, the price mechanism achieves this. It is through the free functioning of the market, he argued, that prices reveal value and thus act as a guide to future action.

What Hayek presented was an epistemic view of the economy. It functioned well to the extent that 'the man on the spot' was enabled to use his knowledge as he saw fit (1948b, p. 85). Hayek's training in the Austrian school of economics was always likely to lead him to view the state as the source of economic irrationality, the force that would frustrate the individual in employing personal knowledge as they wished, compelling them instead to do so on behalf of some politically defined goal. Yet it was his engagement in two debates during the 1920s and '30s that gave form to his critique of public power: that concerning the role of government and central banks in the business cycle; and the exchange known as the socialist calculation debates, to which 'Economics and Knowledge' was a direct contribution, and within which the theoretical viability of planning was contested. In order to arrive at this book's core concern, Hayek's concept of liberty, it will first be necessary to provide an overview of these two episodes in order to establish the basis for his aversion to state power. Chapters 1 and 2 address the two debates respectively.

According to Hayek's epistemic economics, the model of static equilibrium upon which neoclassical economics is based is nothing but an abstraction, useful to economists but also dangerously seductive to governments that may seek to plan the economy (Caldwell, 1988). Instead, Hayek viewed the economy as tending towards equilibrium over time. This realisation led him almost immediately to a consideration of the social conditions necessary for this to occur. The market coordination necessary for the equilibrating tendency to prevail requires that market actors are led by price signals and able to form their own plans and use their own knowledge as they wish. Consequently, by the end of the 1930s, what he termed 'freedom in economic life' had become Hayek's central concern and a prerequisite for this was the rule of law. It is here that we can identify Hayek's transition from formal economics to political economy.

For Hayek, freedom is instantiated when one steps as into the market as an actor; when, guided by a price, one decides to purchase a good either for consumption or investment, or indeed to put it to some productive use in pursuit of future profit. Equally, the point of sale is also a moment when freedom becomes possible. We can be said to be free to the extent that we are not compelled to buy or to sell and the rationality of the transaction – the degree to which it is epistemically efficient – depends on the extent to which prices have not been distorted by non-market pressures. Freedom of choice in such matters, with all the risks of error and ruin as well as reward, is the essence of liberty. It is from this, for Hayek, that all other cultural and intellectual freedoms flow.

Hayek (2001, p. 89) was writing to resist those who sought to 'direct economic life'. There is, however, something not quite right about his insistence that he was concerned with freedom in 'economic life'. His focus was firmly on the market and not on the wider economy. He rejected the socialist version of 'economic freedom' which he portrayed as being concerned with equality of outcome, thus opening the door to authoritarian direction of the economy. Yet, Hayek's intent focus on market processes, rather than on what occurs in the productive sectors of the economy, means that he failed to develop a theory of liberty equal to the profound implications of his epistemic economics.

Hayek insisted on the importance of rules and not commands because rules provide a space within which each can make use of their personal knowledge as they wish, whereas commands involve individuals being told what to do with that knowledge. Rules promote freedom, whereas commands run counter to it. Yet he insisted on rules only in the context of the market. He did not insist on them in the realm of production. He was quite willing to allow a regime based on commands in the productive sector, particularly in the workplace. Command-based planning is acceptable at the level of the private firm because, like a nation in wartime, there is an assumption of a common goal. This may be so, although there will of course be competing interests in any firm. Nonetheless, according to his own epistemic economics, it must still involve knowledge losses. After all, it is the woman or man 'on the spot' who knows best how to use their knowledge. It therefore follows that if we wish to limit these losses, decision-making must be decentralised as much as possible, and this decision-making process must take place under a regime of rules and redress, akin to the rule of law. Furthermore, those rules should not be decided in isolation from those who work under them.

If individual liberty is epistemically important, as Hayek insisted that it is, this should hold true even when we are engaged in non-market economic activities. This, however, was not Hayek's position. His view that liberty is realised or frustrated in the market, rather than in the rest of economic life, led Hayek to frame his writing on liberty with reference, almost exclusively, to threats to market freedom, rather than more broadly conceived economic freedom. His participation in the two key debates of the 1920s and '30s told him that this threat was posed by the state. He does not therefore consider threats to freedom that sit throughout the rest of the economy, which are invariably constituted by private forms of power.

Hayek and republicanism

The problem with liberalism, Hayek believed, was that since the 19th century it had turned increasingly towards state power to try and make people freer. Yet in order to define how liberalism ought to be perceived it was first necessary to detail the manner of its decline. In the years during and after the Second World War, this became Hayek's major research objective and it involved a sustained period of study in the history of political thought. It consisted, above all, in an attempt to disentangle the tradition from what he regarded as its 19th century encumbrances, misconceptions it had accrued in its long world-historical struggle against arbitrary royal and aristocratic rule. Many were the product of tactical alliances with distinct traditions such as nationalism and socialism. Still others, the product of continental importations into true 'liberalism in the English sense' (Hayek, 1948a, p. 28). Particularly injurious had been the fetishisation of democracy, a thing that went hand in hand with the belief that government had the capacity and the right to redesign social institutions in the name of popularly endorsed ends. Hayek's work to distinguish between 'true' and 'false' liberalism is the focus of Chapter 3.

If one wishes to demonstrate deviation, it is by definition necessary to show what went before and, in Hayek's case at least, why it was better. For true liberalism, therefore, Hayek was forced to look back beyond what is commonly considered the liberal era of the late 18th and 19th centuries, first to the republicanism of the early modern period and then, as he became acquainted with the influences upon those who engaged in the great struggles against state authority in this period, to classical sources. At this stage, we must return to a consideration of the confusion of political language. Hayek never claimed to be a republican. Instead, he drew on certain elements of the republican tradition in an attempt to demonstrate the antique provenance of his own version of liberalism. It was through an engagement with that tradition that he arrived at the concept of liberty that is also distinct from that most commonly associated with the liberal tradition. In short, Hayek adopted the concept of liberty as non-domination, which has its origins in the law of republican Rome, rather than that of non interference, which originated with the work of Thomas Hobbes and was subsequently developed by liberals in the 19th century. The first insists that freedom requires the absence of arbitrary power, whereas the second is willing to accept that the absence of physical interference alone renders one free. Hayek found the republican concept of non-domination particularly useful, as his epistemic economics insisted that the existence of arbitrary power alone, carrying with it the threat of future interference, was enough to compromise the effective use of individual knowledge. Demonstrating that Hayek draws on republican resources and establishing his use of the concept of non-domination is this book's core critical contribution, and it is the focus of Chapter 4.

Originally, the republican concept had recognised two potential sources of un-freedom: the first is *imperium* – the dominating power of the state; and the second is *dominium* – the dominating power of private individuals (Pettit, 1997, p. 13). I have already argued how, for Hayek, freedom inheres in the market and that it was state power that threatened it. He was unconcerned with threats posed to the use of knowledge in the wider economy. In a liberal economy, those threats are inevitably private in nature because those who own property and run firms are private individuals and not the state, at least in the main. In his adoption of non-domination Hayek, therefore, jettisoned *dominium*, as he did not regard it as posing a threat to the effective use of knowledge.

Hayek found significant historical support for this partial rendering of non-domination, particularly among the early modern anglophone writers on whom he heavily drew. Like him, their concern was not private power – the Whigs and others were generally wealthy and powerful men who certainly did not wish to have their *dominium* over their servants and tenants questioned. They were, however, greatly alarmed by the growth of royal power. Whereas writers such as Thomas Harrington and Thomas Jefferson in the main represented the landed interest, over the course of the 18th century a new element entered into republican thought: commercial republicanism (Kalyvas and Katznelson, 2008). It regarded commerce, and indeed production and the increased division of labour, as providing a new means of decentring power, reducing the influence of the crown and countering the arbitrary rule of the state. It is this strand of historic republican thought – which counts among its number David Hume, Adam Smith, Thomas Gordon and John Trenchard – with which Hayek has most in common. Yet unlike the commercial republicans, he did not just view the market as a buttress to individual liberty understood in some broader sense. For Hayek, the market was the arena of liberty, it was where one became free. Hence my description of Hayek as a 'market republican'. This market republicanism is best understood as a form of thought that applies the criterion of non-domination to market relations alone. It is not applied to relations within other spheres of economic or social life. Furthermore, it views state power, *imperium*, as the dominating influence that is always and everywhere to be countered.

I argue that if we are to move towards a form of political economy that takes Hayek's epistemic economics seriously, we must look beyond the field of the market and apply his insistence on the rule of law to the economy as a whole. There can be no space afforded to islands of tyranny. In the market we are largely protected from the arbitrary power of the state. When we enter the workplace, we are not protected from the arbitrary power of the employer. I will suggest that this has immediate consequences, in Hayek's own terms, for the efficient use of knowledge in society. The proper instrumentalisation of Hayek's 'great discovery', for the purposes of modern political economy, therefore, requires the full development of his concept of liberty. In republican terms, we must move beyond the limits he imposed upon it, incorporating both *dominium* and *imperium* into our thinking in order to realise an epistemically efficient economy.

The nature of the emergency

Having examined the theoretical basis of Hayek's writing on liberty and his interpretation of the liberal tradition, it will then be necessary to turn to an analysis of why Hayek regarded the political economy of his own time as being inimical to liberty as he had come to define it and hence unsuited to his epistemic conception of the economy. In the modern western context, since at least the end of the First World War, government has been subject to democratic principles. 'Unlimited government', which Hayek identified as having posed the primary threat to market freedom as far back as ancient Rome, has thus, since that time, taken the form of what he termed 'unlimited democracy'. It had been one of liberalism's chief errors, he believed, to become too closely aligned with the ideal of popular sovereignty. They were in fact distinct ideas. While the opposite of democracy is authoritarianism, Hayek argued, liberalism's reverse is totalitarianism. Furthermore, democracy in its unlimited form tended to bring about totalitarian regimes, by which Hayek meant those that sought to socialise the economy. His primary political objective, therefore, was to limit it.

Chapter 5 examines how Hayek's position regarding unlimited democracy developed and how it was largely the product of his analysis of the decline of the German Weimar Republic which came to an end when Adolf Hitler was appointed Chancellor in January 1933. This followed two elections, in July and November 1932, in which his Nazi's had been returned to parliament as the largest party. A particular influence on Hayek's analysis was the work of Carl Schmitt, who himself joined the Nazi Party in May 1933 (Scheuerman, 1999; Cristi, 1998). Yet although Hayek took from Schmitt the manner in which unlimited democracy could lead to totalitarianism, their politics, and most of all their view of what constituted effective political economy, differed radically. Hayek's epistemic economics rendered Schmitt's 'decisionist' model of dictatorship, according to which the regime would oversee the economy, and the dictator would stand as final arbiter in economic matters, entirely intolerable.[2]

I argue that Hayek turned to a second group of German-speaking theorists to find an alternative to the decisionist end point of Schmitt's evolutionary analysis of the decline of unlimited democracy For Hayek, the model of a clear legal framework, as developed by ordoliberal theorists such as Walter Eucken, offered the best context in which market freedom could be realised. Individuals would be able to plan their actions in the market, making use of their own personal knowledge, in a stable legal environment assured that the state would not step in and frustrate their efforts. That Hayek, as an Austrian, should seek to situate his own economics in relation to some of the most influential analyses of the state in the German-speaking world is hardly surprising. What was less predictable, and also struck his peers as peculiar, was that he should seek to apply this theoretical frame directly to Britain. The concept of the legal framework was particularly unsuitable. The ordoliberals had developed it in the context of dictatorship and under dictatorial conditions it is conceivable that it could be imposed, maintained and updated when necessary. In the context of British parliamentary democracy, in the absence of a written constitution and where the fundamental constitutional principle is parliamentary sovereignty, even if such a self-limiting framework could be agreed upon, it could always be almost instantly undone. Hayek would come to recognise parliamentary sovereignty as the acme of unlimited democracy, and this would result in his ultimate rejection of the viability of self-imposed restrictions in the form of a legal framework under democratic conditions such as those in Britain. The chapter closes by examining Hayek's theory of unlimited democracy in light of the market republicanism that came to characterise his thought from the 1950s onwards.

It was inflation that enabled the practice of unlimited democracy, and it was what Hayek referred to as the 'mirage of social justice' that lent it moral legitimacy. Chapter 6 examines these two issues together. For Hayek, it was the power wielded by the trade unions within a system of unlimited democracy that held government to its commitment to full employment even when greater flexibility in the labour market was desirable. In the long run, he argued, this was bound to have inflationary consequences. Ultimately, however, governments were to blame for the inflationary trend. Hayek's political position was, for the majority of his career, similar in form to that which he offered in response to unlimited government. He urged self-imposed restraint. Central banks, invariably under the close influence or direct control of elected governments, should seek to calm rather than excite unwarranted expansions of credit. During the 1970s, inflation became the prism through which all other political issues were viewed. The politics of deflation is therefore also addressed within the chapter as is the manner in which Hayek's critique of social justice was informed by his market republican ideas.

Intellectual emergency equipment and liberal authoritarianism

Over the 1960s and '70s Hayek became radicalised. Having witnessed the steady advance of trade union influence, the growing hold of social justice over the popular mind, and a steep rise in inflation during the early '70s, he gradually lost faith in the capacity of governments to act with restraint with regard to either legislation or money. The system of unlimited democracy made it virtually impossible, he believed, and the existing institutions and practices of western political economy could no longer be relied upon to preserve the liberal economic order. It was in this context, that Hayek (1982d, p. 152) proposed two pieces of 'intellectual emergency equipment': his Model Constitution and a scheme for the denationalisation of money. He regarded these as the 'two inventions' of his career and they were intended to safeguard his 'one discovery', his epistemic economics (Caldwell, 2004, p. 206). They were intended as a response to what he perceived as nothing less than the civilisational emergency posed by unlimited democracy and the inflationary pursuit of social justice. Chapters 7 and 8 consider these innovations in turn.

Although each piece of the equipment has received some, albeit relatively little, attention in the Hayek scholarship, there has not been a consideration of the role they play within Hayek's long-term intellectual project when taken together as intended. If anything, they have been viewed as something of a curiosity. Although proposed during the closing years of Hayek's career, it is certainly not the case that they are merely the distracted detour of an elderly man – rather, each had been in development to some degree since the 1960s and the Model Constitution serves as the *dénouement* of his magnum opus, *Law, Legislation and Liberty*. I propose instead that they constitute the culmination of Hayek's political economy. Their design was informed by his interpretation of liberty as non-domination and in them, Hayek provides us with the fundamentals, the two pillars, of a new market republic in which democracy will be curtailed and control of money will be handed to the heads of large financial institutions, effectively insulated from popular will. The market republic will then take an oligarchic form.

In Chapter 7 I will examine the origins of Hayek's Model Constitution and how it is rooted in his distinction between true and false liberalism and framed with reference to his history of political thought. Initially, it was ostensibly designed for implementation in the 'new nations' during the period in which former colonies were winning their independence. However, the model is in fact a response to a pathology he identified at the heart of the British constitution, namely the unlimited reach of parliamentary sovereignty and what he regarded as the confusion between law-making and legislation. Here again, the influence of Schmitt can be discerned. It is then unsurprising that in the context of increasing inflation and rising trade union militancy, Hayek became willing to advocate the model's imposition not only on the former colonies, but also on Britain itself. The rest of the chapter proceeds to examine the details of the constitution and the manner in which it was intended to dethrone politics and enthrone a legalistic order overseen by a judicial and senatorial elite. The market republican nature of the constitution is addressed throughout.

Chapter 8 will demonstrate the market republican nature of Hayek's scheme for the denationalisation of money. For Hayek, national monies were akin to the nationalised industries that played such a large role in western economies in the decades after the Second World War. What he proposed instead was capitalist money for a capitalist system (Hayek, 1999j, p. 237). By removing government control of the money supply and allowing banks to issue their own currency, Hayek's money scheme would have transferred enormous economic power away from politicians and placed it in the hands of a financial elite. Again, this was a form of republicanism that did not embrace, but sought to frustrate, the political and economic claims of the *demos*.

I will show how Hayek's plan was informed by his engagement with the republican, rather than the liberal, political tradition and was fundamentally concerned with termination of *imperium* over the monetary framework. In doing so, I will examine the details of the scheme and consider its viability along with its reception by Hayek's contemporaries. I will also consider the broader social, political and economic impact that a successful denationalisation of money would have. During his lifetime at least, ultimate control over the money supply was a power no government, even those led by figures who respected Hayek's work, such as Margaret Thatcher, was willing to give up.[3] Instead, Milton Friedman's recommendation of a strictly rule-based expansion of the money supply was preferred, before it too became politically inconvenient. Although Hayek disagreed with Friedman's theory, the readiness of governments to dispense with Friedman's monetarism could be said to confirm his suspicion that even governments intending to act with what he regarded as restraint were unable to do so because of the political pressures of unlimited democracy. As Hayek's scheme retreated further into obscurity with the decreasing rate of inflation, so it seemed that the issue of non-national monies had been pushed to the libertarian margins of debate. The chapter closes, however, with some brief reflections on the actual emergence of such monies in the form of online cryptocurrencies. Again, the broader social implications of this new development are considered from the perspective of republican political theory.

The process by which Hayek envisaged the implementation of his intellectual emergency equipment is absent from his major published works. It emerges, however, in his letters and interviews. Hayek's long-standing distinction between liberalism and democracy led him to an endorsement of liberal authoritarianism as the vehicle for bringing about the radical political and economic change he desired. In a number of instances, Hayek regarded a period of dictatorship as necessary in order to arrest the slide into social democratic totalitarianism, brought about as a result of the electoral victories by left-wing parties. He again referred to the classical world and the republican canon when making the distinction between *isonomia*, the rule of law, and *demokratia*, democracy, which provided the intellectual basis for his endorsement of dictatorship (1953a, pp. 518–519). The invocation of republicanism is apposite. Dictatorship has its origins as an office of republican Rome, and Hayek (1960a, pp. 39, 428, 464, 530) could also point to Cromwell, the most notable early modern republican dictator, as an exemplar of resistance to state power.

Hayek's enthusiasm for authoritarianism has been considered in terms of the influence Schmitt, notoriously one of the foremost theorists of dictatorship, had on his work. I, however, will argue that it was once again the ordoliberal influence that was decisive in this respect. Hayek could never allow the type of economic intervention and oversight Schmitt envisaged a dictator having. Ordoliberalism had instead insisted on a form of dictatorship that would respect the legal framework with regard to the economy and refrain from interfering in the market. Indeed, it was the very essence of the authoritarianism that Hayek endorsed that it remained respectful of the liberal economic order and did not slide into Schmittian totalitarianism. What is more, Hayek did not endorse dictatorship as a long-term solution. In keeping with Roman traditions, he insisted it should be time limited. Classically, however, the dictator was charged with rescuing the existing order from internal or external threat, what Schmitt termed 'commissarial' dictatorship. Hayek, however, hoped the liberal authoritarian would usher in an entirely new constitutional order, Schmitt's 'sovereign' dictatorship. It should not surprise us that the constitutional order that he had in mind was the one he himself had sketched, that of the oligarchic market republic.

Methodology, context and parameters

My chief methodological influence is Michael Freeden's (1998) work on ideology. For him liberalism should be understood as one type of ideology. Although I adopt much of his methodological thinking, I prefer the term tradition. Freeden has shown how ideologies, or traditions, can be interpreted as being composed of concepts; a central core concept with other auxiliary concepts arranged around the core. The overall composition of the concepts will affect what a particular interpretation of the ideology looks like. For example, liberalism will have liberty at its core, but various types of liberalism will emerge depending on the auxiliary concepts: a composition that stresses self-development, community and equality will look very different from one that stresses free market action, individualism and competition. It should also be understood, argues Freeden (1998, pp. 77–87), that ideologies are contested. He regards works of history or political theory that claim to define an ideology as being efforts of 'decontestation', attempts to establish the terms on which an ideology will be widely understood. We can regard Hayek's campaign to establish a true and a false liberalism as just such an attempt at decontestation.

In establishing the republican nature of Hayek's thought, the approach I have taken can also be described as genealogical. It seeks to trace the line of descent of the concept of liberty Hayek employs and how that descent shaped its partial nature. Friedrich Nietzsche (2011), with whom genealogy as a method is most strongly associated, used the approach to undermine the claim of naturalness of a belief and in so doing undermine acceptance of the belief itself. In this spirit, I aim to show how the most prominent and influential reflection on liberty within free market circles relied not on classical liberalism for its basic theoretical support, but on the earlier republican tradition. This should disturb the 'naturalness' of the connection between a belief in market freedom and liberalism and also challenge the prevailing assumption that the employment of a conception of liberty as non-domination naturally leads to a generally progressive form of political economy. In keeping with Freeden's insights, I suggest that if republicanism wishes to inform a new and emancipatory form of political economy, it must do more to stress its radical auxiliary concepts – such as popular sovereignty and equality of power – in order to extend our application of non-domination beyond the lofty heights of the law and the constitution, and into the workplace.

The historical contextualisation of Hayek's work performs an important function in this book, as it throws into relief the nature and progress of his intellectual development. It is always the British context I have chosen to stress. This is because when Hayek sought an empirical grounding for his ideas it was almost always to Britain, of both the 19th and 20th centuries, that he turned. Furthermore, when he was spurred to take up his pen by contemporary political and economic developments, they were also invariably developments that were taking place in Britain.

Hayek moved to Britain in 1931 and from that time forward, despite moving on to Chicago in 1950 and then to Freiberg in 1962, Britain remained the focus of his writing. It is not possible to say with certainty why this was the case. He had been a British citizen since 1938 and spent what were probably the most exciting years of his professional life in London. It may be that his personal experience of England made such a deep impression that it seemed natural for him to frame his thought in relation to British issues. As he reflected:

> Culturally, I feel my nationality now is British and not Austrian. It may be due to the fact that I have spent the decisive, most active parts of my life between the early 1930s and the early 1950s in Britain. But it was really from the first moment arriving there that I found myself for the first time in a moral atmosphere which was completely congenial to me and which I could absorb overnight.
>
> (Hayek, 1994, p. 87)

During his later years Hayek would make regular trips from his home in Freiberg to England to visit his children and grandchildren where they would often holiday in Devon (Ebenstein, 2001, p. 298). He would even remark that for many years the Reform Club in London was the only real home he knew. It was also in Britain that he was, eventually, received with the greatest respect and admiration by those in circles of power, being made a Companion of Honour by the Queen in 1984, after which time he preferred the anglicised 'Frederick' (Griffiths, 2014, pp. 5–6). Perhaps most intellectually pertinent, however, is that 19th century Britain functioned in his thought as the high point of liberal political economy, even as the tenets of liberalism were themselves being undermined. Whatever the case, despite leaving the country physically, it remained his intellectual home.

The period covered by the thesis comes to a close in the early 1980s despite Hayek living until 1992 and the last work ascribed to him, *The Fatal Conceit*, being published in 1988. There are two reasons for this. First, there has been some dispute about the extent to which it can properly be claimed that Hayek was the sole author of that final work. His biographer Alan Ebenstein (2005) has claimed that 'Hayek's last words were written by someone else'. Less forthrightly but with marked circumscription, Bruce Caldwell (2004, p. 316), an editor of Hayek's collected works, has written that 'because it was his last book, some might be tempted to view it as containing the final distillation of Hayek's mature thought. The temptation should be avoided'. This is owing to the fact that William Warren Bartley III, who helped to edit it during Hayek's final years, seems to have at least co-authored the work. It is unlikely, for example, that Hayek would have begun engaging with the work of scholars such as Foucault and Marcuse at such an advanced age having not done so previously. Second, I regard Hayek's two inventions as providing the best, most complete description of the institutions that would ideally emerge from his economic and political theory. Hence, after a final consideration of how this Hayekian political economy might be brought into being, an examination of them provides a convenient point at which to close. It is also worth saying briefly that in this book I do not attempt to examine Hayek's social theory or explore his role within the broader free market movement of the 20th century.

My primary aim in this book can be described as an attempt to prise open what Andrew Gamble (1996, p. x) has referred to as Hayek's 'ideological closures'. When we recognise the centrality of the concept of non-domination to his work, we are also then able to perceive that he does not develop the concept to its fullest. This is, as we have seen, a product of his epistemic economics which was focussed exclusively on market freedom rather than more global economic freedom. I am making the case that we must extend the limits of Hayek's concept of liberty so that it applies both *dominium* and *imperium* to a more comprehensive account of economic life. My purpose is to push forward what is genuinely valuable in Hayek's work, so that it can illuminate the construction of new, radical and emancipatory forms of political economy appropriate for the promotion of liberty in the 21st century.

Notes

1 I use the terms freedom and liberty interchangeably in keeping with common practice.
2 Decisionism is 'a term of art coined by Carl Schmitt in his Political Theology', it 'refers to the rule of a personal will as opposed to the rule of impersonal norms' (Cristi, 2014).
3 The willingness of European nations to join the European Monetary Union does stand as an example of when governments have decided to transfer this power to another authority.

Works cited

Caldwell, B. 1988. 'Hayek's Transformation', *History of Political Economy* 20:4, pp. 513–548.
Caldwell, B. 2004. *Hayek's Challenge: An Intellectual Biography of F.A. Hayek*. Chicago: University of Chicago Press.
Cristi, R. 1998. *Carl Schmitt and Authoritarian Liberalism: Strong State, Free Economy*. Cardiff: University of Wales.
Cristi, R. 2014. 'Decisionism' in M.T. Gibbons (Ed.), *The Encyclopedia of Political Thought*. Accessed at http://onlinelibrary.wiley.com/doi/10.1002/9781118474396.wbept0244/references
Ebenstein, A. 2005. 'The Fatal Deceit', *Liberty* 19:3. Accessed at http://web.archive.org/web/20080622201757/http://libertyunbound.com/archive/2005_03/ebenstein-deceit.html#3
Freeden, M. 1998. *Ideologies and Political Theory: A Conceptual Approach*. Oxford: Clarendon Press.
Griffiths, S. 2014. *Engaging Enemies: Hayek and the Left*. London: Rowman and Littlefield.
Hayek, F.A. 1948a. 'Individualism: True and False' [1945] in Friedrich Hayek (Ed.), *Individualism and Economic Order* (pp. 1–33). Chicago: University of Chicago Press.
Hayek, F.A. 1948b. 'Economics and Knowledge' [1936] in Friedrich Hayek (Ed.), *Individualism and Economic Order* (pp. 33–56). Chicago: University of Chicago Press.
Hayek, F.A. 1953a. The Decline of the Rule of Law', *The Freeman*, 20 April, pp. 518–520.
Hayek, F.A. 1960a. *The Constitution of Liberty*. Chicago: University of Chicago Press.

Hayek, F.A. 1982d. 'The Political Order of a Free People' [1979] in *Law, Legislation and Liberty: A New Statement of the Liberal Principles of Justice and Political Economy* [3 Volume edition]. London: Routledge Kegan Paul.

Hayek, F.A. 1983. 'Nobel Prize Winning Economist', Armen Alchian UCLA Charles E. Young Research Library (Ed.). Department of Special Collections, Oral History Transcript no. 300/324.

Hayek, F.A. 1994. *Hayek on Hayek: An Autobiographical Dialogue*. Stephen Kresge and Leif Warner (Eds.). Chicago: University of Chicago Press.

Hayek, F.A. 1999j. 'The Future Unit of Value' [1981] in Stephen Kresge (Ed.), *Good Money Part Two: The Collected Works of F.A. Hayek, Vol. 6* (pp. 238–252). Chicago: University of Chicago Press.

Hayek, F.A. 2001. *The Road to Serfdom*. London: Routledge.

Kalyvas, A. and Katznelson, I. 2008. *Liberal Beginnings: Making a Republic for the Moderns*. Cambridge: Cambridge University Press.

Nietzsche, F. 2011. *On the Genealogy of Morality*. Cambridge: Cambridge University Press

Pettit, P. 1997. *Republicanism: A Theory of freedom and Government*. Oxford: Oxford University Press. Accessed at http://onlinelibrary.wiley.com/doi/10.1002/9781118474396.wbept0244/references

Scheuerman, W. 1999. *Carl Schmitt: The End of Law (20th Century Political Thinkers)*. Lanham, MA: Rowman and Littlefield.

Skinner, Q. 2008. 'Freedom as the Absence of Arbitrary Power' in Cécile Laborde and John Maynor (Eds.), *Republicanism and Political Theory* (pp. 83–101). Hoboken, NJ: Blackwell-Wiley.

1 Government and the business cycle

Hayek's understanding of freedom emerged from his economic theory. For the first 20 years of his career he worked as an economist, concerned with technical issues relating to the role of money in the business cycle. Hayek (2014) conceived of the economy in abstract terms and considered it to be self-correcting and tending towards equilibrium over time: that in the absence of exogenous shocks, supply and demand would gravitate towards a balanced state, even if they never reached the idealised perfect state of equilibrium central to neoclassical economics (Hayek, 1948b; Caldwell, 1988).

Over the 1920s and '30s, Hayek argued that it was not possible to model economic activity based on data and aggregates of the sort that had begun to be compiled by governmental organisations and bodies associated with the League of Nations (Slobodian, 2018, pp. 55–90). Hayek did not regard this information as a reflection of the real economy at any given point and so rejected the conclusion of the 1923 Annual Report of the US Federal Reserve which stated that 'control of the quantity of money could be used to assure the stabilisation of economic activity' (Kresge, 1999). If the data could not be relied upon to present an accurate depiction of the economy, then any attempt to pursue policies of stabilisation were bound to be misguided from the start. It was, therefore, ill-advised to attempt to use monetary policy to stimulate the economy during an economic downturn, as to do so would only lead to further distortions. It is not the case, however, that Hayek regarded the economy as stable or as always yielding beneficial outcomes. The business cycle was an unfortunate but inevitable aspect of a money economy. Crucially, over this period, Hayek became convinced that it was governments that posed the greatest threat to the effective functioning of this cycle as a result of their growing desire to intervene in it.

Hayek's early work

Having lived through the inflationary crises of the period after the First World War, Hayek was well aware of the impact that fluctuations in the value of money can have on society. Austria's inflationary wartime policies, combined with a move from a gold to a dollar standard, had rendered the war bonds, bought primarily by families of an upper middle class standing similar to the von Hayeks, worthless.[1] On his return from the Italian front in 1918, Hayek enrolled at the University of Vienna. Although his degree was in jurisprudence, with some courses on Roman law under Moriz Wlassak leaving a lasting impression, 'the decisive point was simply that you were not expected to confine yourself to your own subject' (Hayek, 1994, p. 43). This willingness, and ability, to write on a range of subjects would remain with him throughout his career. Nonetheless, Hayek's primary interests lay in psychology and economics. Indeed, he had only turned to the law in order to proceed to one of these subjects, but the war had left no psychology professors teaching at the university. Recognising also that 'economics at least had a formal legitimation by a degree, while in psychology you had nothing', when he completed his jurisprudence degree in 1921, he began a second in the study of economics under the broadly Fabian professor, Friedrich von Wieser, which he completed in 1923. Despite Wieser's deep personal impression on Hayek as a teacher, he was later to recall,

> I now realize – I wouldn't have known it at the time – that the decisive influence was just reading Menger's *Grundsätze*. I probably derived more from not only the *Grundsätze* but also the *Methodenbuch*, not for what it says on methodology but for what it says on general sociology.
>
> (Hayek, 1994, p. 49)

Although Carl Menger, the founder of Austrian School of economics, was bound to have been an influence, it was at some remove. Instead, it was Ludwig von Mises who played the major role in Hayek's early personal and professional development. In later discussions, Hayek remembered how his first economic ideas, along with those of many others of his generation, were of a socialist or semi-socialist nature and how he even found himself in trouble at the *Gymnasium* for reading a socialist pamphlet during his divinity lesson (Hayek, 1994, p. 40). After the war socialism seemed to be in the ascendant. In Hungary, separated from Austria following the revolution brought on by the pressures of war, Béla Kun established a short-lived Soviet Republic (Borsányi, 1993). Hayek's home city would become known as 'Red Vienna' over the course of the 1920s because of the dominance of socialists in local government (Beniston, 2006). In the university itself, he recalled, most of the students were, at least initially, strongly inclined towards socialism. Hayek recognised that it was Mises's (1981) work, *Socialism: An Economic and Sociological Analysis* that 'gradually but fundamentally altered the outlook of many of the young idealists returning to their University studies after World War One. I know' he remembered, 'for I was one of them.' (Hayek, 1992, pp. 126–159).

After graduating, it was Mises who helped Hayek secure his first job in the temporary government agency the Austrian Office of Accounts. One of the great advantages of the job was that his salary was indexed to inflation. (Hayek, 1994, p. 60). This enabled him, despite the crisis, to save enough money by the beginning of 1923 to travel to the US in order to work as a research assistant to Jeremiah Jenks, whom he had met in Vienna in 1922, at New York University.

When he arrived, he found 'that Professor Jenks had left for a vacation and given instructions that he was not to be disturbed'. Hayek was forced to look for work. 'I was finally accepted as a dishwasher in a Sixth Avenue restaurant – but I never actually started on it' he recalled, 'since an hour before I was to report to work a telephone call came through saying that Professor Jenks had returned and was prepared to employ me'. (Hayek, 1994, p. 56)

One of Hayek's reasons for wanting to spend time in America was the advanced state of its mathematical economic models, based upon the belief, expounded by Wesley Clair Mitchell, and before him Thorstein Veblen (1899, 1915), that the acquisition of facts could explain economic phenomena. Such 'institutionalism' was in many regards the American inheritance of the *Methodenstreit*. This had been the 19th century confrontation between the younger German Historical School, led by Gustav Schmoller and those they dismissively referred to as the Austrian School, led by Menger. Fundamentally the dispute was about the nature of economics: whether it is a science based on atemporal precepts, as held by the Austrians or, rather, a form of historical enquiry, as maintained by the Historical School. The implications of either position remain far reaching. If it is a science, following its own inherent rules, then the state must recognise definite limits on the extent to which it is possible to direct the economy. Yet, if economic order is always historically contingent, as much the product of politics as its own motive force, then it might be possible to shape and direct it. Hayek regarded the American Institutionalists as the 'spiritual successors' of the German Historical School, drawing on Joseph Schumpeter's 1926 observation that all that was necessary was to 'change the relative emphasis put upon statistical and historical materials in this picture and we have even to details, the position that Schmoller held throughout his life' (Mitchell, 1937, pp. 37–38).

The Austrian position was heavily informed by the work of the classical economists such as David Hume, Adam Smith and Claude-Frédéric Bastiat. Yet Menger's greatest legacy is his critique of the labour theory of value, so central to classical political economy. Instead, he posited the concept of marginal utility which holds that the utility, and hence the amount an individual is willing to pay for a unit of a particular good, declines the more one consumes. According to this theory, rather than value inhering in some objective quality, such as labour time expended it is, by contrast, entirely subjective. Manger arrived at the position that marginal utility was the determinant of value at the beginning of the 1870s, at approximately the same time as William Stanley Jevons in Britain and Leon Walras in Switzerland and all seem to have arrived at the position independently (Stigler, 1950a, 1950b).

Despite this departure from the classical school, Menger's work conforms to Adam Smith's conception of the economy as the product of interaction between economic actors according to the division of labour. Economic development occurs over time, the result of humanity's innate propensity to 'truck, barter and exchange' (Smith, 1976b, p. 25). This is Smith's famous concept of 'the invisible hand', a force that seemingly guides the market towards beneficial outcomes.

The concept constitutes perhaps Smith's most famous phrase although he uses it only three times (Smith, 1976a, p. 184, 1976b, p. 456, 1980, p. 4; Rothschild, 1994). It is an idea to which Menger (1985) subscribed although unlike Smith who, contrary to the interpretations of much 19th century German scholarship, had maintained the importance of sympathy as set out in his *The Theory of Moral Sentiments* (Haller, 2000; Tribe, 2008), Menger held that self-interest alone would result in invisible hand type outcomes. Hayek certainly regarded Menger as an inheritor of Smith's logic and it is a comparison he draws repeatedly. (Hayek, 1967c, p. 94, 1982b, p. 22, 1978h, pp. 267–269).[2] From an Austrian perspective the great contributions of Smith, his contemporary David Hume, and before them Bernard Mandeville, had been their conceptions of the economy, and thus society more broadly, as the product of an evolutionary development brought about by freely interacting individuals (Hayek, 1978g; Petsoulas, 2001).

Given that Hayek's own work was firmly of the Austrian tradition, his desire to go to America, where the influence of the institutionalists was ascendant, reveals a level of intellectual curiosity. It seems reasonable to assume that he went to familiarise himself with the ideas of his intellectual adversaries. 'What I found most interesting and instructive' he later reflected 'was the work done on monetary policy and the control of industrial fluctuations connected on the one hand with the Harvard Economic Service and on the other with the new experiments in central banking policy of the Federal Reserve System.' (Hayek, 1984a). With the money from Jenks and a studentship he was able to register for a PhD at New York University entitled 'Is the Function of Money Consistent with an Artificial Stabilization of Purchasing Power?' (Kresge, 1999, p. 5). Hayek brought academic habits from the University of Vienna, with its loosely structured timetables and study patterns, with him to America. Rather than work on his thesis he instead attended lectures at Columbia given by Wesley Clair Mitchell (1913), who had founded the National Bureau of Economic Research in New York and whose work, *Business Cycles*, had influenced much of the profession. He also used the time to work on his first article, which examined recent American approaches to monetary theory (Hayek, 1999a).

Hayek's (1999b) second article, 'Monetary Policy in the United States after the Recovery from the Crisis of 1920', introduced German readers to new American approaches to the question. The US Federal Reserve had been established in 1913 and already Hayek was raising the question, 'did the central banking system really offer the best possible remedy for the known weaknesses of the credit organization in the United States?' (Hayek, 1999b, pp. 145–146). Based upon aggregated data of the sort produced by the institutionalists around Mitchel, it was widely argued that the Fed should make full use of a discretionary monetary policy. As Bruce Caldwell has explained, 'If the price level (as measured by some statistically constructed index number) rose beyond a certain point, the Fed banks would follow restrictive policy in order to slow economic activity. If it fell they would do the reverse' (Caldwell, 2004, p. 152). In his 1928 article, 'Intertemporal Price Equilibrium and Movements in the

Value of Money', Hayek built upon his earlier objections to such ambitions and sought to 'provide a theoretical argument against a monetary policy of stabilisation' (Kresge, 1999, p. 30). This article also led him to consider the now largely forgotten work of William Trufant Foster and Waddill Catchings who advocated the concept of underconsumption. Hayek's critique of their work in 'The Paradox of Saving' foreshadowed his later criticisms of Keynes (Hayek, 1995a, p. 74–120). In the article, he emphasised the way in which the general price level lags behind the overall cycle, rendering it an 'unhelpful, potentially destabilising, guide to monetary policy' (Caldwell, 2004, p. 152; Arena, 2002).[3] Hayek's American doctorate was never completed, but the question of whether prices should be stabilised by means of government and central bank measures to alter domestic monetary arrangements was one that occupied him for the rest of his life. By the end of the 1920s, therefore, Hayek had developed the fundamentals of an economic theory that stressed that it was the self-correcting tendencies of the market that must be relied upon and warned against government intervention.

The gold standard and the central banks

On returning from the United States, Hayek reoccupied his position at the Office of Accounts, until Mises was able to establish the Austrian Institute for Business Cycle Research, which Hayek was to head from 1927 until 1931, when he was invited by Lionel Robbins, who had been impressed by 'The Paradox of Saving', to the London School of Economics to deliver a series of lectures (Hayek, 1994, p. 67; Howson, 2011). The lectures, published together as *Prices and Production*, developed Hayek's earlier critique of discretionary monetary policy and were in large part a response to John Maynard Keynes's 1930 work *A Treatise on Money*. In it, Keynes (2012b) had argued that there was no automatic correction mechanism within the economy that would balance saving and investments. When savings became too high, often in response to social and economic uncertainty, economic downturns would occur, and it was this that had produced the persistent mass unemployment Britain had experienced in the 1920s. Although the book was written with the economic sluggishness of 1920s Britain in mind, its logic underpinned his subsequent explanation of the depression of the early 1930s, presented in *The General Theory of Employment Interest and Money*. Prompted by that later crisis, however, Keynes began to think that there might be something intrinsically deficient in the capitalist system, rather than downturns being the result of exogenous shocks. What government must do, he argued, is adopt counter cyclical measures, such as higher public spending, which might reduce unemployment and kick-start the economy.

In the 1929 general election, David Lloyd George, who had been first Chancellor and then Prime Minister during the First World War, and was once again head of the Liberal Party following a decade of internal turmoil, made a 'pledge' to do just this. Both Keynes (2012d) and Hubert Henderson, economists and

Liberal members, wrote in support of a plan to borrow £250 million for a two-year programme of public works. For Keynes, the vital aspect of the plan was that such a huge amount of borrowing by the government would increase bank assets and thus encourage them to make loans available to businesses and the public (Skidelsky, 2016, pp. 4–19). An economist at the Treasury accurately referred to the public works aspect as merely 'a piece of ritual', the use of a policy approach that the public was familiar with as a cover for a much more radical and innovative response to the deepening malaise.

The existing orthodoxy, in both the Conservatives and Labour parties, however, was that adherence to a gold standard and to balanced budgets was essential for the national economy and the maintenance of the empire (Eichengreen, 1996). Moreover, the reintroduction of the gold standard across European economies during the 1920s, in the wake of the First World War, was strongly associated with agreements on arms limitation. Any attempt to use state power to boost the economy by any particular nation risked being viewed as an effort to gain a national advantage and concomitantly being perceived as insufficiently committed to a lasting peace (Tooze, 2014, pp. 394–407). The gold standard had been effectively suspended by Britain during the First World War in order to meet the costs of the conflict. Keynes (2012e) had been opposed to its reintroduction in 1925, when the Treasury, under Chancellor Winston Churchill, valued sterling at pre-war levels. This resulted in a decline in exports and an increase in unemployment. For Keynes, the gold standard was nothing more than a 'barbarous relic' of the 19th century (2012a) under which those who hold the gold have the power with the result being that the scope for politics is severely circumscribed.

For Keynes, the gold standard's critical deficiency, with regard to the business cycle, was that it restricted the capacity of government to affect credit and therefore counter downturns. Despite the re-imposed restraints, he did not, however, give up on urging central banks to do more to counter the entrenched unemployment that characterised the British economy of the 1920s, particularly in those areas, such as Scotland and northern England, where the old heavy industries of the 19th century predominated. The most important means by which governments could make more money available in the general economy was not via the 'ritual' of public works, but by lowering the rate at which banks borrowed overnight from the central bank, consequently encouraging them to lend more to businesses. As Keynes (2012f, pp. 420–427) described it, 'a central bank, which is free to govern the volume of cash and reserve money in its monetary system by the joint use of bank rate policy and open-market operations, is . . . in a position to control not merely the volume of credit but the rate of investment, the level of prices and in the long run the level of incomes'. This was even possible under the gold standard 'provided that the objectives it sets before it are compatible with . . . maintenance of gold convertibility'.

It was precisely this sort of central bank policy Hayek had countered while in the US. In his L.S.E. lectures, Hayek (1931) argued, contrary to Keynes, that attempts to counter the trade cycle would only lead to a further disruption of the overall economic order. The lectures were elegant and seemed to impress his audience. The idealised market, possessed of self-correcting tendencies that he presented did not, however, reflect global economic realities. The UK had already undergone four consecutive quarters of negative growth by the time the lectures were published in September 1931, and the number of unemployed was approaching three million (Mitchell et al., 2009). September was also the first month of the new coalition National Government, formed in the face of a mounting international financial crisis. One of the government's first actions, as the Bank of England's gold reserves reached the point of exhaustion, was to again bring Britain off the gold standard (Eichengreen and Temin, 2000) For Hayek (2001, p. 12), this marked the beginning of the 'inglorious years' during which Britain 'transformed its economic system beyond recognition'. Following the National Government's re-election with an increased majority in October, its primary policy concern was maintaining a balanced budget by cutting spending and increasing trade within the Empire (Booth and Pack, 1985, p. 58). Although he was supportive of balanced budgets, this 'empire preference' involved a further measure that undermined Hayek's vision of a healthy economic system: the introduction of tariffs to favour the colonies and dominions, that emerged from the 1932 Ottawa conference. Thus, the two pillars of classical liberal political economy, free trade and the gold standard, were both conclusively rejected within a year of each other. The abandonment of gold by countries across most of Europe in 1932, then the US in 1933, and eventually France in 1936, resulted in what Hayek referred to as a widespread 'monetary nationalism', undermining any last remnants of a 19th century liberal order.

It should be noted, in light of the later turn his thoughts took, that Hayek's resistance to counter cyclical measures did not at this stage of his career amount to an opposition to the existence of central banks in themselves.[4] Rather, he believed that they should exert a restraining influence during periods of credit expansion and certainly not be looking to stimulate demand during a downturn. Their central aim ought to be to exercise 'beneficial regulatory influence' to act as 'a stabilising influence', applying 'the necessary braking effect' when the economy was overheating (White, 1999). 'And so, we arrive' wrote Hayek at the end of his third lecture 'at results which only confirm the old truth that we may perhaps prevent a crisis by checking expansion in time, but that we can do nothing to get out of it before its natural end, once it has come'. Although Keynes encouraged government action through credit expansion and fiscal stimulus, Hayek warned that we 'must leave it to time to effect a permanent cure by the slow process of adapting the structure of production to the means available for capital purposes' (Hayek, 1931, p. 99).

Hayek's opposition to government intervention was underpinned by his commitment to the gold standard. For him, it had served as the fundamental means by which government influence over money had been limited, as the requirement of specie payment in gold had prevented governments from simply issuing fiat money in whatever amount they might have wished (Hayek, 1999c, 1999h).[5] According to David Hume's famous price-specie flow mechanism countries on the gold standard effectively import gold relative to the amount that the value of exports exceeds imports. Consequently, without any need for central bank action the amount of money would increase and decrease as required resulting in commensurate rises and falls in the value of gold. Higher prices would make exports more expensive and so the international system would tend again towards equilibrium, all without the need for government or central bank action.

Hayek was not an unqualified supporter of the gold standard. He regraded one of its key deficiencies to be the fact that increases in the amount of gold mined, rather than solely the demands of business, impacted the amount of money in circulation. Furthermore, the fundamental drawback of the system as it had operated was that it had been incomplete, 'a mixed system . . . better called a gold nucleus standard' where gold had only underpinned national currencies (Hayek, 1999e, p. 50). The ideal, for Hayek (1999e, p. 44) would have been a 'homogeneous international monetary system . . . only an international gold standard with exclusive gold circulation in all countries would conform to this picture.' But, he added, 'this has never existed'. Nevertheless, the gold standard had ultimately reflected real movements in trade because 'the final result, the change in the relative value of the total quantities of money', once affected by shifts in the availability of credit, 'is brought about by a corresponding change in the quantity of money, the number of money units, in each country' (Hayek, 1999e, p. 50). Thus, the global system tracked Hume's specie–flow theory even if it did not tightly conform to it. Remarkably, given the decentralised nature of his later thought, in 1937 Hayek was of the opinion that 'a really rational monetary policy could be carried out only by an international monetary authority', but he concluded that, at least the standard as it had operated was 'far preferable to numerous independent and independently regulated national currencies' (Hayek, 1999e, p. 99).

Hayek (1999f) subsequently shifted ground somewhat from his qualified support of the gold standard to an endorsement of a 'commodity reserve currency'. Rather than have the value of money tied to gold, he advocated that the standard could instead be set by a basket of production goods, 'the basic idea is that currency should be issued solely in exchange against a fixed combination of warehouse warrants for a number of storable commodities and be redeemable in the same "commodity unit"' (Hayek, 1999f, p. 109). This unit could then function in an international, effectively self-contained and self-correcting system of international trade where transfers of money across borders would have an equivalent effect on the value of currencies. He again made the point that his fundamental concern was that government should not be able to alter the value of money as it chose and he insisted that the 'great need' was 'for a system under which these controls are taken from the separate bodies which can but act in what is essentially an arbitrary and unpredictable manner and to make the controls instead subject to a mechanical and predictable rule'(Hayek, 1999f, p. 114). Here, we see a concern with government 'arbitrariness' that would inform Hayek's subsequent political theory.

The exchange with Keynes

So successful were Hayek's initial lectures at the L.S.E. that he received an almost immediate invitation from Lionel Robbins to teach there, albeit initially as a visiting professor. It seems that Robbins wanted allies in confirming the position of the School as a bastion of classical liberalism, in opposition to the new economics emanating out of Cambridge under the direction of Keynes (Shearmur, 1997, pp. 68–82; Wapshott, 2011). Certainly, Robbins and Keynes had disagreed (Skildelsky, 2010), somewhat acrimoniously, over the appropriate government response to the deepening economic crisis as members of the Economic Advisory Committee, established in 1930 by the Labour government (Caldwell, 2004, pp. 170–171). Hayek was clear that the root cause of the crisis was the expansion of cheap credit, rather than, as Keynes argued, underinvestment. Hayek's recollections of Robbins's motives for bringing him to London were clear: 'this is the thing we need at the moment, to fight Keynes. So I was called in for this purpose' (Hayek, 1994, 67). Furthermore, the newly appointed Robbins sought to establish the L.S.E. as an international, cosmopolitan institution in contrast to the established English centres of economics at Manchester and in Cambridge. In this respect Hayek was a good fit and his lectures were well received, introducing to his English audience an Austrian theoretical structure much as Robbins must have intended (Burgin, 2012, pp. 12–32).

Susan Howson (2011), however, has suggested that rather than Robbins seeking continental reinforcements for a campaign against Keynes, it was the young Austrian who was most eager to enter the fray. She notes that according to the date on which Hayek's lectures were announced, Robbins must have invited him prior to his disagreement with Keynes (Howson, 2001, p. 370). By the time of Hayek's lectures, Keynes's *Treatise on Money* had been published and Hayek had heard Keynes's radio broadcast, 'Saving and Spending' shortly before travelling to England. Also, he preceded his visit to London with one to Cambridge, where he stayed with Denis Robertson at Trinity, gave a lecture to the Marshall Society and attended Keynes's Monday Club. Richard Khan, who was present at the Marshall Society meeting, attributed the 'breach' between L.S.E. and Cambridge economists to Hayek, not to Robbins (Howson, 2009, p. 10) It may then be that Hayek felt he had the tools in his hands, shaped by his experience in the United States, to take on one of Britain's leading public intellectuals and argue against a role for governments and experts in shaping the economy or attempting to intervene to alter the business cycle. Most likely the various intentions of both Hayek and Robbins coincided, initiating a close personal and professional relationship between the two.[6]

Within six months of Hayek's initial lectures at the L.S.E. he had further sought to engage Keynes with the first part of a critical review of the *Treatise* published in the August 1931 issue of *Economica*. Hayek (1995b) criticised Keynes for misapplying the early work of Knut Wicksell, upon whose theory of the natural rate of interest Keynes had based his equations (Caldwell, 1995). Keynes's reaction was robust. In the November issue of *Economica*, whilst largely granting Hayek's criticism, Keynes (1931) proceeded to archly dismiss *Prices and Production*, just out in print, as

> one of the most frightful muddles I have ever read, with scarcely a sound proposition in it beginning with page 45, and yet it remains a book of some interest, which is likely to leave its mark on the reader. It is an extraordinary example of how, starting with a mistake, a remorseless logician can end up in Bedlam.

In the following months, the pair exchanged correspondence. Keynes's colleague Piero Sraffa (1995) kept up the criticism of Hayek issuing from Cambridge in a further review, but Keynes himself never responded to the second half of Hayek's review, out in February 1932, preferring instead to improve his own theory. The final result would be the most influential economic treatise since Smith's *The Wealth of Nations*, his *General Theory of Employment, Interest and Money* published in 1936 (Keynes, 2012c).

Hayek (1939) returned to the controversy surrounding Keynes's review of *Prices and Production* and sought to respond to some of the criticisms levelled at him in his volume of essays, *Profits, Interest and Investment*. This, however, only confused the situation further, with his adversaries claiming he had simply altered his theory to such an extent that it no longer conformed to his original thesis. The theoretical details have been explored in greater detail than is possible here by Gerald O'Driscoll (1978). Relevant for our purposes is that Hayek never chose to review Keynes's *General Theory*. Why, has been the subject of some conjecture (Howson, 2001). A variety of reasons have been offered for the apparent oversight, chief among them that Keynes was so apt to change his mind on theory that it hardly seemed worth the effort (Hayek, 1994, p. 79). Certainly, Keynes was a mercurial mind, but the actual reason may be that Hayek was far from clear about his own theory, and so unable to offer the comprehensive criticism of Keynes' book that it undoubtedly warranted. As Hayek later recognised, the invitation to his initial L.S.E. lectures had arrived

> when I had for the first time a clear picture of this theory but had not yet gone into all the complicated details. If I had progressed in working out an elaborate treatise, I would have encountered any number of complications and would have produced a very difficult treatise
>
> (Hayek, 1994, p. 67).

He would struggle on with the complications and 'under the pretext that the ongoing war might make completion of the work impossible' Hayek (2007) sent *The Pure Theory of Capital* for publication in 1941. It went largely unnoticed and remains relatively little read. In contrast *The General Theory* set in place the foundations of respectable economic thought for the post-war world.[7]

Fundamental to the disagreement between Hayek and Keynes and his followers was their conception of the economy. For Hayek, although the business cycle was an unfortunate reality, it was best left to take its own course. For Keynes, it was entirely possible that the economy could enter a state in which unemployment would remain high and output low in the absence of government action. As he wrote in *The General Theory* 'The right remedy for the trade cycle is not to be found in abolishing booms and thus keeping us permanently in a quasi-slump, but in abolishing slumps and thus keeping us in a quasi-boom' (Keynes, 2012c, p. 322). For Hayek, the economy tended towards equilibrium over the long run, for Keynes there was no reason to assume it would.

Despite the acrimonious nature of the disagreement between Hayek and Keynes during the 1930s, it is important to recognise the fundamental similarities in their general outlooks. Both were liberals who disliked the schemes for government planning that were increasingly fashionable during the period (Cornish, 2013). Hayek, in particular, was keen to stress his respect for his adversary. Keynes was the older, more established, and in many respects more commanding figure of the two. He had also been the author of the *Economic Consequences of the Peace* which had condemned the economic clauses of the peace treaties of 1919, making him a 'hero . . . long before he achieved fame as an economic theorist' to central Europeans of Hayek's generation (Hayek, 1978j, p. 283). Despite theoretical disagreements, the two had arrived at friendly terms, as evidenced by Keynes finding rooms for Hayek and his family at King's College Cambridge during the L.S.E.'s wartime evacuation from London. Even at the height of their theoretical fall-out, and Hayek's association of Keynes's doctrines with 'monetary nationalism' he stressed 'that when I describe the doctrines I am going to criticise . . . I do not mean to suggest that those who hold them are actuated by any sort of narrow nationalism. The very name of their leading exponent, J.M. Keynes testifies that this is not the case' (Hayek, 1999c, p. 40).

Certainly, Hayek's engagement with Keynes was one of the defining features of his intellectual life. Disagreements with his theoretical heirs would feature over his entire career. Remarkably, however, Hayek believed that had Keynes not died of a heart attack in April 1946, he would have reacted against some of the more mechanical ways in which 'Keynesians' began to apply his theory in the post-war world. 'I had asked him' remembered Hayek of their last meeting,

> whether he was not getting alarmed by the use of which some of his disciples were putting his theories. His reply was that these theories were greatly needed in the 1930s; but if these theories should ever become harmful, I could be assured that he would quickly bring a change in public opinion. What I blame him for is that he had called such a tract for the times the *General Theory*.
>
> (Hayek, 1978j, p. 287)

What Keynes may have said in response to this recollection we can of course never know, although one imagines it is unlikely he would have quietly concurred.

Conclusion

In this chapter I have provided a brief overview of Hayek's writing on the business cycle, his defence of the gold standard and his debates with Keynes. Taken together, these strands constitute the first of his major intellectual engagements. Fundamental to Hayek's Austrian economic training was an opposition to government playing a role in influencing economic processes – this was the prime inheritance of the *Methodenstreit*. From an early point in his career, he rejected the possibility of aggregated data giving an accurate depiction of the real economy. Furthermore, he was troubled that such stores of information could be used to legitimate government interventions in the business cycle. According to his Austrian theoretical perspective, this had to be resisted. Demonstrating the inadequacy of aggregates therefore became a central concern.

A major bulwark against governments' ability to stimulate – and thus in Austrian terms distort – the business cycle was the existence of the gold standard. Over the 1930s, Hayek maintained a defence of a specie standard. While it continued to function, he defended gold, despite its various deficiencies. When it ceased to exist, he offered a new and improved scheme for a commodity-based standard. John Maynard Keynes was his chief intellectual adversary across these related debates. Hayek would ultimately come to regard the legacy of the man he later referred to with loaded humour as 'St Maynard' as an existential threat not merely to economic order but, as we shall see in Chapter 6, to western civilisation and individual liberty itself. What emerges clearly out of the earliest major intellectual engagement of Hayek's life is that he regarded governments as posing the cardinal threat to liberal economic order.

Notes

1 Hayek dropped the minor aristocratic appellation 'von' from his name after the Austrian republican government banned the use of hereditary titles in 1919.

2 For a very different perspective on Smith which laments his influence on the practice of economics, primarily for his labour theory of value, but one which also condemns his 'plagiarism' of Francis Hutcheson see Rothbard (1995).

3 Hayek's relationship to quantity theory of money is complex. Irving Fisher, whose work on the theory Hayek considered important also made use of aggregated data. Hayek commented in *Prices and Production* that though he felt aggregates were inherently misleading, it would be a disaster for economics if people forgot about the quantity theory. Hayek was later to disagree with the subsequent generation of monetarists, influenced by Fisher, and led by Milton Friedman.

4 See Chapter 8.

5 Despite a keen awareness of the history of British economic thought, Hayek makes no reference to an ongoing issue of 19th century economics: the viability of a bimetallic standard. The matter was not of direct theoretical relevance to his basic concern to limit government control of money. He would later write that 'The possibilities of bimetallism are irrelevant for our present problems' (Hayek, 199h p, 140).

6 The relationship was to break down after Hayek divorced his first wife with whom the Robbins's were also friendly after the Second World War. This may also partly have prompted his move to the University of Chicago. The relationship would eventually recover during the 1970s.

7 There has been significant debate about the extent to which the government came to adopt what might loosely be called Keynesian, rather than planning, responses to the depression. The most fruitful period of this lengthy debate was from the mid-1970s to early '90s, following the collapse of the 'Keynesian consensus'. For an early in-depth work from this period see Howson (1975).

Works Cited

Arena, R. 2002. 'Monetary Policy and Business Cycles: Hayek as an Opponent of the Quantity Theory Tradition' in Thierry Aimar, Jack Birner and Pierre Garrouste (Eds.), *F.A. Hayek as a Political Economist* (pp. 81–96). London: Routledge.

Beniston, J. 2006. 'Culture and Politics in Red Vienna', *Austrian Studies* 14, pp. 1–19.

Booth, A. and Pack, M. 1985. *Employment, Capital and Economic Policy: Great Britain 1918–1939*. New York: Wiley-Blackwell.

Borsányi, G. 1993. *The Life of a Communist Revolutionary, Béla*. Mario Fenyo (Trans.). Boulder, CO: Social Science Monographs.

Burgin, A. 2012. *The Great Persuasion: Reinventing Free Markets Since the Depression*. Cambridge, MA: Harvard University Press.

Caldwell, B. 1988. 'Hayek's Transformation', *History of Political Economy* 20:4, pp. 513–548.

Caldwell, B. 1995. 'Introduction' in Bruce Caldwell (Ed.), *Contra Keynes and Cambridge: The Collected Works of F.A. Hayek, Vol. 6* (pp. 1–48). Chicago: University of Chicago Press.

Caldwell, B. 2004. *Hayek's Challenge: An Intellectual Biography of F.A. Hayek*. Chicago: University of Chicago Press.

Cornish, S. 2013. 'The Hayek Literature' in Robert Leeson (Ed.), *Hayek: A Collaborative Biography, Part 1 Influences from to Bartley* (pp. 74–89). London: Palgrave Macmillan.

Eichengreen, B. 1996. *Gold Fetters: The Gold Standard and the Great Depression, 1919–1939*. Oxford: Oxford University Press.

Eichengreen, B. and Temin, P. 2000. 'The Gold Standard and the Great Depression', *Contemporary European History* 9:2, pp. 183–207.

Gamble, A. 1996. *Hayek: The Iron Cage of Liberty*. Cambridge: Polity Press.

Haller, M. 2000. 'Carl Menger's Theory of Invisible Hand Explanations', *Social Science Information* 39:4, pp. 529–565.

Hayek, F.A. 1931. *Prices and Production*. London: Routledge & Kegan Paul.

Hayek, F.A. 1939. *Profits, Interest, and Investment*. London: Routledge & Kegan Paul.

Hayek, F.A. 1948b. 'Economics and Knowledge' [1936] in Friedrich Hayek (Ed.), *Individualism and Economic Order* (pp. 33–56). Chicago: University of Chicago Press.

Hayek, F.A. 1967c. 'Kinds of Rationalism' [1964] in Friedrich Hayek (Ed.), *Studies in Philosophy, Politics and Economics* (pp. 82–95). London: Routledge & Kegan Paul.

Hayek, F.A. 1978g. 'Dr Bernard Mandeville' [1967] in Friedrich Hayek (Ed.), *New Studies in Philosophy, Politics and the History of Ideas* (pp. 249–266). London: Routledge & Kegan Paul.

Hayek, F.A. 1978h. 'Adam Smith's Message in Today's Language' [1976] in Friedrich Hayek (Ed.), *New Studies in Philosophy, Politics, Economics and the History of Ideas* (pp. 267–269). London: Routledge & Kegan Paul.

Hayek, F.A. 1978j. 'Personal Recollections of Keynes and the Keynesian Revolution' [1966] in Friedrich Hayek (Ed.), *New Studies in Philosophy, Politics, Economics, and the History of Ideas* (pp. 283–289). London: Routledge & Kegan Paul.

Hayek, F.A. 1982b. *Rules and Order* [1973] in Friedrich Hayek (Ed.), *Law, Legislation and Liberty: A New Statement of the Liberal Principles of Justice and Political Economy* [3 Volume edition]. London: Routledge Kegan Paul.

Hayek, F.A. 1984a. 'Introduction' in Roy McCloughrey (Ed.), *Money, Capital and Fluctuations: Early Essays.* Chicago: University of Chicago Press.

Hayek, F.A. 1992. 'Ludwig von Mises' [composed of several essays 1951/73/78] in Peter Klein (Ed.), *The Fortunes of Liberalism: The Collected Works of F.A. Hayek, Vol. 4* (pp. 126–159). Chicago: University of Chicago Press.

Hayek, F.A. 1994. *Hayek on Hayek: An Autobiographical Dialogue.* Stephen Kresge and Leif Warner (Eds.). Chicago: University of Chicago Press.

Hayek, F.A. 1995a. 'The Paradox of Saving' [1929] in Bruce Caldwell (Ed.), *Contra Keynes and Cambridge: The Collected Works of F.A. Hayek, Vol. 6* (pp. 74–120). Chicago: University of Chicago Press.

Hayek, F.A. 1995b. 'Reflections on the Pure Theory of Money of Mr. J.M. Keynes' in Bruce Caldwell (Ed.), *Contra Keynes and Cambridge: The Collected Works of F.A. Hayek, Vol. 6* (pp. 121–146). Chicago: University of Chicago Press.

Hayek, F.A. 1999a. 'A Survey of Recent American Writing: Stabilisation Problems in Gold Exchange Standard Countries' [1924] in Stephen Kresge (Ed.), *Good Money Part One: The Collected Works of FA Hayek, Vol. 5* (pp. 39–66). Chicago: University of Chicago Press.

Hayek, F.A. 1999b. 'Monetary Policy in the United States after the Recovery from the Crisis of 1920' [1925] in Stephen Kresge (Ed.), *Good Money Part One: The Collected Works of FA Hayek, Vol. 5* (pp. 71–152). Chicago: University of Chicago Press.

Hayek, F.A. 1999c. 'The Fate of the Gold Standard' [1932] in Stephen Kresge (Ed.), *Good Money Part One: The Collected Works of FA Hayek, Vol. 5* (pp. 153–168). Chicago: University of Chicago Press.

Hayek, F.A. 1999e. 'Monetary Nationalism and International Stability' [1937] in Stephen Kresge (Ed.), *Good Money Part Two, The Collected Works of FA Hayek, Vol. 6* (pp. 37–105). Chicago: University of Chicago Press.

Hayek, F.A. 1999f. 'A Commodity Reserve Currency' [1943] in Stephen Kresge (Ed.), *Good Money Part Two: The Collected Works of FA Hayek, Vol. 6* (pp. 106–114). Chicago: University of Chicago Press.

Hayek, F.A. 1999h. 'The Denationalisation of Money' [1976] in Stephen Kresge (Ed.), *Good Money Part Two: The Collected Works of F.A. Hayek, Vol. 6* (pp. 128–229). Chicago: University of Chicago Press.

Hayek, F.A. 2001. *The Road to Serfdom.* London: Routledge.

Hayek, F.A. 2007. *The Pure Theory of Capital: The Collected Works of FA Hayek, Vol 12* [1941], Ed. Lawrence White. Chicago: University of Chicago Press.

Hayek, F.A. 2014. *John Stuart Mill and Harriet Taylor: Their Friendship and Subsequent Marriage: The Collected Works of F.A. Hayek, Vol. 12.* Sandra Peart (Ed.). Chicago: University of Chicago Press.

Howson, S. 1975. *Domestic Monetary Management in Britain, 1919–38.* Cambridge: Cambridge University Press.

Howson, S. 2001. 'Why Didn't Hayek Review Keynes's *General Theory*? A Partial Answer', *History of Political Economy* 33:2, pp. 369–74.

Howson, S. 2009. 'Keynes and the LSE Economists', *Journal of the History of Economic Thought* 31:3, pp. 257–280.

Howson, S. 2011. *Lionel Robbins.* Cambridge: Cambridge University Press.

Keynes, J.M. 1931. 'The Pure Theory of Money. A Reply to Dr. Hayek', *Economica* 34, pp. 387–397.

Keynes, J.M. 2012a. 'A Tract on Monetary Reform' [1923] in Elizabeth Johnson and Donald Moggridge (Eds.), *The Collected Writings of John Maynard Keynes, Vol. 4* (online). London: MacMillan.

Keynes, J.M. 2012b. 'A Treatise on Money' [1930] in Elizabeth Johnson and Donald Moggridge (Eds.), *The Collected Writings of John Maynard Keynes, Vol. 6* (online). London: MacMillan.

Keynes, J.M. 2012c. *The General Theory of Employment, Interest and Money* [1936] in Elizabeth Johnson and Donald Moggridge (Eds.), *Collected Writings of John Maynard Keynes, Vol. 7* (online). London: MacMillan.

Keynes, J M. 2012d. 'Can Lloyd George Do It?- The Pledge Examined' [1929] in Elizabeth Johnson and Donald Moggridge (Eds.), *The Collected Works Writings of John Maynard Keynes, Vol. 9* (online) (pp. 86–125). London: MacMillan.

Keynes, J.M. 2012e. 'The Economic Consequences of Mr. Churchill' [1925] in Elizabeth Johnson and Donald Moggridge (Eds.), *The Collected Works Writings of John Maynard Keynes, Vol. 9* (online) (pp. 207–230). London: MacMillan.

Keynes, J.M. 2012f. 'Credit Control' in Elizabeth Johnson and Donald Moggridge (Eds.), *The Collected Works Writings of John Maynard Keynes, Vol. 11* (online) (pp. 420–427). London: MacMillan.

Kresge, S. 1999. 'Introduction' in Stephen Kresge (Ed.), *Good Money Part One: The Collected Works of FA Hayek, Vol. 1* (pp. 1–38). Chicago: University of Chicago Press.

Menger, C. 1985. *Investigations into the Method of the Social Sciences with Special Reference to Economics*. L. Schneider (Ed.), F. Nock (Trans.). New York: New York University Press.

Mises, L. 1981. *Socialism: An Economic and Sociological Analysis*. J Kahane (Trans.). Indianapolis: Liberty Fund.

Mitchell, J., Solomou, S.N. and Weale, M. 2009. 'Monthly and Quarterly GDP Estimates for Interwar Britain', *National Institute of Economic and Social Research Discussion Paper* 348.

Mitchell, W.C. 1913. *Business Cycles*. Berkeley: University of California Press.

Mitchell, W.C. 1937. *The Backward Art of Spending Money*. New York: McGraw – Hill Book Company.

O'Driscoll, G.P. 1978. *Economics as a Coordination Problem: The Contributions of Friedrich A. Hayek*. New York: New York University Press.

Petsoulas, C. 2001. *Hayek's Liberalism and its Origins: The Idea of Spontaneous Order and the Scottish Enlightenment*. London: Routledge.

Rothbard, M. 1995. *Economic Thought Before Adam Smith: An Austrian Perspective on Economic Thought, Vol. 1*. Cheltenham: Edward Elgar.

Rothschild, E. 1994. 'Adam Smith and the Invisible Hand', *The American Economic Review* 84:2, pp. 319–322.

Shearmur, J. 1997. 'Hayek, Keynes and the State', *History of Economics Review* 26, pp. 68–82.

Shearmur, J. 2006. 'Hayek, The Road to Serfdom and the British Conservatives', *Journal of the History of Economic Thought* 28:3, pp. 309–314.

Skildelsky, R. 2010. *Keynes: The Return of the Master*. London: Allen Lane.

Skidelsky, R. 2016. 'How Keynes Came to Britain' *Review of Keynesian Economics Review of Keynesian Economics* 4:1, pp. 4–19.

Slobodian, Q. 2018. *Globalists: The End of Empire and the Birth of Neoliberalism*. Cambridge, MA: Harvard University Press.

Smith, A. 1976a. *The Theory of Moral Sentiments*. Oxford: Oxford University Press.

Smith, A. 1976b. *An Inquiry into the Nature and Causes of the Wealth of Nations*. Oxford: Oxford University Press.

Smith, A. 1980. 'The History of Astronomy' in *Essays on Philosophical Subjects*. Oxford: Oxford University Press.

Sraffa, P. 1995. 'Dr Hayek on Money and Capital' in Bruce Caldwell (Ed.), *Contra Keynes and Cambridge: The Collected Works of FA Hayek, Vol. 9* (pp. 198–209). Chicago: University of Chicago Press.

Stigler, G.J. 1950a. 'The Development of Utility Theory 1', *Journal of Political Economy* 58:4, pp. 307–327.

Stigler, G.J. 1950b. 'The Development of Utility Theory 2', *Journal of Political Economy* 58:5, pp. 373–396.

Tooze, A. 2014. *The Deluge: The Great War, America, and the Remaking of the Global Order, 1916–1931*. London: Allen Lane.

Tribe, K. 2008. '"Das Adam Smith Problem" and the Origins of Modern Smith Scholarship', *History of European Ideas* 34:4, 514–525.

Veblen, T. 1899. *Theory of the Leisure Class*. New York: Macmillan.

Veblen, T. 1915. *Imperial Germany and the Industrial Revolution*. New York: Macmillan.

Wapshott, N. 2011. *Keynes Hayek: The Clash that Defined Modern Economics*. New York: W.W. Norton and Company.

White, L. 1999. 'Why Didn't Hayek Favor Laissez Faire in Banking', *History of Political Economy* 31:4, pp. 754–69.

2 The socialist calculation debates

The second intellectual dispute that gave form to Hayek's concept of liberty has become known as the Socialist Calculation Debate. In his disagreements with Keynes and his supporters, the core concern was how best to maintain the capitalist system. In this second engagement with the advocates of socialism, however, the very desirability of that system was contested. The debate had two distinct phases. In the first, which arose after then end of the First World War, the chief protagonists were Mises and Otto Neurath. It centred on the viability of direct planning and the abolition of markets. In the second phase, during the mid-1930s, Hayek sought to counter the response of 'market socialists', such as Oskar Lange and Abba Lerner, who argued, in response to the earlier contest, that competition could still function as a guide to investment even under conditions of common ownership.[1] What emerged from the debate was the forceful equation, on Hayek's part, of freedom in the market with individual liberty. By contrast, he came to view economic planning, and increasingly government economic intervention of any kind, as the essence of tyranny.

In 1932, only a year after being invited to the L.S.E. as a visiting professor, Hayek took up the long vacant Tooke Chair of Economic Science. In his inaugural address, 'The Trend of Economic Thinking', delivered in the spring of 1933, he set out his assessment of how the discipline had developed, and where it might be headed (Hayek, 1991). In doing so he touched on many of the methodological issues that would exercise him for the rest of his career, even as his focus expanded beyond purely economic matters. In his address Hayek observed that 'it is probably no exaggeration to say that economics developed mainly as the outcome of the investigation and refutation of successive Utopian proposals' and,

> From the time of Hume and Adam Smith, the effect of every attempt to understand economic phenomena – that is to say, of every theoretical analysis – has been to show that, in large part, the coordination of individual efforts in society is not the product of deliberate planning, but has been brought about, and in many cases could only have been brought about, by means which nobody wanted or understood, and which in isolation might be regarded as some of the most objectionable features of the system. . . .

The recognition of the existence of this organism is the recognition that there is a subject-matter for economics.

(Hayek, 1991, p. 15)

Hayek's lecture delivered a call to recognise the importance of theory, rather than the piling up of statistics, to any understanding of the economy. From his perspective, the belief in the all-encompassing accuracy of such data lent itself not only to the relatively restrained, if misguided, attempts to shape the business cycle, in the manner advocated by Keynes, but also to the more radical schemes that sought to plan the economy as a whole.

From economics to political economy

Worryingly for Hayek, as the economic depression of the early 1930s deepened, the greater the appeal of economic planning seemed to become (Ritschel, 1997, pp. 97–143; Thorpe, 2008, pp. 86–101). In the Labour Party, a commitment to common ownership was enshrined in Clause IV of the party's 1918 constitution. Following the marginalisation of guild socialists and those who wished to see a general democratisation of the economy, such as G.D.H. Cole and R.H. Tawney, by those of a more Fabian outlook, common ownership was always likely to take a statist form. Indeed, the famous Clause IV had first been drafted by Sidney and Beatrice Webb, two of the earliest and most influential members of the Fabian Society who, somewhat ironically, had also founded Hayek's new employer. Along with others on the left, they looked to the apparent economic success of the Soviet Union under Stalin's Five Year Plans, as standing in stark contrast to western failings. Yet among conservatives also, there were growing calls for greater state economic involvement. In 1938 Harold MacMillan reflected on the effect of the economic crisis, in a book revealingly entitled *The Middle Way*, writing that 'throughout the whole of the post-war period there had been growing an uneasy consciousness of something radically wrong with the economic system' and that 'one of the consequences of the crisis was to confirm these suspicions and to liberate men's minds from a continued subservience to the economic orthodoxy of the pre-war world' (Macmillan, 1938, pp. 7–8; Thorpe, 2010, pp. 89–146). Although his ideas were by no means mainstream within the party at this time, MacMillan would go on to become Conservative Prime Minister in 1957. Even in liberal circles, around Lloyd George and 'The Next Five Years Group', there was an expectation that government must do more. Other organisations also promoted the idea, such as the 'Council of Action for Peace and Reconstruction' and the leftist 'Popular Front'. All proposed some form of planning as a way out of the prevailing economic slump and as a means of preventing future calamities (Ritschel, 1997, pp. 20–59; Pugh, 2006; Barberis et al., 2005, p. 353).

Despite the appeal of planning as a concept, the actual economic policies of the coalition National Government remained almost entirely orthodox. Nonetheless, in the intellectual and policy making circles within which

Hayek moved, planning was increasingly perceived as a progressive middle way between *laissez-faire* capitalism and Soviet style communism (Marwick, 1964, pp. 285–298). Neither could Hayek, Robbins and others necessarily find allies in business for their vision of the market. Since the end of the First World War many of the measures put in place to protect British businesses during the conflict had not been removed. Some were even extended, for example the 1920 Dyestuffs Act, preventing the import of substances applicable to the textile trade (Aldcroft, 2001, pp. 4–61; Booth and Melvyn, 1985, p. 58; Carpenter, 1976). For Hayek (1935a, pp. 22–24) this was all dangerous nonsense, a form of 'interventionist chaos'. According to the duality of his thought, which held that there could either be a free market or an unfree one, there could be no middle way and the tragedy of 1930s British politics was that no significant group was arguing the liberal case any longer. Moreover, if some advocates of planning took encouragement from Russia or Italy or Germany then they must also accept the concomitant consequences for individual freedom.[2]

In order to support his case, Hayek introduced his English audience to the continental critique of planning in his 1935 edited volume, *Collectivist Economic Planning*. In addition to arguing against direct planning, the book had a second purpose, which was to address more recent schemes for market socialism. These Hayek dismissed as poor imitations of the free market, yet such ideas were nascent at best and not widely known. The book then had its greatest impact in taking to task direct planning, building upon Mises's 1920 essay, 'Economic Calculation in the Socialist Commonwealth' This was largely because, in Britain at least, popular notions of planning remained hazy, and still owed more to that older influence.

The central concern of the volume is rationality: whether it is more rational to plan an economy, or whether the allocation of resources should be left to competition. In the introduction Hayek outlined the history of the debate and he rehearsed his version of the various forms in which socialism has been proposed. In addition to Mises, he noted that both Max Weber and the Russian economist Boris Brutzkus, arrived at similar conclusions about 'the impossibility of rational calculation in a centrally directed economy' at around the same time as Mises (Hayek, 1935a, p. 35). The Bolshevik revolution of 1917, followed by a number of failed communist revolutions throughout Europe following the defeat of Germany and Austria–Hungary, meant that the question was not simply one of technical debate but one of immediate political importance.

The arguments in Mises's 1920 essay had been arrived at in opposition to those of Otto Neurath (1973), who had served in one of these uprisings, as the President of the Central Planning Office in the Bavarian Soviet Republic. He argued that the methods of planning and war economy developed during the First World War could be fruitfully pursued during peacetime. There are three key elements to Mises's critique of socialism. First, that it is not possible to calculate what a worker should be paid in labour time alone as 'labour is not a uniform and homogeneous quantity', as such 'the remuneration of labour cannot but proceed on an arbitrary basis' (Mises, 1935, p. 94). Remuneration must therefore become a political decision to be taken by government. Second, moving on to the more important issue of exchange, Mises conceded that even under socialism where, for example, 'each comrade receives a bundle of coupons, redeemable within a certain period against a definite quantity of certain specified goods' it would not be necessary 'that every man should consume the whole of his portion'. Exchanges of consumer goods could still be allowed to take place according to people's preferences, even perhaps retaining money as the medium of exchange. Yet although some veneer of rationality may still pertain at the level of lower order consumption goods, this merely conceals the irrationality brought about by the fact that 'under socialism all the means of production are the property of the community' (Mises, 1935, pp. 90–91). As such there can be no market for higher order production goods such as iron or coal or heavy machinery. Instead they must be allocated *in natura*, in kind. Accordingly,

> All transactions which serve the purpose of meeting requirements will be subject to the control of a supreme authority. Yet in place of the economy of the "anarchic" method of production, recourse will be had to the senseless output of an absurd apparatus. The wheels will turn, but will run to no effect.
>
> (Mises, 1935, p. 106)

The best a socialist economy can hope for is to proceed upon the basis of 'vague estimates' as change can neither be appraised in advance nor retrospectively determined. 'There is only groping in the dark' Mises argued and 'socialism is the abolition of rational economy' (Mises, 1935, p. 110) The lack of rational calculation in production goods also resulted in Mises (1935, p. 125) dismissing Lenin's (1934) recent pronouncements that Russian communism's most pressing task is 'the organisation of bookkeeping and control of those concerns, in which the capitalists have already been expropriated'. In the absence of money prices for production goods this is entirely superfluous, Mises insisted, as the numbers on the page bear no relationship to reality. Curiously, he noted how Lenin's (1934) prioritisation of proper accounting revealed him to be a socialist not a syndicalist. Lenin of course never claimed to be syndicalist and would likely have been surprised to hear the revolution described in such terms. This, perhaps, should serve as a reminder of how recent the 1917 revolution was, and how incomplete were popular and expert understandings of it.

A third criticism Mises made of socialism is that without the profit motive there is no pressure for the 'reform and improvement of production' and that as conditions change existing procedures become 'a dead limb in the economic organism. All attempts to breathe life into them have so far been in vain.' He based this on the claim that 'we are in the position to survey decades of state and socialist endeavour'. However, he did not specify to which endeavours he was referring (Mises, 1935, p. 118). Hayek argued that many socialists and planners had ignored Mises' criticisms and continued to think, if they thought at all beyond the generality, that to plan must be better than not to plan, in the terms offered by Neurath some sixteen years previously (Hayek, 1935a, pp. 1–3). In contrast to the Webbs, Hayek insisted Russia had suffered many economic problems and offered them as evidence that an embrace of crude planning there confirmed the arguments Mises made in 1920.

There were, however, other socialists, primarily Oskar Lange and Abba Lerner, who had taken up the challenge offered by Mises's criticisms and had sought to outline how a socialist market economy might function. Their position was succinctly summed up by Joseph Schumpeter when he recounted the history of the debate.[3] He effectively agreed that socialist planning could in fact be guided by consumer tastes. In essence,

> Exactly as today every firm in a perfectly competitive industry knows what and how much to produce and how to produce it as soon as technical possibilities, reactions of consumers (their tastes and incomes) and prices of means of production are given, so the industrial managements in our socialist commonwealth would know what to produce, how to produce and what factor quantities to 'buy' from the central board as soon as the consumers have revealed their 'demands'.
>
> (Lavoie, 1981, 47)

It was this competitive solution to the problem posed by Mises that Hayek (1935b) took to task in his conclusion to the volume. Regarding schemes to introduce a competitive element into socialism he concluded that,

> it will at best be a system of quasi competition where the person really responsible will not be the entrepreneur but the official who approves his decisions and where in consequence all the difficulties will arise in connection with freedom of initiative and the assessment of responsibility that are usually associated with bureaucracy.
>
> (Hayek, 1935b, p. 237)

Indeed, Hayek maintained that any such attempts at 'pseudo competition' would simply combine the most problematic aspects of full central planning and a system of free competition. Essentially, 'so effective is the system of free competition', based upon the myriad actions of individuals within the system, that even if it were possible for a dictator to control the entire economy, 'the best the dictator could do in such a case would be to imitate as closely as possible what would happen under free competition' (Hayek, 1991, p. 30).

There is a significantly body of literature that examines the theoretical nuances of the socialist calculation debate that it is beyond the scope of this book to address. (Lavoie, 1985; Cottrell and Cockshott, 1993; O'Neill, 1996; Boettke, 2000). Inevitably, there are varying interpretations of its true nature and alternative accounts of which side won. What many early reviewers of the debate, including Schumpeter, failed to recognise was the significance of Hayek's shift to a dynamic model of equilibrium. The prevalence of the static neoclassical model had allowed proponents of planning to maintain at least the theoretical possibility of carrying out all the simultaneous equations necessary to achieve equilibrium at any given point in time. Lavoie (1981) has stressed that although this may apply under static conditions, the dynamic nature of the model offered by Hayek in particular renders the data for such calculations inaccessible. What is significant for our purpose is that Hayek's move to a dynamic model necessarily occasioned, as Bruce Caldwell has argued, a broader shift in his thought towards an attempt to understand the social conditions necessary for economic coordination to occur *over time*.[4]

It was in the context of the debate that Hayek (1948b) made his most significant contribution to the socialist calculation debate and indeed to economic theory in general, his paper, 'Economics and Knowledge'. The work was also to prove a central consideration in the award of his Nobel Memorial Prize in Economics almost forty years later.[5] If Hayek's concept of liberty emerged out of his economics, then this was the point at which his move towards political economy began. The fundamental question he sought to address was how economic coordination is possible under conditions of constant change, and it is in this paper that his epistemic conception of the economy first emerged (Hayek, 1948b, 1983).

Hayek (1994, p. 206) would recall that it 'was with a feeling of sudden illumination, sudden enlightenment that I . . . wrote that lecture'. The paper claimed that economic theory should be primarily concerned not with the allocation of scarce resources or the division of labour, but with the utilisation of knowledge. 'I was aware', he remembered, 'that I was putting down things which were fairly well known in a new form. And perhaps it was the most exciting moment in my career when I saw it in print'. In the paper he reflected that, 'I have long felt that the concept of equilibrium itself and the methods which we employ in pure analysis have a clear meaning only when confined to the analysis of the action of a single person' and he continued that, 'we are really passing into a different sphere and silently introducing a new element of altogether different character when we apply it to the explanation of the interactions of a number of different individuals' (Hayek, 1948b, p. 35). In a real economy, people change their plans either because of their own subjective revisions, or owing to an objective change in circumstances. Of course, plans will often be changed and 'equilibrium connections will be severed' (Hayek, 1948b, p. 52). Overall, however, the tendency towards equilibrium over time will prevail, hence the new dynamism of his theory.

Hayek argued that economists had made the mistake of assuming that the economic data they use in their modelling had also been given to all the economic agents within the model, but this was not at all the case. Instead, knowledge was divided and 'the division of knowledge, which is quite analogous to, and at least as important as, the problem of the division of labour', so that,

> The problem which we pretend to solve is how the spontaneous interaction of a number of people, each possessing only bits of knowledge, brings about a state of affairs in which prices correspond to costs, etc., and which

could be brought about by deliberate direction only by somebody who possessed the combined knowledge of all those individuals.

(Hayek, 1948b, p. 51)

The recognition of subjective ignorance of the overall economic whole meant that the proper role for the economist was to address 'propositions about the acquisition of knowledge'. The object of economic study ought therefore to be, 'how can the combination of fragments of knowledge existing in different minds bring about results which, if they were to be brought about deliberately, would require a knowledge on the part of the directing mind which no single person can possess?' (Hayek, 1948b, pp. 46–54). In 1945, Hayek expanded on the consequences of his shift to a dynamic model of equilibrium for our thinking about prices, social rules and institutions. Reflecting on both his debate with Keynes and with the advocates of planning, he wrote that 'the sort of knowledge with which I have been concerned is knowledge of the kind which by its nature cannot enter into statistics and therefore cannot be conveyed to any central authority in statistical form' (Hayek, 1948c, 83).

Essentially, knowledge has two characteristics that prevent such a conveyance: it is always dispersed, Hayek's main focus in 1936, and it is often tacit in nature. Tacit knowledge is 'the knowledge of the particular circumstances of time and place.' It can be compared to skill or technique and for this reason is essentially inarticulable. Consequently, insisted Hayek, knowledge is always best employed by the 'man on the spot'. 'But' he wrote,

> the 'man on the spot' cannot decide solely on the basis of his limited but intimate knowledge of the facts of his immediate surroundings. There still remains the problem of communicating to him such further information as he needs to fit his decisions into the whole pattern of changes of the larger economic system.
>
> (1948b, p. 85)

The question of how economic coordination is able to take place on the grand scale and across great distances, therefore remains, because 'experience shows us', he wrote,

> that something of this sort does happen, since the empirical observation that prices do tend to correspond to costs was the beginning of our science. But in our analysis, instead of showing what bits of information the different persons must possess in order to bring about that result, we fall in effect back on the assumption that everybody knows everything and so evade any real solution of the problem.
>
> (Hayek, 1948b, p. 51)

However, having recently read Karl Popper's (2002) *The Logic of Scientific Discovery*, he conceded that verification of this is highly problematic. 'I am afraid' he admitted, 'that I am now getting to a stage where it becomes exceedingly difficult to say what exactly are the assumptions on the basis of which we assert that there will be a tendency toward equilibrium and to claim that our analysis has an application to the real world. I cannot pretend that I have as yet got much further on this point' (Hayek, 1948a, p. 48). He never got much further with it yet maintained that the tendency existed and thus remained faithful to his conception of the economy as tending towards equilibrium over the long term.

We can, nonetheless, identify two elements to Hayek's explanation of how coordination occurs. The first develops the Misesian emphasis on the price mechanism. For Hayek it was a 'marvel' condensing information relating to a vast number of economic variables into a single symbol. 'We must look at the price system as such a mechanism for communicating information if we want to understand its real function' he wrote:

> The most significant fact about this system is the economy of knowledge with which it operates, or how little the individual participants need to know in order to be able to take the right action. In abbreviated form, by a kind of symbol, only the most essential information is passed on and passed on only to those concerned.
>
> (Hayek, 1948c, p. 86)

In the absence of this marvel, 'one of the greatest triumphs of the human mind' – though not of human design – effective coordination over time would be an impossibility.

The second element in establishing the conditions that enable a tendency towards equilibrium over time is the existence of stable rules and institutions. For prices to function effectively, a whole range of other conditions must be in place. A degree of socio-economic stability is necessary such that realistic plans can be expected to be met. Firms and individuals simply cannot plan for the future in highly unstable conditions. Fundamental is that everyone should act according to the 'rules of the game'. Some of these will be cultural, with individuals being expected to behave in a certain way under certain conditions. Also crucial are the explicit rules – or laws – of society. It is only the presence of such rules and laws, which like prices serve as a guide to action, that renders economic coordination over time possible.

It was this insight that would occasion Hayek's transformation, not simply from a static to a dynamic model of equilibrium, but from economics to political economy and his new intellectual project of 'a re-examination of the age old concept of freedom under the law, the basic conception of traditional liberalism' (Hayek, 1967c, p. 92; Caldwell, 1988). In the context of Hayek's new epistemic economics, individual liberty became paramount, as the dispersed and tacit nature of knowledge means that coordination necessarily depends upon the individual's ability to make use of their knowledge as they see fit within a rule-based order. From this epistemic perspective, freedom itself becomes understood in economic terms as the freedom to act within the market. He therefore came to consider planning not only as irrational, but also as inimical to liberty.

Planning vs freedom

An explicit portrayal of planning in these terms was signalled by Hayek's (1997a, 1997b) pamphlet 'Freedom and the Economic System'.[6] In it, it becomes clear that by freedom, Hayek meant 'freedom in economic affairs' or 'economic freedom'. In using the term economic freedom, I wish to stress that Hayek regarded the economy, or as we shall see more specifically the market, as the field of social life where freedom is realised, or else is thwarted. It is therefore a very different rendering of the phrase from that presented by socialists for whom it was associated with freedom from want. Indeed, we can view Hayek's adoption of the term as discursively subversive, as he sought to disassociate it from its more widely held socialist connotations.

In addition to marking Hayek's first sustained writing on freedom, the pamphlet is interesting for the way in which he approaches the issue. The argument is framed in such a way that the intellectual and cultural benefits of freedom are portrayed as paramount. This sounds very much like the ethical New Liberal concern for self-development, espoused by thinkers such as T.H. Green and by influential liberals in the late 19th and early 20th century. Yet, as we shall see in the next chapter, Hayek regarded New Liberalism as deeply injurious to the longer liberal tradition. Later in his career he would stress the importance of economic freedom on other grounds, such as the size of the population it can support. However, here Hayek went on to assert that the benefits of free intellectual life can only be enjoyed if first there is control over one's 'economic life'. Only when freedom is conceived of in this way, and government kept as far out of economic life as possible, will all other freedoms, cultural, intellectual and artistic, become possible. 'State control over economic life, which is so generally wanted', insisted Hayek, must 'necessarily lead to the suppression of intellectual and cultural freedom' as only ideas that promoted the official plan of the day would be tolerated (Hayek, 1997b, p. 191). As such, although still engaging with the issue on the same intellectual terrain as the New Liberals, his political recommendations are the reverse. Government could not extend freedom, rather it should be considered primarily as a source of threat.

At the outbreak of the Second World War, the Ministry for Economic Warfare moved into the L.S.E.'s Houghton Street campus and the School itself was relocated to Cambridge where it occupied Peterhouse College (Dahrendorf, 1995).[7] By the middle of 1940, the majority of Hayek's colleagues in the economics profession had been called upon by the government to participate in the war effort. Being of Austrian birth and only having become a British citizen in 1938, Hayek was prevented from doing so.[8] His lack of official war work would only distance him further from many others in the profession who were impressed by what planning could achieve when a clear goal was set, whether it was aircraft production or the allocation of scarce resources under rationing. Lionel Robbins provides perhaps the best example of just such a convert to the potential power of government to achieve socially desirable ends. During the war he served at the head of the economists advising the coalition government and subsequently accepted the basics of the new creed of Keynesian demand management that came to the fore following victory and even renounced the Austrian inspired advice he offered the government during the economic crisis of the 1930s (Howson, 2011). Hayek's relative isolation and reduced teaching hours because of the enlistment of potential students left him with time to fill. It was during this period that he set about what he envisaged would become a single multivolume work on 'the abuse and decline of reason' designed to answer the question that had begun to pose itself in 'Freedom and the Economic System': how had liberalism lost its way so badly?

The project was never completed in the manner Hayek had envisioned. Partly, this was because he became alarmed at the hold planning had taken of the official mind during the war and so he rushed his central thesis out in print in 1944's *The Road to Serfdom*.[9] It is in this book that 'the conflict between planning and freedom' emerges most starkly (Hayek, 2001, p. 227). That distinction could be witnessed, argued Hayek, by observing developments in Germany under Hitler's National Socialists. Although we will examine the veracity of this claim further in Chapter 5, for him the country was a planned economy in much the same way as Soviet Russia, and the defining feature of the regime was its desire to shape the economy, a desire that rendered it truly 'socialist' in his terms as much as in the Nazi's own. Hayek did nothing to draw out the different ways in which the two economies operated. For him, both were examples of his monolithically conceived 'planning'.[10]

Nineteenth century liberals like Alexis de Tocqueville and the historian Lord Acton had 'warned' wrote Hayek (2001, p. 13) 'that socialism means slavery', and yet society had 'steadily moved in the direction of socialism' ever since. Further warnings were cited: A.V. Dicey (2008) had written of the dangers to individual liberty associated with socialism. Hillaire Belloc (1912) had also worried that the reforms associated with the New Liberal government would lead in due course to *The Servile State* in a manner that George Orwell (2001) regarded as prescient. In the 1920s Lord Hewert (1929), the Lord Chief Justice of England, had decried the rise of *The New Despotism* associated with the expansion of state bureaucracy. The message of the book is clear: planning, and more specifically socialism,

> the great utopia of the last few generations . . . is not only unachievable, but . . . to strive for it produces something so utterly different that few of those who now wish it would be prepared to accept the consequences,

These included, above all, the rise of regimes such as Nazism (Hayek, 2001, p. 32).

Given the cross-party support for 'planning', Hayek provocatively dedicated his book to 'the socialists of all parties'. There was no reason to assume, he insisted, that Britain was immune to the totalitarian outcomes witnessed elsewhere. Although planning was a legitimate goal in wartime, with the entire nation set on a single end, a material victory over Germany would mean little if German ideas were allowed to set the direction of public policy when the war came to a close. Indeed, those ideas are presented as a more enduring and dangerous threat than German weapons.[11] The book pleads with its English readership to rediscover 'the rule of freedom which had been achieved in England' and 'seemed destined to spread throughout the world' but which 'by about 1870. . . began to retreat' in the face of the new ideals of planning and organisation that had been emanating from the newly unified *Kaiserreich* (Hayek, 2001, p. 21). Only under conditions of that older economic liberalism would it become possible to make the best use of knowledge in society. A full understanding of this older liberalism therefore became central to Hayek's intellectual project.

The limits of Hayek's epistemic economics

Despite the fundamental importance of individual liberty to Hayek's new epistemic conception of the economy, he did not pursue a consideration of the conditions necessary to allow the woman or 'man on the spot' to make optimum use of their knowledge within the most prevalent unit of economic cooperation – the private firm. He was clear that although state planning at the level of an entire economy is irrational, all economic activity is in a sense planned activity. The critical issue, he reflected, is 'who is to do the planning', and whether it is 'to be done centrally, by one authority for the whole economic system, or is to be divided among many individuals' (Hayek, 1948c, p. 79). For him, it was emphatically the latter. There is, however, an ambiguity in the term 'many individuals' and Hayek does not offer further specifics regarding who these planners ought to be.

Although almost all individuals will have personal long-term plans, which will predominantly involve choice of occupation and even place of work – crucial elements in Hayek's conception of market freedom – this does not mean every individual will be a constant and active participant in the plan-making processes that underpin market coordination. This sort of radical epistemic individualism would require economic collaboration based only on contracts with each act of collaboration subject to a specific and well-defined agreement. This, however, is not how individuals function as actors in the real economy. Instead, those with capital usually prefer to form private firms that employ individuals on the basis of a more expansive, less tightly defined, form of contract. Those who must work to support themselves generally prefer to work for such private firms, as the period of employment, and hence their income, is assured for longer than if they were entirely autonomous market actors entering into a contract with another party for each discrete service as is generally necessary when self-employed.

There are many good reasons why firms are formed. As Ronald Coase (1937) argued, it is simply often cheaper to direct tasks via command to a retained workforce than it is to negotiate and enforce contracts for every necessary process.[12] The ability of firms to issue commands by fiat is enabled by the incompleteness of employment contracts. The non-contractual nature of relationships and processes within the firm renders it an essentially non-market sphere within which the 'marvel' of the price mechanism cannot function. Therefore, this method of communicating knowledge does not exist inside such enterprises. Although the existence of effective prices in the market can guide action within the firm, those who plan on its behalf, deciding where to allocate resources internally, are subject to the same 'groping in the dark' that Mises had associated with planned national economies. In Austrian terms, this, inevitably, is a major barrier to rationality within the firm.

In addition to the lack of prices, the dispersed and tacit nature of knowledge also creates problems within the planned enterprise that constitutes a private firm. Inevitably, those who follow commands within firms – namely employees – are not generally involved in the planning process. The problems associated with state planning are therefore again mirrored within the firm. The impossibility of the full conveyance of knowledge to the planners results in a reduction of epistemic effectiveness. Hayek, however, chose not to apply the insights of his epistemic economics to the planned economy of the firm. Given that his commitment to freedom was a product of his belief in the beneficial effects it had for the use of knowledge, this omission was to have a fundamental impact on how he conceived of liberty itself.

Conclusion

In this chapter I have shown how, following his appointment at the L.S.E., Hayek embarked upon his second major intellectual engagement of the inter-war years: his opposition to 'planning'. In his inaugural address he invoked the founders of the classical tradition in his opposition to the 'utopian' schemes associated with socialism. What concerned Hayek and Robbins during this period was the pervasive popularity of the idea of planning, even if its economic ramifications had, they argued, rarely been thought through. One product of Hayek's participation in the socialist calculation debates was his explicit shift to a dynamic model of equilibrium. This almost immediately provoked a consideration on his part of the conditions necessary for economic coordination over time to occur; they were twofold: effective prices and a stable framework of rules and laws.

These two conditions were necessary because of the dispersed and tacit nature of knowledge. This renders it incommunicable in its totality to a central planner. Even market socialist schemes would fall down, Hayek argued, because they are unable to communicate changes in circumstance quickly enough to allow changes to decisions on investment to take place in the way that the price mechanism can. Ultimately, all such schemes could do would be to impersonate the market system and eventually individuals would have to be directed into certain occupations by those in authority. Therefore, not only was planning irrational, the absence of economic freedom would also result in restrictions on a range of other personal freedoms. From the late 1930s onwards, Hayek starkly equated common ownership and planning with tyranny and private property

The socialist calculation debates 43

and the free market with liberty. However, he did not apply the insights of his epistemic turn to an analysis of relationships within the firm. In effect, only those economic processes under the direction of the state, rather than of private individuals, were presented as epistemically compromised. As in the first of his major intellectual engagements regarding the business cycle, out of his opposition to planning emerged a depiction of government as the force that jeopardises market freedom.

Notes

1 Although not taking issue with the periodisation of the debates, John O'Neill (1995, 1996) has argued that Hayek and Neurath share a similar methodological position – being concerned with the way knowledge is used in society whereas for Mises and the market socialists the fundamental concern is the most effective means of accounting. Nonetheless, substantively, both Hayek and his mentor defended a market predicated on private property whereas their opponents advocate common ownership

2 These were not few in number and included Oswald Mosley, at the time a radical Labour Party Member of Parliament who would go on to form the British Union of Fascists, see Skidelsky (1981). Also, Sidney and Beatrice Webb (1936). Even Lloyd George was to visit Hitler and approve of his oversight of the German economy in 1936.

3 For an alternative reading of Schumpeter as providing an ironic caricature of the market socialist position see (Boettke et al., 2017),

4 This section of the book is indebted to Caldwell's (1988, 2004) crucial work on Hayek's transformation in this regard.

5 The prize was established in 1969 by the Sveriges Riksbank. It was not established by Alfred Nobel in his will in 1895 and should not, therefore, be considered a Nobel Prize proper.

6 The piece was published in both short and expanded form.

7 It was Keynes who helped Hayek to find rooms at Kings and Hayek's son Laurence recalled the two patrolling the college roofs at night to check the blackout was being enforced (Ebenstein, 2001, p. 106). After some months Hayek found a property with more space on Malting Lane to which he moved his family (Hayek, 1994, p. 46).

8 Nonetheless, he did try to offer his service to the war effort. He wrote 'Some Notes on Propaganda in Germany' advising the BBC regarding how best to appeal to a German audience (Hayek, 1939a). He also wrote offering his services to the Ministry of Information suggesting he was especially qualified to help organise and advise the propaganda effort, though he apparently received no reply (Hayek, 1939b).

9 The other elements of the project were published as 'Scientism and the Study of Society' and 'The Counter-Revolution of Science'. These appeared in the pages of *Economica*, from 1941 to 1943. Some four decades later, Hayek intended his last work *The Fatal Conceit* as a final completion of the endeavour. (Caldwell, 2004, p. 219).

10 The literature on the German economy under Nazism is vast. For an introductory overview see Tooze (2008).

11 Germany and German thinkers are discussed almost exclusively in a negative fashion. The brief exceptions are passing references to Goethe and von Humboldt, and also a quote from Hölderlin. Even Emmanuel Kant, whose concept of the *Rechtsstaat* informs the basic argument of the book is mentioned only once (Hayek, 2001, pp. 7, 24, 85).

12 Alchian and Demsetz (1972) take a different position, on the basis that an employment contract is 'subject to continuous renegotiation' and therefore the employer cannot be regarded as holding an autocratic position. For my counter argument, see the third section of chapter 4 and also the book's conclusion.

Works cited

Aldcroft, D. 2001. *The European Economy 1914–2000.* London: Routledge.

Alchian, A. and Demsetz, H. 1972. 'Production, Information Costs, and Economic Organization', *The American Economic Review* 62:5, pp. 777–795.

Barberis, P., McHugh, J. and Tyldesley, M. (Eds.) 2005. *Encyclopaedia of British and Irish Political Organisations, Parties, Groups and Movements of the 20th Century.* London: Continuum.

Belloc, H. 1912. *The Servile State.* London: T.L. Foulis.

Boettke, P. (Ed.). 2000. *Socialism and the Market: The Socialist Calculation Debate Revisited* (9 volumes). London: Routledge.

Boettke, P., Solomon, S.M. and Storr, V.H. 2017. 'Schumpeter, Socialism, and Irony', *Critical Review* 29:4, pp. 415–446.

Booth, A and Melvyn, P. 1985. *Employment, Capital and Economic Policy: Great Britain, 1918-1939.* Oxford: Basil Blackwell.

Caldwell, B. 1988. 'Hayek's Transformation', *History of Political Economy* 20:4, pp. 513–548.

Caldwell, B. 2004. *Hayek's Challenge: An Intellectual Biography of F.A. Hayek.* Chicago: University of Chicago Press.

Carpenter, L.P. 1976. 'Corporatism in Britain', *Journal of Contemporary History* 11:1 pp. 3–25.

Coase, R.H. 1937. 'The Nature of the Firm', *Economica* 4, pp. 386–405.

Cottrell, A. and Cockshott, P. 1993. 'Calculation, Complexity and Planning', *Review of Political Economy* 5:1, pp. 73–112.

Dahrendorf, R. 1995. *LSE: A History of the London School of Economics and Political Science, 1895–1995.* Oxford: Oxford University Press.

Dicey, A.V. 2008. *Lectures on the Relation between Law and Public Opinion in England During the Nineteenth Century.* R. VandeWetering (Ed.). Indianapolis: Liberty Fund.

Ebenstein, A. 2001. *Friedrich Hayek: A Biography.* New York: Palgrave, St Martin's Press.

Hayek, F.A. 1935a. 'The Nature and History of the Problem' in Friedrich Hayek (Ed.), *Collectivist Economic Planning* (pp. 1–40). London: Routledge & Kegan Paul.

Hayek, F.A. 1935b. 'The Present State of the Debate' in Friedrich Hayek (Ed.), *Collectivist Economic Planning* (pp. 201–243). London: Routledge & Kegan Paul.

Hayek, F.A. 1939a. 'Some Notes on Propaganda in Germany'. Friedrich A. von Hayek papers, Box no. 61, Folder no. 3, Hoover Institution Archives.

Hayek, F.A. 1939b. 'Correspondence with F.W Ogilvie'. Friedrich A. von Hayek papers, Box no. 61, Folder no. 5, Hoover Institution Archives.

Hayek, F.A. 1948a. 'Individualism: True and False' [1945] in Friedrich Hayek (Ed.), *Individualism and Economic Order* (pp. 1–33). Chicago: University of Chicago Press.

Hayek, F.A. 1948b. 'Economics and Knowledge' [1936] in Friedrich Hayek (Ed.), *Individualism and Economic Order* (pp. 33–56). Chicago: University of Chicago Press.

Hayek, F.A. 1948c. 'The Use of Knowledge in Society' [1945] in Friedrich Hayek (Ed.), *Individualism and Economic Order* (pp. 77–91). Chicago: University of Chicago Press.

Hayek, F.A. 1967c. 'Kinds of Rationalism' [1964] in Friedrich Hayek (Ed.), *Studies in Philosophy, Politics and Economics* (pp. 82–95). London: Routledge & Kegan Paul.

Hayek, F.A. 1983. *Nobel Prize Winning Economist.* Ed. Armen Alchian UCLA Charles E. Young Research Library, Department of Special Collections, Oral History Transcript no. 300/324.

Hayek, F.A. 1991. 'The Trend of Economic Thinking' [1933] in W.W. Bartley III and Stephen Kresge (Eds.), *The Trend of Economic Thinking: The Collected Works of FA Hayek, Vol. 3* (pp. 13–30). Chicago: University of Chicago Press.

Hayek, F.A. 1994. *Hayek on Hayek: An Autobiographical Dialogue.* Stephen Kresge and Leif Warner (Eds.). Chicago: University of Chicago Press.

Hayek, F.A. 1997a. 'Socialist Calculation: The Competitive "Solution"' [1940] in Bruce Caldwell (Ed.), *Socialism and War: The Collected Works of F.A Hayek, Vol. 10* (pp. 117–140). Chicago: University of Chicago Press.

Hayek, F.A. 1997b. 'Freedom and the Economic System' [1938] in Bruce Caldwell (Ed.), *Socialism and War: The Collected Works of F.A Hayek, Vol. 10* (pp. 189–212). Chicago: University of Chicago Press.

Hayek, F.A. 2001. *The Road to Serfdom*. London: Routledge.

Hewert, G. 1929. *The New Despotism*. London: Ernest Benn.

Howson, S. 2011. *Lionel Robbins*. Cambridge: Cambridge University Press.

Lavoie, D. 1981. 'A Critique of the Standard Account of the Socialist Calculation Debate', *The Journal of Libertarian Studies* 5:1, pp. 41–87.

Lavoie, D. 1985. *Rivalry and Central Planning: The Socialist Calculation Debate Reconsidered*. Cambridge: Cambridge University Press.

Lenin, V.I. 1934. 'The Immediate Tasks of Soviet Government' in *Collected Works, Vol. 27* (pp. 235–278). New York: International Publishers.

Macmillan, H. 1938. *The Middle Way*. London: Macmillan.

Marwick, A. 1964. 'Middle Opinion in the Thirties', *English Historical Review* 79:311, pp. 285–298.

Mises, L. 1935. 'Economic Calculation in the Socialist Commonwealth' in Friedrich Hayek (Ed.), *Collectivist Economic Planning* (pp. 87–130). London: Routledge & Kegan Paul.

Neurath, O. 1973. 'Through War Economy to Economy in Kind' in R.S. Cohen and M. Neurath (Eds.), *Empiricism and Sociology* (pp. 123–157). Dordrecht: Reidel.

O'Neill, J. 1995. 'In Partial Praise of a Positivist: The work of Otto Neurath', *Radical Philosophy* 74, pp. 29–58.

O'Neill, J. 1996. 'Who Won the Socialist Calculation Debate?' *History of Political Thought* 17:3, pp. 431–442.

Orwell, G. 2001. 'Second Thoughts on James Burnham' in Peter Davison (Ed.), *Complete Works, Volume 18* (pp. 268–284). London: Secker and Warburg.

Popper, K. 2002. *The Logic of Scientific Discovery*. London: Routledge.

Pugh, M. 2006. 'The Liberal Party and the Popular Front', *English Historical Review* 121:4, pp. 1327–1350.

Ritschel, D. 1997. *The Politics of Planning. The Debate on Economic Planning in Britain in the 1930s*. Oxford: Oxford University Press.

Skidelsky, R. 1981. *Oswald Mosley*. London: Papermac.

Thorpe, A. 2008. *A History of the British Labour Party*. London: Palgrave Macmillan.

Thorpe, D.R. 2010. *Supermac: The Life of Harold MacMillan*, London: Random House.

Tooze, A. 2008. 'The Economic History of the Nazi Regime' in Jane Caplan (Ed.), *Short Oxford History of Nazi Germany* (pp. 168–194). Oxford: Oxford University Press.

Webb, S. and Webb, B 1936. *Soviet Communism: A New Civilisation?* London: Charles Scribner's Sons.

3 Liberalism true and false

Even though Hayek had insisted that 'probably nothing has done so much harm to the liberal cause as the wooden insistence of some liberals on certain rough rules of thumb, above all the principle of *laissez-faire*', he struggled to convince many readers of the *Road to Serfdom* that he really was offering something new, with a fresh, positive role for government in creating the framework within which economic freedom could flourish. In the United States in particular, Hayek was regarded as an unsophisticated champion of the old school, often by allies and enemies alike. A review in *The Nation* was revealingly entitled 'Back to Grandfather: Dr Hayek's Guide to the Pre-War Era' (Chase, 1945; Finer, 1945). Likewise, an editorial in the *New Republic* (1945) wrote that Hayek's book 'found an enthusiastic response in the United States among those who are using the economic theories of the 1880s to justify the business practices of the 1940s.' Yet even his allies, the long-standing opponents of Franklin Delano Roosevelt's New Deal, who regarded the work as offering their position strong intellectual support, also understood it as signalling a call for a return to an older 'common sense' approach to the economy.[1]

In Britain Hayek's admittedly political book also caused a stir. On the 4th June 1945, in his first post-war general election campaign broadcast, Winston Churchill suggested that planning might result in a British Gestapo (Shearmur, 1996). In this he was inspired, according to Macmillan (1969, p. 32), by *The Road to Serfdom*. The claim caused some controversy and created the impression that Churchill was labelling his wartime colleagues in the Cabinet as potential Nazis. The following night Clement Attlee, the leader of the Labour Party, in his own broadcast, responded that Churchill's speech consisted of 'the second-hand version of the academic views of an Austrian professor, Friedrich von Hayek.' (Ebenstein, 2001, p. 138). The subsequent Labour landslide indicates that Attlee's promise of democratic oversight of a larger section of the economy appealed more to the British people than the warnings of Churchill or Hayek.

What most worried Hayek was that many of those who considered themselves liberals did not recognise the dangers his book had signalled. Even Robbins found it difficult to accept Hayek's description of the dangers facing post-war Britain. Ronald Coase recalled that 'in Britain, living in what is a very tolerant society, few people could imagine that this was going to be the result. I remember Lionel Robbins saying to me this is a very fine book from the continental point of view. It just wasn't British.' (McPhail and Farrant, 2013, p. 974).[2] John Maynard Keynes (2012g) wrote to Hayek with a sympathetic reading but maintained that 'moderate planning will be safe if those carrying it out are rightly orientated in their own minds and hearts to the moral issue . . . what we need' he wrote, 'is the restoration of right moral thinking – a return to proper moral values in our social philosophy. If only you could turn your crusade in that direction you would not feel quite so much like Don Quixote.' For Hayek, however, such arguments were further evidence of the extent to which such 'liberals' had become unmoored from the tradition's original principles.

The British/continental binary

Hayek came to feel that for a successful case to be made against planning and economic intervention, it would first be necessary to disentangle liberalism from some of the political and ideological alliances it had formed over the course of the 19th century. 'That nineteenth-century liberalism did not succeed more fully' he insisted (1948d) was 'due largely to . . . historical accidents' as 'it successively joined forces first with nationalism and later with socialism' in its great struggle against arbitrary royal rule. Yet 'both forces' were 'equally incompatible with its main principle'. Its alliance with socialism in particular had led certain liberals to espouse an unreflective commitment to 'unlimited democracy', which, as we shall see in Chapter 5, Hayek believed constituted the major threat to market freedom in the western world. In his lecture, 'Individualism: True and False', delivered just months after the end of the Second World War, Hayek argued that:

> The difficulty which we encounter is not merely the familiar fact that the current political terms are notoriously ambiguous or even that the same term often means nearly the opposite to different groups. There is the much more serious fact that the same word frequently appears to unite people who in fact believe in contradictory and irreconcilable ideals. Terms like "liberalism" or "democracy," "capitalism" or "socialism," today no longer stand for coherent systems of ideas. They have come to describe aggregations of quite heterogeneous principles and facts which historical accident has associated with these words but which have little in common beyond having been advocated at different times by the same people or even merely under the same name.
>
> (Hayek, 1948a, pp. 2–3)

Hayek therefore attempted to dispel this confusion in political language by describing what he believed 'liberalism' should really stand for. In Michael Freeden's terms, he embarked on a campaign to 'decontest' the liberal tradition.

The 19th century occupies an ambivalent position in Hayek's work. It was the period in which market freedom was most closely realised particularly, he believed, in Britain. Yet, the century also witnessed a dangerous decline in respect for the conditions required for that freedom to flourish. This pertained among certain liberals just as much as anyone else. We are faced then with the counter-intuitive fact that a figure strongly associated with classical liberalism rejected the prevailing intellectual legacy of the century most closely associated with it. The frequent characterisation of Hayek's work as an 'effort to provide a comprehensive restatement of nineteenth-century liberalism' (Spieker, 2013, p. 920) is, therefore, as erroneous today as it was when advanced by the unfavourable reviewers of *The Road to Serfdom*.

Hayek's explanation for the disconnect between the economic realities and the intellectual direction of the 19th century is to be found in his theory of discursive change. It simply took time, he argued, for the great ideas of an age to find purchase in politics and the popular mind, and thus impact lived experience. Hayek (1960a, p. 445) approvingly quoted Keynes, sharing his belief that 'practical men, who believe themselves to be quite exempt from any intellectual influence, are usually the slaves of some defunct economist.' (Hayek, 1960a, p. 445). It was clearly the case, he felt, that,

> People rarely know or care whether the commonplace ideas of their day have come to them from Aristotle or Locke, Rousseau or Marx, or from some professor whose views were fashionable among the intellectuals twenty years ago.
>
> (Hayek, 1960a, p. 113)

So it was that only in the 19th century that the 'true individualism' necessary for market freedom took hold. It had, however, begun 'its modern development with John Locke, and particularly with Bernard Mandeville and David Hume, and achieved full stature for the first time in the work of Josiah Tucker, Adam Ferguson, and Adam Smith' as well as in the work of 'Burke, and the English Whigs' (Hayek, 1948a, p. 4). Although the relationship of these theorists to Whiggism as a political movement is complex and contested (Forbes, 1975; Burrow, 1988), Hayek considered them prime exemplars of the Whig intellectual tradition. True individualism, which Hayek regarded as primarily a phenomenon of the market, was, for him, the core tenet of authentic, true liberalism.[3]

This individualism conceived of social development as being, in the words of Adam Ferguson, the product of 'human action but not of design'. It was in the work of Ferguson, along with that of Hume and Smith, that Hayek locates the origins of the concept of spontaneous order. Drawing on this 'Whig' tradition, Hayek depicted spontaneous orders as developing over time, the product of myriad interactions. They are social processes and institutions that emerge gradually to meet particular needs. Developing largely on the basis of trial and error, evolving based on experience, knowledge of best practice inheres in such processes and institutions in a way that it cannot in those that are rationally designed. Hayek quoted Michael Polanyi (1951) as providing the best contemporary articulation of the concept:

> When order is achieved among human beings by allowing them to interact with each other on their own initiative – subject only to the laws which uniformly apply to all of them – we have a system of spontaneous order in society
>
> (Hayek, 1960a, p. 160).[4]

The sum of all economic processes and interactions, which Hayek later termed the *catallaxy*, could be considered the acme of spontaneous order. Hayek was uncomfortable with the word 'economy' on the basis that in its Aristotelian origins it referred to the expenditure and organisation of the household, or *oikos*. What is generally referred to as the economy was, for him, the very opposite of this, not an organization to be overseen by a head, but a spontaneous order. Furthermore, it is important to note that for Hayek there were not simply two types of order: natural and constructed. A spontaneous order was in fact a third type of order: it was something grown in the absence of human direction, but that growth could only occur because of the existence of human-made rules. It was important that these laws themselves, however, were evolved, in the manner of the English Common Law, rather than designed.

Hayek identified this respect for evolved institutions with 'liberalism in the English sense' (unfortunately, the confusion of English and British is a recurrent error in his work). Crucially, it did not look to state power for institutional design, thus averting that particular threat to market freedom. True individualism understood, Hayek (1948b, p. 6) argued, 'that there is no other way toward an understanding of social phenomena but through our understanding of individual actions directed toward other people and guided by their expected behaviour'. It therefore gave rise to a liberalism that recognised the importance of abstract rules that would guide individuals in their actions but would not compel them to act in a certain manner. Hayek's endorsement of British liberalism was closely linked to his epistemic economics. 'Our submission to general principles is necessary' he wrote, 'because we cannot be guided in our practical action by full knowledge and evaluation of all the consequences. So long as men are not omniscient, the only way in which freedom can be given to the individual is by such general rules to delimit the sphere in which the decision is his' (Hayek, 1948a, p. 19).

In contrast, 'the liberalism prevalent on the continent' was characterised by 'false individualism' (Hayek, 1948a, p. 28). This individualism imagined it was within the power of the individual, or the individual and a group of collaborators, to plan social society in order to achieve a particular set of outcomes. It was, therefore, entirely at odds with the market freedom Hayek had placed at the centre of his thought. False individualism was the product, he maintained, of the misapplication of methods appropriate to the natural sciences to the study of society. It originated with the French Enlightenment, being ultimately a product of René Descartes' distinction between mind and matter, which gave rise to the mistaken belief that the physical world could be comprehended in its entirety.[5] The 17th century saw the ascendancy of a 'favourite idea of positivist sociology' propagated by men such as Condorcet, d'Alembert and Lagrange: 'that of an observer to whom physical and social phenomena would appear in the same light, because "a stranger to our race . . . would study human society as we study those of the beavers and bees."' (Hayek, 2010b, p. 173). The success of the natural sciences in explaining the physical world was such 'that they soon came to exercise an extraordinary fascination on those working in other fields, who rapidly began to imitate their teaching and vocabulary. Thus was established the 'tyranny' which 'the methods and technique of the sciences in the narrow sense of the term have ever since exercised over the other subjects' (Hayek, 2010a, p. 78). Hayek termed this intellectual imperialism 'scientism'.

Subsequently, the French revolution 'swept away the old system of colleges and universities' and 'thus a whole generation grew up to whom that great storehouse of social wisdom . . . the great literature of all ages, was a closed book' (Hayek, 2010b, pp. 175–176). Even more significantly, he wrote, the Revolutionary Convention established an institution that was to become 'the source of the scientistic hubris' and 'a model imitated by the whole world': the *Ecole Polytechnique*.[6] Science, rather than the arts or humanities, informed the practices and ethos of the *Ecole*, and it was here, argued Hayek, that those who would formulate some of the most grandiose 'scientistic' designs were tutored:

> it was in this atmosphere that Saint-Simon conceived some of the earliest and most fantastic plans for the reorganisation of society . . . it was at the *Ecole Polytechnique* where, during the first twenty years of its existence, Auguste Comte, Prosper Enfantin, Victor Considérant, and some hundreds of later Saint- Simonians and Fourierists received their training, followed by a succession of social reformers throughout the century down to Georges Sorel.
>
> (Hayek, 1948b, p. 181)[7]

So it was that 'the present popularity of "economic planning" is directly traceable to the prevalence of the scientistic ideas' and forms of thought that significantly predated economics (Hayek, 1948a, p. 156).[8] Later in his career, he would term this mindset 'constructivism'.

Hayek's dismissal of 18th century French thought as overly rationalistic is supported by more recent work by Pierre Rosanvallon (2002). Conversely, Helena Rosenblatt (2018) has argued for the centrality of France to the development of the liberal tradition as a whole, thus rejecting Hayek's analysis. The manner in which Hayek is forced to incorporate figures such as Montesquieu and Tocqueville into liberalism in the English poses a serious problem for his binary. Given the many exceptions Hayek had to make to his genealogy we must consider why he was so intent on thinking in national terms. One reason is indicated by subsequent interviews conducted with Hayek by his intended biographer, William Warren Bartley III. Hayek reflected that while in the US he would read alone and,

> It was then that I discovered my sympathy with the British approach, a country I did not yet know but whose literature increasingly captivated me. It was this experience which, before I had ever set foot on English soil, converted me to a thoroughly English view on moral and political matters, which at once made me feel at home when I later first visited England three and a half years later. . . . In the sense of that Gladstonian liberalism, I am much more English than the English.
>
> (Caldwell, 2010, p. 23)

It may simply have been that Hayek was sentimentally attached to the idea of England or Britain as the true home of liberalism, with its geographical discreteness contributing to the impression that it offered a distinct alternative to what he regarded as the continental model. A second related explanation is that Hayek, with good reason, sincerely regarded Britain as a country that had pursued more liberal economic policies than its European counterparts. This was at least the case until what he regarded as the ignominious year of 1931, when Britain finally abandoned the path of 'true' liberalism in the face of global economic crisis. A further explanation may be the extent to which he was influenced by the French historian Élie Halévy (1967). Hugh Stuart Jones (2002) has argued that Hayek's interpretation of socialism as originating with French Saint-Simonianism owes much to Halévy's paper 'The Age of Tyrannies'. It was published posthumously in *Economica*, in 1941, during which time Hayek was editor of the journal and working on his 'Abuse of Reason' project.[9] The similarities are significant. Halévy's 'discovery' of the French, non-Marxist origins of socialism, with organisation rather than class conflict the central concern is indeed the key theme of Hayek's argument in 'The Counter Revolution of Science'. Although Halévy's influence may well have been significant, he would not have gone on to say that, because it was French in origin, socialism was essentially un-British in the manner Hayek maintained.

Mill and rationalism

Despite his wish to maintain a British/Continental binary, Hayek nonetheless recognised that the 'true' individualism of Smith and Hume came under almost instant attack from the utilitarianism of their English contemporary, Jeremy Bentham, and subsequently his philosophical radical followers. They sought to use the power of legislation to create the conditions that would secure the 'greatest happiness for the greatest number'. It was, however, John Stuart Mill who, having been rendered susceptible to ideas of design by exposure to the utilitarianism of his father James Mill, did most to transmit the continental infection into the mainstream of 'true' British liberalism.

Hayek's relationship with John Stuart Mill was complex (Caldwell, 2008; Légé, 2008). 1951 saw the publication of Hayek's (2014) edited collection of the letters exchanged between Mill and his friend and eventual wife Harriet Taylor, with an introduction that identified Taylor as influencing Mill in his turn towards socialism.[10] Hayek regarded much of Mill's work as overly rationalistic. He also considered his reliance on the labour theory of value as problematic and his theoretical separation of economic production and distribution, in combination with his chapters on socialism, as having proved profoundly injurious to the British liberal tradition. Hayek had been exposed to Wesley Clair Mitchell's interpretation of Mill as an early institutional socialist during his time in the United States, yet it was Mises's work, *Liberalismus*, which had the enduring influence on Hayek. In it, Mill is dismissed as 'an epigone of classical liberalism' and 'the great advocate of socialism'. In typically emphatic style Mises even went so far as to insist that 'all the arguments that could be advanced in favour of socialism are elaborated by him with loving care. In comparison with Mill all other socialist writers – even Marx, Engels, and Lassalle – are scarcely of any importance' (Mises, 2005, p. 155).

Wherever Mill may come in the order of importance of socialist thinkers, for Hayek his greatest disservice to liberalism lay in his introduction of European ideas of organisation into British liberal thought (Caldwell, 2008, pp. 692–693). The view of Mill as a point of departure or development, depending on one's political standpoint, was standard for the interwar period. As Caldwell indicates it was one shared by Sidney Webb, L.T. Hobhouse and Hayek's colleague Harold Laski and stems from Mill's (1990) description of himself and Taylor as being 'decidedly under the general designation of Socialists' in his *Autobiography* as well as his influence on a subsequent generation of New Liberals more willing to use state power to achieve their ends.

Taking his cue from Mises, Hayek ascribed the growing influence of socialism and collectivist ideas in Mills' work to the influence of Harriet Taylor. Although Taylor's influence may have been decisive, it was Mill's youthful attraction to intellectual developments on the continent that rendered him vulnerable to socialism's appeal, especially his interest in the work of Saint Simon and Auguste Comte, the very archetypes of the engineers and planners Hayek had written about:

> In his *Autobiography* he describes them as "the writers by whom, more than by any others, a new mode of thinking was brought home" to him and recounts how particularly one of their publications, which seemed to him far superior to the rest, Comte's early *System of Positive Policy*, "harmonised well with my existing notions, to which it seemed to give a scientific shape. I already regarded the methods of physical science as the proper models for the political. But the chief benefit which I derived at this time from the trains of thought suggested by the Saint-Simonians and by Comte, was, that I obtained a clearer conception than ever before of the peculiarities of an era of transition in opinion, and ceased to mistake the moral

and intellectual characteristics of such an era, for the normal attributes of humanity".

(Hayek, 2010b, p. 238)

Quoting further from Mill's *Autobiography*, Hayek went on to recount that:

> although he lost sight for a time of Comte, he was kept *au courant* of the Saint-Simonians' progress by Gustave d'Eichthal (who had also introduced Carlyle to Saint-Simonism), how he read nearly everything they wrote and how it was "partly by their writings that eyes were opened to the very limited and temporary value of the old political economy, which assumes private property and inheritance as indefeasible facts, and freedom of production and exchange as the *dernier mot* of social improvement".
>
> (Hayek, 2010b, p. 239)

We have here, Hayek wrote 'undoubtedly the first roots of J. S. Mill's socialist leanings'. Despite the underlying influence of Henri de Saint-Simon, it was Comte (1998), Saint Simon's collaborator and eventual adversary, that Mill did the most to propagate. Comte developed a positive sociology that sought to discover the natural laws according to which society should be organized.[11] 'Mill's *Logic*,' wrote Hayek 'Buckle's and Lecky's historical works, and later Herbert Spencer, made Comte's ideas familiar to many who were often completely unaware of their source' (Hayek, 2010b, p. 279).[12] Moreover, it was Mill who had 'by his advocacy of distributive justice and a general sympathetic attitude towards socialist aspirations ... prepared the gradual transition of a large part of the liberal intellectuals towards socialism' (Hayek, 1978d, pp. 129–130).

Given Mill's later repudiation of Comte as a 'liberticide', Hayek's ascription of Mill's socialism to this earlier influence is problematic (Hayek, 2010b, p. 279). Moreover, Mill's variant of socialism, based upon cooperation and a decentralisation of power, bears no resemblance to the schemes espoused by Saint Simon or Comte (Mill, 1989, pp. 219–280). Mill had advocated free competition on the basis of a system of worker ownership *and* the price mechanism. (Claeys, 1987; Sarvasy, 1985) Hayek's unwillingness to engage with Mill on these terms, and to simply dismiss him as an advocate of organisation, is telling. A similar oversight is evident in relation to other forms of socialised ownership (Hayek, 1967k, 1967m), such as syndicalism, some of whose leading exponents, such as Arturo Labriola, had advocated entirely unrestricted market competition within a structure of reformed ownership (Landa, 2010, p. 200).

Questions of history

As part of his efforts to delineate a true and false liberalism Hayek also indicted Mill for the rise of New Liberalism. In this instance, another aspect of Mill's thought was at fault, namely his high regard for personal development. In prioritising this over the classical regard for market freedom, his work had allowed

T.H. Green and others to make the case, not for socialism itself, but for an inter-ventionist state that would seek to ensure the prerequisites for 'self-realisation'.

Historians of the 19th century agree with Hayek that it was a period of con-current discourses. Donald Winch (1996) and John Burrow (1998) have also been keen to stress the continuities between 18th century Whiggism and 19th century Liberalism. However, it is doubtful whether the sort of true liberalism Hayek attempted to recover was ever a historical reality. In seeking histori-cal grounding for it, rather than restraining himself to a normative theoretical statement of what he believed liberalism *ought* to be, Hayek was always bound to run into the type of difficulties he encountered with his British/continental binary. Mark Bevir (2001) has argued that liberalism as a coherent and dynamic political movement was distinct from Whiggism, being based on a combina-tion of Whig inflected political economy and Benthamite ethical rationalism. This intellectual combination was, however, short-lived enduring only from the mid-1830s through to the mid-1860s. He ascribes its decline to the collapse of two central tenets of the classical political economy: Malthusian thinking, and the associated wage fund doctrine which held that wage levels are in an inverse relation to increases in population. However, despite the population boom in Victorian England wages continued to rise into the 1860s thanks both to Britain's global dominance in trade combined with the campaigns of trade unions to ensure remuneration increased as well as profits. Furthermore, even at its apogee, Victorian liberalism, despite its rationalist core, always maintained an evangelical inflection that left it periodically suspicious of inroads made by the market into other areas of social life. Looked at from this perspective, it is far from clear that 'true liberalism' ever had a manifest historical existence. Instead it appears as a set of commitments Hayek sought to reconstruct in order to support his own intellectual project of resisting arguments for greater state oversight of the economy.

Such was the inability of classical political economy to explain the evident realities of industrial society that by the closing decades of the 19th century Walter Bagehot confidently insisted that it was 'dead in the public mind'. Bage-hot (1885) also noted that its collapse was accompanied by a precipitous decline in regard for the doctrine of free trade. This was due more to the emergence of international competitors, particularly Germany and the United States, than it was to intellectual inroads made by continental schemes of organisation, par-ticularly those associated with Saint-Simon, Comte, or Fourier which were by this period approaching antique. Certainly, Marxism's appeal in Europe was growing, but it only made a minor impact in Britain. Indeed, the first English edition of *Das Kapital* was not published until 1887. In the closing decades of the century, political economy experienced something of a rebirth, thanks to the marginal revolution. However, this 'neo-classical' economics now modelled itself as a positive science centred on the concept of competitive equilibrium rather than as a way of thinking about the relationship between the state and society. Its relationship to liberalism was, therefore, changed. As we have seen in Chapter 2, neo-classical economics even lent credence to certain strains of socialist thought. Hayek, and subsequent generations of Austrian scholars, wished to return to a consideration of the institutional framework in the manner of the classical political economy even as they rejected its theory of value.

By the 1870s then, with their socio-economic worldview under threat, liberals were questioning both the nature and purpose of their movement. This was the context in which the New Liberalism, and its receptiveness to the social and ethical responsibilities of government, emerged to give liberal intellectuals and politicians a new direction. Inspired by the work of T.H. Green who had done the most to develop Mill's emphasis on self-development, New Liberals insisted that the object of liberal policy should be enabling all individuals to realise their own inner potential and ambition. The corollary of this was that obstacles to such realisation should be minimised, if not removed, and that it was the role of the state to do so. It was this ethical liberalism that, as we have seen in Chapter 2, Hayek had first felt compelled to engage with in 'Freedom and The Economic System'. J.A. Hobson on the left of this new movement, argued that,

> Liberalism is now formally committed to a task which certainly involves a new conception of the State in its relation to the individual life and to private enterprise.... From the standpoint which best presents its continuity with earlier Liberalism, it appears as a fuller appreciation and realisation of individual liberty contained in the provision of equal opportunities for self-development. But to this individual standpoint must be joined a just apprehension of the social, viz., the insistence that these claims or rights of self-development be adjusted to the sovereignty of social welfare.
>
> (Hobson, 1909, p. xii)[13]

Similarly, L.T. Hobhouse held that liberalism had developed beyond its negative stage, during which time its primary focus had been combatting corruption and privilege, and moved into a positive phase in which it created the conditions for self-development and even 'self-realisation'. The introduction of National Insurance contributions and old age pensions by the New Liberal governments of 1906–14 constituted the legislative manifestation of this new movement. The common good, liberalism's key concern according to Hobhouse's organic conception of society is one 'founded on personality and postulates free scope for the development of personality in each member of the community. This is the foundation not only of equal rights before the law, but also of what is called equality of opportunity' (Hobhouse, 1964, p. 56). No longer was the state a 'necessary evil'; instead it had become a 'vital instrument' of liberty (Greenleaf, 1983, p. 27).

During the 1920s, the prevailing sense was that the liberal movement had moved on from the 19th century and its supposedly narrow focus on the economic agency of the individual. For Hayek, this meant that 'when the First World War ended, the intellectual tradition of liberalism was well-nigh dead', (Hayek, 1952, p. 729). Yet, as I have argued, the intellectual foundations of Hayek's true liberalism had already been undermined even before the catastrophe of the world war and the post-war appeal of economic planning. Although Keynes (1926) declared the 'End of Laissez Faire' in the interwar period, it seems more likely that the 19th century attitude of government to the economy was not as *laissez-faire* as the generation of liberals writing in the 1920s and '30s assumed (Frankel Paul, 1980).[14] To the extent that it existed as a principle of government rather than a popular ideology, it lasted only briefly, perhaps in Britain over the 1830s and '40s (Tinbergen, 1952) Although Hayek rejected *laissez-faire*, this corresponds to his own position that 'for a comparatively short time in the middle of the last century the degree to which the economic problems were seen and understood by the general public was undoubtedly much higher than it is at present' (Hayek, 1935a, p. 8). This in itself must lead us to conclude that Hayek in fact appreciated that his version of liberalism had never in fact enjoyed a period of unquestioned intellectual dominance, even before the advent of the New Liberalism. To assert a fleeting period of ideological prevalence, based upon an already unstable coalition of interests, as the manifestation of a true and transhistorical liberalism was always historically untenable. This in itself, of course, does not invalidate his claims about what liberalism *ought* to be. Yet Hayek's understanding that liberalism had always been a contested discourse did not deter him from demarcating what was 'true' and what was 'false' in the tradition in a manner that reveals the essentially political, rather than scholarly, nature of his project.

Conclusion

Hayek ascribed the reaction of many liberals to *The Road to Serfdom* to the fact that the liberal tradition had itself become hopelessly confused. In order to win the battle for liberalism and establish market freedom as being at the core of how the tradition was popularly understood – to 'decontest' it – he embarked upon a sustained period in the study of intellectual history. Authentic liberalism, Hayek insisted, was British liberalism. This British/continental binary was, however, at best dubious. Frequently, he was unable to sustain it. Nevertheless, he maintained that it was the preference for rational design, or 'constructivism' which originated in France before migrating to Germany, that threatened true individualism. The critical point of transition of continental rationalism into the British liberal tradition was to be found, Hayek argued, in the work of John Stuart Mill. Having imbibed the utilitarianism of his father James Mill, he was always likely to be susceptible to rationalism. This first manifested itself in his interest in Comteanism and then, under the influence of his wife Harriot Taylor, in his espousal of socialism. Hayek's attempt to identify true liberalism with a concrete historical moment was, however, highly problematic. His inter-war work in economics had led him to view freedom in an exclusively market sense and to regard government as the primary and enduring threat to that freedom. Liberalism had therefore gone astray, he argued, when it began to look to government as an aid rather than as a danger to liberty.

Notes

1 In the 1966 Foreword to the 1956 edition of *The Road to Serfdom* Hayek (1967g) noted that he had given little thought to the book's possible appeal in America, yet the University of Chicago Press had licensed the serialisation of the book in the *Reader's Digest* free of charge. Founded in 1922, the magazine carried an anti-communist message and also reproduced pieces that criticised President Franklin Delano Roosevelt's 1930s New Deal (Sharp, 2000). Hayek (1994, p. 91) approved of the simplified serialisation carried out by Max Eastman and it resulted in a planned lecture tour of the U.S, drawing crowds in excess of expectations.

2 It was another 'continental mind', one which would come to occupy a place at the heart of the British establishment and help define modern British liberalism, who was, perhaps, the least impressed by *The Road to Serfdom*. Isaiah Berlin (2004), then a diplomat in the British Embassy in Washington, wrote to a friend in April 1945 that he was 'still reading the awful Dr Hayek.'

3 Hayek steadfastly insisted that David Hume was a Whig, despite Hume's complex and often frustrated relationship with the Whig party. See Friedrich Hayek, 'The Legal and Moral Thought of David Hume' in *Studies In Philosophy, Politics And Economics Philosophy* (Chicago, 1967) 106–121. For an article in support of Hayek's position see Eugene Miller, 'David Hume: Whig or Tory?', *New Individualist Review* 1:3 (1962), 165–174. For a study that is less eager to claim Hume for Whiggism and that draws out the ambivalence of his position see Pocock (1985).

4 It also seems to be Polanyi who coined the term (Polanyi, 1951, pp. 111–137).

5 Although at odds with their political positions, for his interpretation of Descartes's influence on the French Enlightenment, Hayek was indebted to Ruggiero (1927) and Laski (1932). See (Hayek, 1982b, p. 146).

6 The distinction between the French and British Enlightenment has influenced a subsequent generation of free market, neo-conservative thinkers. See Himmelfarb (2008).

7 It is curious Hayek includes Sorel here who, with his emphasis on the importance of myth, hardly fits the rationalist template Hayek is suggesting. It is again perhaps part of his determination to suggest a French/British binary with the *Ecole* playing an important role.

8 The inapplicability of limited models to complex phenomena remained a central concern for Hayek informing his criticisms of attempts by authority to shape the overall order of economy and society. For a detailed theoretical exposition of his position, see Friedrich Hayek (1967b). At this stage of his career Hayek believed that positivist techniques, although inappropriate to the study of society were appropriate to the natural sciences. Under the influence of Karl Popper, who Hayek assisted in obtaining a position at the L.S.E., he subsequently changed this view, see Hayek, (1967b) For Hayek's relationship with Popper see Ebenstein (2001, pp. 155–166).

9 For example, both considered the Webbs, with their Fabian Socialism as 'exponents of the Prussian model' who 'were obviously fascinated by the success of the Bismarckian State- Socialism' Halévy regarded this as 'one of the most important intellectual "discoveries"'. Halevy's method 'which typically proceeded by identifying two antinomical principles at work within a given movement or set of ideas, and tracing the consequences of the tension between the two principles' is also highly reminiscent of Hayek's (Jones, 2002, p. 62). However, Hayek had been prone to think in dualities since at least the mid-1930s.

10 Cass Sunstein (2015) has described Hayek's work on the subject as 'an enormous, uncharacteristic, and somewhat obsessive undertaking'. For a critical reading of Hayek's work see Gray (2015).

11 For the part played by Comte in the development of positivism and positivism's subsequent influence in western thought see Melissa Lane (2003, pp. 321–342).

12 Herbert Spencer, whose evolutionary sociology is somewhat similar to Hayek's own ideas of social development, is equally dismissed as a representative of continental rationalism. Hayek (1948a, p. 11).

13 Hobson was keen to note, however, that many of the moves in this direction taken by the Liberal Party, such as the introduction of old age pensions and the proposed introduction of National Insurance, were as much born of political expediency as intellectual reflection. See Freeden (1988).

14 John Bartlet Brebner (1948) subsequently argued that *laissez-faire* had been a myth. He was supported in this conclusion, albeit with some variations, regarding the role of Benthamite Utilitarians, by a number of other historians (MacDonagh, 1958; Parris, 1960; Hart, 1965).

Works cited

Bagehot, W. 1885. *The Postulates of English Political Economy*. London: G.P Putnam's Sons.

Berlin, I. 2004. 'Letter to Elizabeth Morrow' [4 April 1945] in Henry Hardy (Ed.), *Isaiah Berlin: Letters 1928–46* (p. 540). Cambridge: University of Cambridge Press.

Bevir, M. 2001. 'The Long Nineteenth Century in Intellectual History', *Journal of Victorian Culture* 6:2, pp. 313–335.

Brebner, B.J. 1948. 'Laissez Faire and State Intervention in Nineteenth Century Britain', *The Journal of Economic History* 8:1, pp. 59–73.

Burrow, J.W. 1988. *Whigs and Liberals: Continuity and Change in English Political Thought*. Oxford: Oxford University Press.

Caldwell, B. 2008. 'Introduction' in Bruce Caldwell (Ed.), *The Road to Serfdom: The Collected Works of FA Hayek, Vol. 2* (pp. 1–33). Chicago: University of Chicago Press.

Caldwell, B. 2010. 'Introduction' in Bruce Caldwell (Ed.), *Studies on the Abuse and Decline of Reason: The Collected Works of FA Hayek, Vol. 13* (pp. 1–45). Chicago: University of Chicago Press.

Chase, S. 1945. 'Back to Grandfather: Dr Hayek's Guide to the Pre-War Era', *The Nation*, p. 565.

Claeys, G. 1987. 'Justice, Independence, and Industrial Democracy: The Development of John Stuart Mill's Views on Socialism', *The Journal of Politics* 49:1, pp. 122–147.

Comte, A. 1998. *Early Political Writing*. H.S. Jones (Ed.). Cambridge: Cambridge University Press.

Ebenstein, A. 2001. *Friedrich Hayek: A Biography*. New York: Palgrave, St Martin's Press.

Finer, H. 1945. *The Road to Reaction*. Boston: Little, Brown and Company.

Forbes, D. 1975. 'Sceptical Whiggism, Commerce and Liberty' in A.S. Skinner and T. Wilson (Eds.), *Essays on Adam Smith* (pp. 79–201). Oxford University Press.

Freeden, M. 1988. *J.A. Hobson: A Reader*. London: Routledge.

Gray, J. 2015. 'How Friedrich Hayek became Fascinated with the Romance of Harriet Taylor and J S Mill', *The New Statesman*, 28 May.

Greenleaf, W.H. 1983. *The British Political Tradition, Vol. 2: The Ideological Heritage the Rise of Collectivism*. London: Routledge.

Griffiths, S. 2014. *Engaging Enemies: Hayek and the Left*. London: Rowman and Littlefield.

Halévy, É. 1967. *The Era of Tyrannies: Essays on Socialism and War*. London: Allen Lane.

Hart, J. 1965. 'Nineteenth-Century Social Reform: A Tory Interpretation of History', *Past and Present* 31, pp. 39–61.

Hayek, F.A. 1935a. 'The Nature and History of the Problem' in Friedrich Hayek (Ed.), *Collectivist Economic Planning* (pp. 1–40). London: Routledge & Kegan Paul.

Hayek, F.A. 1948a. 'Individualism: True and False' [1945] in Friedrich Hayek (Ed.), *Individualism and Economic Order* (pp. 1–33). Chicago: University of Chicago Press.

Hayek, F.A. 1948b. 'Economics and Knowledge' [1936] in Friedrich Hayek (Ed.), *Individualism and Economic Order* (pp. 33–56). Chicago: University of Chicago Press.

Hayek, F.A. 1948d. 'The Economic Conditions of Interstate Federalism' in Friedrich Hayek (Ed.), *Individualism and Economic Order* (pp. 225–272). Chicago: University of Chicago Press.

Hayek, F.A. 1952. 'Rebirth of Liberalism', *The Freeman* (Orange, Conn.) 28 July, pp. 729–731

Hayek, F.A. 1960a. *The Constitution of Liberty*. Chicago: University of Chicago Press.

Hayek, F.A. 1967a. 'Degrees of Explanation' [1955] in Friedrich Hayek (Ed.), *Studies in Philosophy, Politics and Economics* (pp. 3–21). London: Routledge & Kegan Paul.

Hayek, F.A. 1967b. 'The Theory of Complex Phenomena' [1964] *in Studies In Philosophy, Politics And Economics Philosophy* (pp. 22–42). London: Routledge & Kegan Paul.

Hayek, F.A. 1967g. 'The Road to Serfdom after Twelve Years' [1956] in Friedrich Hayek (Ed.), *Studies in Philosophy, Politics and Economics* (pp. 216–228). London: Routledge & Kegan Paul.

Hayek, F.A. 1967k. Unions, Inflation and Profits' [1959] in Friedrich Hayek (Ed.), *Studies in Philosophy, Politics and Economics Philosophy* (pp. 280–294). Chicago: University of Chicago Press.

Hayek, F.A. 1967m. 'The Corporation in Democratic Society: In Whose Interest Ought It To And Will It Be Run?' [1960] in Friedrich Hayek (Ed.), *Studies in Philosophy, Politics and Economics Philosophy* (pp. 300–312). Chicago: University of Chicago Press.

Hayek, F.A. 1978d. 'Liberalism' [1973] in Friedrich Hayek (Ed.), *New Studies in Philosophy, Politics, Economics and the History of Ideas* (pp. 119–151). London: Routledge & Kegan Paul.

Hayek, F.A. 1982b. 'Rules and Order' [1973] in *Law, Legislation and Liberty: A New Statement of the Liberal Principles of Justice and Political Economy* [3 Volume edition]. London: Routledge Kegan Paul.

Hayek, F.A. 1994. *Hayek on Hayek: An Autobiographical Dialogue*. Stephen Kresge and Leif Warner (Eds.). Chicago: University of Chicago Press.

Hayek, F.A. 2010a. 'Scientism and the Study of Society' [1942/43/44] in Bruce Caldwell (Ed.), *Studies on the Abuse and Decline of Reason: The Collected Works of FA Hayek, Vol. 13* (pp. 77–168). Chicago: University of Chicago Press.

Hayek, F.A. 2010b. 'The Counter Revolution of Science' [1941] in Bruce Caldwell (Ed.), *Studies on the Abuse and Decline of Reason: The Collected Works of FA Hayek, Vol. 13* (pp. 167–282). Chicago: University of Chicago Press.

Hayek, F.A. 2014. *John Stuart Mill and Harriet Taylor: Their Friendship and Subsequent Marriage: The Collected Works of F.A. Hayek, Vol. 12*. Sandra Peart (Ed.). Chicago: University of Chicago Press.

Himmelfarb, G. 2008. *The Roads to Modernity: The British, French, and American Enlightenment*. London: Vintage.

Hobhouse, L.T. 1964. *Liberalism*. Oxford: Oxford University Press.

Hobson, J.A. 1909. *The Crisis of Liberalism: New Issues of Democracy*. London: P.S. King & Son.

Jones, H.S. 2002. 'The Era of Tyrannies: Élie Halévy and Friedrich von Hayek on Socialism', *European Journal of Political Theory* 1:1, pp. 53–69.

Keynes, J.M. 1926. *The End of Laissez Faire*. London: Hogarth Press.

Keynes, J.M. 2012a. 'A Tract on Monetary Reform' [1923] in Elizabeth Johnson and Donald Moggridge (Eds.), *The Collected Writings of John Maynard Keynes, Vol. 4* (online). London: MacMillan.

Keynes, J.M. 2012g. 'Letter to Hayek' [1944] in in Elizabeth Johnson and Donald Moggridge (Eds.), *The Collected Works Writings of John Maynard Keynes, Vol. 27* (online) (pp. 385–388). London: MacMillan.

Lane, M. 2003. 'Reactions to Positivism', in R. Bellamy and T. Ball (Eds.), *The Cambridge History of Twentieth-Century Political Thought* (pp. 321–342). Cambridge University Press.

Laski, H. 1932. *Studies in Law and Politics*. London: Allen & Unwin.

Légé, P. 2008. 'Hayek's Readings of Mill', *Journal of the History of Economic Thought* 30, pp. 199–215.

MacDonagh, O. 1958. 'The Nineteenth-Century Revolution in Government: A Reappraisal', *The Historical Journal* 1:1, pp. 52–67.

Macmillan, H. 1969. *Tides of Fortune*. London: Macmillan and Company.

McPhail, E. and Farrant, A. 2013. 'Hayek and the Sorcerer's Apprentice: Whither the Hayekian Logic of Intervention?', *American Journal of Economics and Sociology* 72:4, pp. 966–982.

Mill, J.S. 1989. *On Liberty and Other Writings*. Stefan Collini (Ed.). Cambridge: Cambridge University Press.

Mill, J.S. 1990. *Autobiography*. London: Random House.

Mises, L. 2005. *Liberalism: The Classical Tradition*. Bettina Bien Greaves (Ed.), Ralph Raico (Trans.). Indianapolis: Liberty Fund.

New Republic. 1945. 'Poor Mr Hayek', 23 April, p. 543.

Parris, H. 1960. 'The Nineteenth-Century Revolution in Government: A Reappraisal Reappraised', *Historical Journal* 3, pp. 17–37.

Paul, E.F. 1980. 'Laissez Faire in Nineteenth-Century Britain: Fact or Myth?', *Literature of Liberty* 3:4, pp. 5–38.

Pocock, J.G.A. 1985. 'Hume and the American Revolution' in J.G.A. Pocock (Ed.), *Virtue, Commerce and History*. Cambridge: Cambridge University Press.

Polanyi, M. 1951. *The Logic of Liberty*. Chicago: University of Chicago Press.

Rosanvallon, P. 2002. 'Political Rationalism and Democracy in France in the 18th and 19th Centuries', *Philosophy Social Criticism* 28:6, pp. 687–701.

Rosenblatt, H. 2018. *The Lost History of Liberalism: From Ancient Rome to the Twenty-First Century*. Princeton, NJ: Princeton University Press.

Ruggiero, G. 1927. *History of European Liberalism*. Oxford: Oxford University Press.

Sarvasy, W. 1985. 'A Reconsideration of the Development and Structure of John Stuart Mill's Socialism', *The Western Political Quarterly* 38:2, pp. 312–333.

Sunstein, C. 2015. 'John & Harriet: Still Mysterious' Review of John Stuart Mill and Harriet Taylor: Their Friendship and Subsequent Marriage, *New York Review of Books,* 2 April.

Sharp, J. 2000. *Condensing the Cold War: Reader's Digest and American Identity*. Minnesota: University of Minnesota Press.

Shearmur, J. 1996. *Hayek and After: Hayekian Liberalism as a Research Programme*. London: Routledge.

Spieker, J. 2013. 'Defending the Open Society: Foucault, Hayek, and the Problem of Biopolitical Order', *Economy and Society* 42:2, pp. 304–321.

Tinbergen, J. 1952. *On the Theory of Economic Policy*. Amsterdam: North-Holland Publishing Company.

Winch, D. 1996. *Riches and Poverty: An Intellectual History of Political Economy in Britain, 1750–1834*. Cambridge: Cambridge University Press.

4   Hayek's market republicanism

Hayek's liberalism might be modern, but the true individualism which he insisted underpinned it certainly was not: he traced its origins back to the classical world. The genealogy of true individualism he constructed is therefore at odds with the influential early 19th century analysis of Benjamin Constant (1819) who, although never using the word 'liberal', distinguished between the positive political liberty of the ancients and the private commercial liberty that had developed among the moderns. It also differs from the dominant mainstream representation of the roots of liberal thinking presented by Isaiah Berlin (1969) who essentially endorsed Constant's distinction.

A direct result of Hayek's engagement with pre-liberal political thought was his adoption of a pre-liberal conception of liberty as non-domination. Given the close association of this interpretation of liberty with historical struggles against royal tyranny, it is also commonly referred to as the republican concept of liberty. It holds that individual freedom requires a legal status that shields them from the arbitrary, and thus dominating, power of others. This conception of liberty as non-domination is more demanding than that held by the negative conception of liberty associated with classical liberalism. According to that later conception, liberty requires the absence of interference; an individual can be said to be free to the extent that they are not directly interfered with by others. Hayek adopts non-domination because it complements his epistemic economics, according to which the existence of arbitrary power alone compromises economic coordination and exerts a deleterious effect on the use of knowledge.

One of the central aims of this chapter is to clarify confusions of terminology. It is true that Hayek never adopted the term 'republican' or employed the language of non-domination. He always remained committed to 'liberalism'. I will show, however, that this does not detract from the republican nature of his writings, nor are republican forms of thought as he employed them incompatible with a commitment to liberal economics.

Hayek and the republican tradition

Hayek had been clear during the 1940s that true 'liberalism in the English sense' had been informed by values and ideas that predated the liberal era.

In a 1953 article, 'The Decline of The Rule of Law', for the libertarian publication *The Freeman*, he insisted that it was necessary to return to 'the source in order to recover the original meaning of the debased verbal coin which we still use' (Hayek, 1953a, p. 519). The task of establishing the origins of true liberalism became his primary research objective during the 1950s and it was one that required looking back beyond the 19th century and all its attendant complications.[1]

'For any Englishman', Hayek (1953a, pp. 518–519) wrote, freedom was synonymous with the conception of the rule of law, though sadly he believed that this identification had been lost. Although he noted that the Common Law tradition made the English receptive to freedom under the rule of law, there was, he wrote, a definite 'rediscovery' and

> there can be little doubt about the source from which the Englishmen of the late Tudor and early Stuart period derived their new political ideal for which their sons fought in the seventeenth century; it was the rediscovery of the political philosophy of ancient Greece and Rome which, as Thomas Hobbes complained, inspired the new enthusiasm for liberty.

Many of the classical texts had been translated during the reign of Elizabeth I, although 'in the course of the seventeenth century the influence of Latin writers largely replaced the direct influence of the Greeks' and, Hayek wrote that 'this spirit of the laws of free Rome has been transmitted to us mainly in the works of the historians and orators of the period, who once more became influential during the Latin Renaissance of the seventeenth century'. So it was that 'to the seventeenth-century Englishmen the Latin authors became increasingly the more important sources of political philosophy'. Although both Tacitus and Livy exercised significant influence, it was in the work of the Roman republican Cicero that the classical tradition achieved its greatest impact. 'The classical inheritance' was important, wrote Hayek in *The Constitution of Liberty*, 'not only because of the great influence it exercised on the political thought of the seventeenth century, but also because of the direct significance that the experience of the ancients has for our time.' Remarkably, he even insisted that it was Cicero who 'became the main authority for modern liberalism' (Hayek, 1960a, p. 166). Hayek's elevation of Cicero is significant and indicates the distinctive nature of his interpretation of liberalism. The Roman viewed the labouring classes as irrational and incapable of ruling. It was only when guided by an elite senatorial class that they became an asset rather than a threat to the republic (Ramgotra, 2014).

Hayek was keen to stress, *contra* Constant, that the true liberty of the ancients was economic, not political, boldly stating that 'this classical period was also a period of complete economic freedom, to which Rome largely owed its prosperity and power.' History, however, was only useful to Hayek insofar as it could support his case against any attempt to plan the economy. So it was that planning and the welfare state make a somewhat anachronistic appearance in the early empire where

> from the second century A.D. . . . state socialism advanced rapidly. In this development the freedom which equality before the law had created was progressively destroyed as demands for another kind of equality arose. During the later empire the strict law was weakened as, in the interest of a new social policy, the state increased its control over economic life'.
>
> (Hayek, 1960a, p. 167)

For another thousand years, Hayek (1960a, p. 4) wrote, the importance of economic and market freedom was lost from the western political tradition until its rediscovery, first among 'the Italians of the early Renaissance' among whom it had never entirely been obliterated, and then among the Dutch and the English.

It was the republicanism of the English Civil War period that provided the context in which the classical tenets of true individualism and its regard for freedom under the law were reframed for application to a modern commercial society. Out of the 'extensive and continuous discussion of these issues during the Civil War' Hayek (1960a, p. 169) wrote, 'emerged all the political ideals which were thenceforth to govern English political evolution'. For an ardent opponent of Marx and an advocate of the importance of ideas to historical change, Hayek's analysis of the reasons for that war do take on a materialist tone; economic concerns were the root cause of the conflict, he argued. However, unlike Marxist histories, for him these concerns were not the product of class struggle, but of 'the King's efforts to regulate economic life' and various other royal affronts to the apparently widely held regard for market and more fundamental economic freedoms, for 'men then seem to have understood better than they do today that the control of production always means the creation of privilege, of giving permission to Peter to do what Paul is not allowed to do' (Hayek, 1953a, p. 519).

Hayek continued to put history to use in support of his political and economic theory, making a direct comparison between the debates regarding the relationship of government to the economy in his own time with those that led to war in the 17th century:

> Nor is it generally remembered today that the decisive struggle between King and Parliament which led to the recognition and elaboration of the Rule of Law was fought mainly over the kind of economic issues which are again the centre of controversy today. To the nineteenth-century historians the measures of James I and Charles I which produced the conflict seemed antiquated abuses without topical interest. Today, some of these disputes have an extraordinarily familiar ring. (In 1628 Charles I refrained from nationalising coal only when it was pointed out to him that it might cause a rebellion!) (Hayek, 1953a, p. 519).[2]

Ultimately however, the King could not be restrained. For Hayek, the constitutional contests and the eventual war were not therefore fundamentally about gaining greater political rights. After the deposition of James II in 1688, a reframing of the legal and constitutional order occurred simply because it was deemed necessary to defend economic freedom.

In the post-revolutionary situation after 1688, the party that best kept alive a high regard for economic freedom was, Hayek believed, the Whigs and he wrote that:

> It was the ideals of the English Whigs that inspired what later came to be known as the liberal movement in the whole of Europe and that provided the conceptions that the American colonists carried with them and which guided them in their struggle for independence and in the establishment of their constitution . . . Whiggism is historically the correct name for the ideas in which I believe. The more I learn about the evolution of ideas, the more I have become aware that I am simply an unrepentant Old Whig – with the stress on the "old"'.
>
> (Hayek, 1960a, p. 409)

The distinction between old and new Whigs is from Edmund Burke's (1992) 'An Appeal from the New Whigs to the Old', the New being Burke's adversaries in the party, led by Charles James Fox, who supported the French Revolution. Stressing the word old also distinguished Hayek from 'the Whig parties of the nineteenth century', in both Britain and the United States, who 'finally brought discredit to the name among the radicals' (1960a, p. 409). However, Hayek does not seem to have been aware of many of the complexities of Whig politics, in particular the split between Country and Court Whigs, or else if he was he chose not to examine them, perhaps because they did not conform to the historical lessons he wished his readers to draw.

In identifying the early modern appearance of core liberal tenets, Hayek was hardly alone. This had, rather, been one of the major tropes of the 'Whig Interpretation of History' that Herbert Butterfield (1931) had criticised in his monograph of that name. The type of history Butterfield complained about presented a complacent narrative of progress, with continuity and the expansion of liberty characterising the British political tradition back at least to the Civil War. Hayek certainly held many of the canonical authors of Whig history, such as Acton, Macaulay and Maitland, in high esteem, citing them repeatedly. Furthermore, in the introduction to his edited volume, *Capitalism and the Historians*, Hayek (1967f, p. 203) took Butterfield to task for dismissing Whig history. We owe a debt to such history, argued Hayek, because 'its beneficial effect in creating the essentially liberal atmosphere of the nineteenth century is beyond doubt and was certainly not due to any misrepresentation of facts . . . it may not stand up in all respects to modern standards of historical research' he continued, but 'it gave the generations brought up on it a true sense of the value of the political liberty which their ancestors had achieved for them, and it served them as a guide in preserving that achievement.' It was no coincidence, therefore, that the decline of this historical perspective had accompanied the decline in respect for true liberalism.[3]

Despite this, and the central role Hayek ascribed to the Whigs themselves, his own intellectual history is far from Whiggish. It could certainly be accused, as we have seen, of instrumentalising the past for contemporary political purposes, one of Whig history's most egregious indulgences, yet his was certainly not a narrative of happy progress. Hayek's history was, rather, one of rupture and jeopardy. For him, the 19th century had not witnessed a stately improvement in either ideas or institutions; quite the reverse. Hence his general rejection of the intellectual legacy of that century. As we have seen, it was not to the statements of classical liberalism, offered by Mill or Constant, that Hayek turned. Instead, he repeatedly cited earlier authorities – those whom modern scholars have identified as belonging to a specifically republican tradition – as providing the best account of the true individualism necessary to create the conditions needed for the effective epistemic functioning of the market.

The 1960s and '70s saw a revival of interest in classical republicanism among writers who were dissatisfied with the prevailing progressivist narratives of the kind Butterfield had warned against.(Arendt, 1958; Pocock, 1975).[4] The tendency in the history of political thought had been to chart the steady rise of Anglophone liberalism from the early modern period through to the practices of the modern English-speaking liberal democracies.[5] This new wave of literature stressed the novelty of liberalism as a 19th century intellectual development. With its focus on commerce and private life, it was contrasted with an earlier republicanism which viewed commerce and private wealth as posing a threat to its primary political value: civic virtue.

For Hannah Arendt (1958), John Pocock (1975) and others, such virtue was to be promoted through political participation in the life of the state, the *vita activa*. They drew on Aristotelian political theory and looked to ancient Greece, in particular the democracy of Athens, for an example of how such a life might be lived. For this reason, they have been referred to as neo-Athenian theorists (Maynor, 2003). During the 1980s and '90s, a new approach began to emerge. Rather than participation in a collective, it emphasised the importance of individual liberty to the republican tradition, understood in terms of a certain legal status, secured by the rule of law. It looked to republican Rome, rather than to Athens, and in particular to the Roman law and its distinction between freeman and slave and insisted on the importance of 'neo-Roman' forms of thought, and specifically the concept of non-domination that issues from Roman law, to early modern republicans, Whigs and others. Those who wish to instrumentalise these insights for application to modern political theory have come to be known as 'neo-republicans' (Pettit, 1997; Dagger, 1997; Brugger, 1999; Honohan, 2002; Honohan and Jennings, 2006; Maynor, 2003; Laborde, 2008; Lovett, 2010).

To its supporters, neo-Roman republicanism is not simply a body of normative political theory; it is a way of thinking about freedom that stretches back to antiquity. In demonstrating the extent to which their work conforms to Hayek's, it is particularly significant that the genealogy of the tradition they offer is essentially identical to his own genealogy of true individualism. Quentin Skinner is the foremost historian of the neo-Roman concept of non-domination. He has demonstrated the persistence of the Roman understanding of liberty in Italy and its resurgence in the Italian states of the early renaissance (Skinner, 1993).[6] It then spread across Europe and particularly to England, aided by the first translations of classical texts in the reign of Elizabeth I. The concept continued to inform political debate throughout the later 17th and 18th centuries, becoming the language through which all parties and factions sought to assert their competing claims to power, although invocations of liberty were particularly prevalent among the Whigs (Skinner, 1974, pp. 198–128). It was also this understanding that influenced the more radical authors of the 18th century, such as the commonwealthmen, and eventually the American revolutionaries who took up arms against the King and their supporters in Britain. Philip Pettit, Skinner's close ally in the field of political theory, whose work *Republicanism: A Theory of Freedom and Government*, remains the foundational statement of neo-republican theory, gives the most convenient historical *précis*:

> In speaking of republicanism, I refer to the long republican tradition – and, indeed, the broad republican tradition – that has become the focus of interest for a recent School of historical scholarship. This tradition had its origins in classical Rome, being associated in particular with the name of Cicero. It was resurrected in the Renaissance, featuring powerfully in the constitutional thinking of Machiavelli, and it played an important role in the self-conception of the northern Italian republics: the first modern European polities. It provided a language which dominated the politics of the modern West and had a particular salience in the Dutch Republic, during the English Civil War, and in the period leading up to the American and French Revolution.
>
> (Pettit, 1997, p. 19)

Although Hayek would wish to exclude the French revolutionaries from his history of true liberalism (and Machiavelli serves no discernible function in his theory) the survival and subsequent migration of these classical ideas from northern Italy to England, the Netherlands and America all bear a striking resemblance to his earlier narrative.

Although republican forms of thought were integral to Whiggism from 1688 onward, the strand of republicanism with which Hayek most closely associated his work has become known as 'commercial republicanism' and it developed towards the end of the 18th century and is evident in the work of David Hume, Adam Smith, Montesquieu, and John Trenchard and Thomas Gordon (MacGilvray, 2011). All of these writers found it necessary to defend commercial society in republican terms such was its discursive dominance during this period (Casassas, 2013). A common theme uniting them was the belief that commerce could, if practiced properly, promote liberty. The general increase in wealth would de-centre power, weakening state authority. Unlike earlier generations of republicans who viewed commerce as a threat to the civic virtue needed to maintain a republic, these thinkers viewed the pursuit of commercial self-interest not only as being consistent with the existing political order, but also as having the potential to promote individual independence within it. Moreover, the personal mobility of the new commercial age, as opposed to the stasis and obligation of feudalism, would allow individuals to escape dependence on local overlords.[7] At times, Skinner's work recognises that republican thinking was a spur to the sort of private industry more commonly associated with liberalism in a manner that elides the sort of clear distinctions he insists upon elsewhere (Skinner, 199b).[8] For the commercial republicans, 'a community living under arbitrary government' he writes,

> will find itself languishing for lack of energy and initiative and restricted above all in its range of economic activities. Among early modern defenders of republican liberty, Trenchard and Gordon place particular emphasis on this argument in *Cato's Letters*, developing self-congratulating contrast between the commercial success of free states such as Great Britain and the poverty of arbitrary regimes such as Turkey and France. . . . The essence of Trenchard and Gordon's argument is that "where there is liberty, there are encouragements to labour, because people labour for themselves: and no one can take from them the acquisitions that the make" whereas in arbitrary countries, men in trade are every moment liable to be undone.[9]
>
> (Skinner, 2008b, p. 91)[10]

Although these commercial republicans are an important influence on Hayek, he goes beyond their insistence that trade and commerce promote freedom. For him, the market is not conceived of as an addition to, and in many respects secondary, to more fundamental productive processes, both agrarian and industrial, as it was for early modern commercial republicans. This is partly a product of the distinction between the marginalism of Hayek's economics as opposed to the labour theory of value that prevailed in the earlier period. For Hayek, the market was where value is subjectively determined and thus serves as a guide to future action in the productive sectors of the economy. According to the labour theory, value is imbued throughout production and then shapes behaviour in the market. On a more fundamental level in relation to our central concern here – which is liberty – for Hayek the market does not stand as a buttress to individual liberty more broadly defined as it did for the commercial republicans. Instead, the market is the arena in which liberty is realised. Market freedom is freedom. Political 'freedoms' or civic virtues, which still ultimately took precedence in the work of the commercial republicans are relevant to Hayek only insofar as they promote market freedom. This is because only market freedom allows for the effective epistemic functioning of the economy. For this reason, and for an additional one relating more closely to Hayek's conception of non-domination to be explored in the next section, it would be inappropriate to regard Hayek as a latter-day commercial republican. His commitment to the market was far more radical than that. Accordingly, I have coined the term 'market republican' to describe the nature of Hayek's particular adoption of republican forms of thought, and to describe the type of institutional and monetary arrangements he regarded as necessary for a truly liberal economy to flourish.

Hayek and non-domination

If the tenets of true liberalism were ancient, then it made sense to look to the ancients and their early modern inheritors for the definition of liberty appropriate to the maintenance of market freedom in the 20th century and beyond. In doing so, Hayek arrived, not at the classical liberal definition of liberty, but at the republican concept of liberty (Irving, 2017). 'Man, or at least European man', he wrote, 'enters history divided into free and unfree . . . the freedom of the free may have differed widely, but only in the degree of an independence which the slave did not possess at all.' The distinction was simple. Whereas being free meant always the 'possibility of a person's acting according to his own decisions and plans', a slave was 'irrevocably subject to the will of another who by arbitrary decision could coerce him to act or not to act in specific ways'. So it was, he wrote, that 'the time-honoured phrase by which this freedom has often been described is therefore "independence of the arbitrary will of another"' (Hayek, 1960a, p. 12).

Hayek's study of intellectual history over the course of the 1940s and '50s had led him to think theoretically about what constituted liberty. A particularly significant period in the development of his thought was a tour, taken with his wife, around the Mediterranean following in the footsteps of Mill. This culminated in a series of lectures delivered in Cairo, published in 1955, which would form the basis of 1960's *The Constitution of Liberty*.[11] Hayek's turn towards a more thoroughgoing engagement with the theory of liberty was first popularly showcased in a 1956 broadcast for the BBC. After discussing the importance of the rule of law, he continued, 'differently expressed the aim of all this is to prevent arbitrary coercion. After all, a man is free if he need not obey the arbitrary will of any other person.' (Hayek, 1956).[12]

It was because the citizens of republican Rome had defined liberty in this way that they had become the finest exemplars of true individualism. An understanding of freedom in terms of non-domination, as the absence of arbitrary power or arbitrary rule, had underpinned the economic freedom that had enriched the republic, only to be subverted by the emperors, setting Rome on the path to decline (Hayek, 1960a, p. 167, 1982b, pp. 82–83). It was this concept of liberty that again took hold during the period of the 'rediscovery' of true individualism in the early modern period as a result of the translation of classical texts, as explored in the previous section, and it informed the ideas and actions of republicans in the English civil war, and revolutionaries in the American colonies. It is for this reason that it has been referred to as both a republican concept of liberty, and as a neo-Roman concept. It is this neo-Roman, republican conception of liberty as non-domination that Hayek employed to make his case for market freedom and to warn against the power of the state.

An important feature of the republican concept is that it is concerned with free status rather than free action alone. For example, a slave might have the most caring and beneficent owner possible, one who never interferes in the business of their chattel. Nonetheless, the slave cannot be considered free, because at any moment the owner may decide to exercise their position of dominance, interfering in the slave's life. As such, living in a state of domination is itself inimical to liberty. This understanding held particular resonance for Hayek as a result of the nature of his epistemic economics. As we have seen in Chapter 2, the efficient use of knowledge requires that plans can be formulated under stable conditions. This is undermined when there is uncertainty regarding the possibility of interference by another party, for Hayek primarily the state. Knowledge inefficiencies will therefore occur even when interference does not take place. The very fact that another could arbitrarily interfere means a certain amount of caution, of self-censorship and deference, will be necessary in order not to provoke the representatives of state power. This is inimical to market freedom and to economic freedom more broadly conceived, and therefore to the efficient use of knowledge. Hayek (1960a, p. 47) referred to the existence of these conditions as coercion. Coercion involves both undue physical interference and the potential for arbitrary interference. It amounts to 'control of the environment or circumstances of a person by another that, in order to avoid greater evil, he is forced to act not according to a coherent plan of his own but to serve the ends of another'. Essentially, this is the condition of the slave, as opposed to that of the free individual who can act independently.

It is significant that Hayek's definition of liberty in neo-Roman terms predates the 20th century's most influential delineation of the understanding of freedom appropriate to a liberal society; Isaiah Berlin's inaugural lecture as Oxford's Chichele professor of social and political theory, 'Two Concepts of Liberty'. In it, Berlin (1969, p. 132) argued that 'I am normally said to be free to the degree to which no man or body of men interferes with my activity'. This, he termed the 'negative concept of liberty' and it was the understanding most suited, he argued, to liberalism. He contrasted it to the positive concept, which he associated with self-realisation. For him this positive second concept lent itself to a less tolerant, more authoritarian type of polity. This was primarily because it was susceptible to the presumption that self-realisation requires a certain pattern of action, with the result that individuals may be 'forced to be free' in a Rousseauvian sense. The critical point for our purposes, however, is that for Berlin, the appropriate way to think about freedom was as the absence of interference. For Hayek, and those in the long republican tradition, this simply fails to take account of the ways in which freedom can be compromised without any actual interference having to take place.

A further significant difference between the negative conception of freedom as non-interference and the republican insistence on non-domination is that the latter does not regard all interference as contrary to individual liberty. This is illustrated by the different approach taken towards the law. For Berlin, any restraint upon action places a limit upon freedom, however necessary such a restraint or law may be socially. Thus, he was led to argue that, 'it remains true that the freedom of some must at times be curtailed to secure the freedom of others' (Berlin, 1969, p. 126). For those in the republican tradition, informed by neo-Roman understandings, the law did not limit freedom but instead secured it, removing the potential for arbitrary rule. For Hayek, 'the rule of law' and 'independence of the arbitrary will of another' were synonymous. As he wrote, 'the principle that coercion should be allowed only for the purpose of ensuring obedience to rules of just conduct approved by most, or at least by a majority, seems to be the essential condition for the absence of arbitrary power and therefore of freedom.' (Hayek 1982d, p. 5). Hence some interference, legal interference, was not problematic. This was because it was not arbitrary. It could be incorporated into the data upon which people based their plans and was not therefore inimical to market freedom and the use of knowledge. Drawing again upon the example of Rome he wrote that,

> During the classical period of the Roman Law, it was once more understood that there was no real conflict between freedom and the law, their generality, certainty, and the restrictions they placed on the discretion of the authority, which was the essential condition of freedom.
>
> (Hayek, 1953a, p. 519)

This difference is partly explained by the differing ideas of liberalism held by Hayek and Berlin. For the latter, a liberal society was a pluralistic society which could accommodate a wide range of differing ideas and lifestyles. Accordingly, freedom understood as the absence of interference seemed appropriate. However, as we have seen, Hayek conceived of liberalism in strictly economic terms. What was crucial was freedom in the market, according to which 'a person pursues his own aims by the means indicated by his own knowledge' and this 'must be based on data which cannot be shaped at will by another' (Hayek, 1960a, p. 20). Hence the need for a conception of liberty that looked beyond interference to the existence of arbitrary power.

The negative concept and the republican concept, or at least Hayek's interpretation of it, do share some common positions. This is partly because of the negative character of many republican concerns. For Berlin (1969, p. 132) there must exist 'a certain minimum area of personal freedom which must on no account be violated'. This is very similar to Hayek's own insistence that liberty 'presupposes the existence of a known sphere in which the circumstances cannot be so shaped by another person'.[13] The difference is that for Berlin there must be an absence of interference, or obstruction, with liberty conceived of in terms of physical action; for Hayek even if there is no physical interference, should the potential for arbitrary interference exist, then the individual living under that threat is still un-free and their sphere of independence infringed. Hayek's distance from earlier 19th century liberalism is further underlined by this distinction.

We have already seen that Hayek arrived at his concept of true individualism through a reading of Roman and 'Whig' authors along with others in the long republican tradition. Berlin, by contrast, was guided by 19th century interpretations. Benjamin Constant's notion that liberal freedom is a particularly modern construct was a fundamental influence upon the lecture. But Berlin also drew, with qualifications, upon both Bentham and John Stuart Mill, two figures whom Hayek believed had undermined the liberal tradition as he sought to portray it. It was the ascendency of the negative concept of liberty – common to Bentham, Mill and Berlin – that, from a Hayekian perspective, had allowed schemes for social organisation to take hold via an increasing body of legislation: so long as there was no physical interference, government's increasing 'control of the environment or circumstances' in which people lived could not be viewed as compromising liberty. For Hayek, however, the manner in which this control might be changed or altered introduced an element of arbitrariness contrary to market freedom.

Such was the success of Berlin's lecture that it effectively obscured Hayek's earlier work. It was Berlin's negative concept of liberty that was recognised as the concept appropriate to modern liberalism by most contemporary political theorists. Such was the general ignorance of the older republican tradition as something distinct from liberalism in the disciplines of history and political theory, that Hayek himself did not recognise the structural difference between his concept of liberty and Berlin's. This would account for his lack of engagement with Berlin in *The Constitution of Liberty*, despite the prominence of the latter's lecture. Nowhere was the tendency of Berlin's work to swallow Hayek's more in evidence than in Lionel Robbins's (1961) review of that book. In it, he simply states, as though a matter of fact, that 'Professor Hayek's conception of liberty, like that of the great liberal thinkers of the past, runs in terms of absence of arbitrary coercion. In Sir Isaiah Berlin's useful classification it is the negative conception.'

Hayek did not use the term non-domination, did not explicitly identify himself with the republican tradition and may not have been fully cognisant of the distinction between his own way of thinking about freedom and that more common within liberalism. Nonetheless, the pre-liberal nature of his conception of liberty is illustrated when his work is read alongside that of Skinner and Pettit, who have delineated its particularities in greater detail. Both contrast it to Berlin's negative concept. 'The negative conception of freedom as non-interference and the positive conception of freedom as self-mastery are not the only available ideals of liberty' Pettit (1997, p. 17). tells us,

> a third alternative is the conception of freedom as non-domination, which requires that no one is able to interfere on an arbitrary basis – at their pleasure – in the choices of the free person. This is the conception espoused

in the long republican tradition. Thus, republicans regarded all of those who are subject to another's arbitrary will as unfree, even if the other does not actually interfere with them; there is no interference in such a case but there is a loss of liberty. And, in cases where a regime of law did not subject people to an arbitrary will, they thought that legal coercion was not a compromise of people's liberty; there is interference in such a case but no loss of liberty.

Whereas Hayek begins *The Constitution of Liberty* with the distinction between the freeman and the slave, Skinner offers us a strikingly similar account of the origins of liberty:

> According to the republican theory, as classically propounded in the rubric *De statu hominum* at the start of the *Digest*, the paramount distinction in civil associations is between those who enjoy the status of *liberi homines* or 'freemen' and those who live in servitude. The rubric opens with the contention that 'the chief distinction in the law of persons is that all men are either free or else are slaves'. As the next chapter explains, the *libertas* enjoyed by free-men consists in their being 'in their own power' as opposed to being 'under the power of someone else'. By contrast, the loss of liberty suffered by slaves arises from living 'under the power of a master' and hence in subjection to his *arbitrium* or arbitrary will'.
>
> (Skinner, 2008a, p. ix)

In terms equivalent to those offered by Hayek, Skinner has explained that according to the republican, or neo-Roman concept:

> If the continuation of your liberties depends upon the arbitrary will of anyone else, then you are not a free-man but a slave, even though you may have the fullest de facto enjoyment of your liberties, and may therefore be able to act entirely as you choose. Knowing that you are free to act or not to act solely because there is someone who has chosen not to hinder you is what reduces you from the standing of a free-man to a state of servitude. The second necessary condition of living as a free-man under a system of positive law is therefore that your capacity to exercise your rights and liberties must never be subject to anyone else's will.
>
> (Skinner, 2006, p. 157)

What makes the *liber homo* free is the 'absence of dependence' (Pettit, 2002) or, as Hayek wrote, 'independence of the arbitrary will of another' (Hayek, 1960a, p. 12). Furthermore, the neo-republican understanding of the relationship between law and liberty also mirror Hayek's. As Pettit writes:

> the law that answers systematically to people's general interests and ideas – represents a form of interference, it does not compromise people's liberty; it

constitutes a non-mastering interferer. Republicans do not say, in the modernist manner, that while the law coerces people and thereby reduces their liberty, it compensates for the damage done by preventing more interference than it represents. They hold that the properly constituted law is constitutive of liberty in a way that undermines any such talk of compensation.

(Pettit, 1997, p. 35)

Indeed, Pettit himself, in a footnote, observes that for Hayek, as for republicans and neo-republicans, the law does not necessarily constitute a 'fetter' as it does for those he describes as classical liberals. Instead he recognises that,

the interference of a certain sort of law – a law that has been produced by a certain process of evolution, or a law that is inherently justifiable in a certain way – does not remove liberty. For Hayek, then, freedom will not be the absence of interference as such but rather the absence of interference by agencies other than those favoured laws.

(Pettit, 1997, p. 50)

Nonetheless, he does not develop this similarity, with all its attendant implications, further.[14]

Hayek's prior use of the republican conception of freedom as non-domination presents a significant challenge to the neo-republican narrative of its development, displacement, and recovery. For Pettit (1997, p. 50), the older concept was displaced and obscured with such effectiveness that liberalism, and its associated concept of non-interference, had 'apparently succeeded in staging this *coup d'état* without anyone's noticing the usurpation that had taken place'. It was only recovered, the neo-republicans maintain, by them towards the end of the 20th century. Clearly, if Hayek employed it during the mid-20th century then the *coup* Pettit writes of was not nearly as complete as he and others have assumed. Bound up with Hayek's use of the concept is the concomitant challenge to the liberal vs republican binary that neo-republicans have sought to maintain. This clear-cut break has already been called into question by theorists such as Cass Sunstein (1988), and Richard Dagger (1997) whereas others, such as Andreas Kalyvas and Ira Katznelson (2008), have demonstrated the various intersections and points of agreement between early liberals and commercial republicans. It would be to misunderstand the manner in which the republican tradition related to liberalism to insist that the two are mutually exclusive. It is therefore the case that Hayek's enduring attachment to the language of liberalism in no way contradicts the republican form his thinking about liberty took on from the mid-1950s onward.

The limits of Hayekian liberty

This section considers how the limits of Hayek's epistemic economics, considered at the end of Chapter 2, informed his development and application of freedom as non-domination. Despite the similarities, the manner in which Hayek and the neo-republicans employ the republican concept differ markedly. This has major consequences for their respective views on the appropriate nature of governance and institutional design. Neo-republicans are concerned about the threats posed by both public and private power to individual liberty. Both are consistently recognised as potential sources of domination that can threaten personal independence. There is an appreciation that arbitrary rule of a more immediate, even intimate, type than that which we associate with the power of the state can manifest itself horizontally in the relationships between individuals in society as well as vertically between the individual and the representatives of state power.

In *Republicanism*, Pettit helpfully distinguishes between the two types of domination that result: domination by private individuals is referred to as *dominium*; state domination is referred to as *imperium*. This distinction we are told was held in antiquity and survived to inform the work of early modern jurists (Kriegel, 1995). The manner in which neo-republicans structure their understanding of the conception of freedom as non-domination around these two pillars leads them to advocate a range of measures that seek not only to limit the power of the state but also to restrict that of potentially dominating private actors. More often than not, the latter will actually require state power, via the actions of government, in the form of legislation. For example, legislation preventing discrimination based on race or gender or sexuality, or laws guaranteeing the rights of spouses. Neo-republicans therefore seek to limit the exposure of one group or member of society to exploitation by another. In Hayek's work, however, there is little concern for the danger of *dominium*.

Although Hayek had stressed the importance of individual liberty since the 1930s, it was primarily regarded as being important because it allowed individuals to formulate and pursue their plans in a manner that enabled the economy to tend towards equilibrium over time. As we have seen in Chapter 2, Hayek's primary concern was not economic freedom *per se*, but freedom in the market. It is for this reason that he applied his insistence on non-domination only to market relations. His engagements against Keynes and planning led him to conclude that it was arbitrary state power, *imperium* in republican terms, that posed the threat to market freedom. To limit exposure to state interference, he advocated a rules-based order. At the same time, however, Hayek was quite happy to allow commands to prevail throughout the productive sectors of the economy, most overtly within the private firm, as he did not regard this as compromising the epistemic functioning of the market. Yet existence under a regime of commands rather than rules is the basis, Hayek tells us, of tyranny. Within the private firm, employees are exposed not to public, but to private arbitrary rule, in republican language *dominium*. This is made possible by the loosely defined and incomplete nature of employment contracts, according to which those employed will often be required to perform tasks to which they have not explicitly consented (Gourevitch, 2013). A consideration of *dominium* is, however, almost entirely absent from Hayek's work despite the fact that he believes that exposure to arbitrary power results in the misuse, or non-use, of knowledge. That Hayek chose to apply the republican conception of freedom as non-domination only to market, rather than economic relations more broadly conceived, is a further, conclusive reason for referring to his thought as 'market republican'. That Hayek viewed only the state as a threat is a result of his ideological closures.

Such a partial application of the concept of non-domination by no means invalidates the claim that Hayek did indeed employ it. He simply did so differently to today's neo-republicans. Yet he is by no means alone within the republican tradition in his partial application. Quite the contrary, for this was how most of the early modern sources on which he drew also made use of it. The leading republicans of the English civil war and their Whig inheritors were wealthy and propertied men. Accordingly, they did not fear falling under the domination of other members of society so much as they feared domination by the crown and, later, a corrupt executive.[15] They were by no means eager to expand the freedoms of those lower down the social scale, to their tenants and servants, the early modern equivalents of what today we might term 'employees' or workers. In fact, they even regarded arbitrary private power as a natural and good thing. Thus, we have Algernon Sidney, a prominent republican thinker to whom Hayek makes recurring reference, insisting that the absence of *imperium* was important precisely because it allowed him to exercise his *dominium* as he saw fit. Limited sovereign power was necessary because it,

> leaves me a liberty to take servants, and put them away at my pleasure. No man ... can tell me whether I am well or ill served by them. Nay, the state takes no other cognisance of what passes between me and them, than to oblige me to perform the contracts I make ... if there be a contest between me and my servant regarding my service, I only am to decide it: He must serve me in my own way, or be gone if I think fit, tho' he serve me never so well; and I do him no wrong in putting him away.
>
> (Sidney, 1996, pp. 548–549)

This was the general position of the Whig authors on whom Hayek drew. Their exclusion of *dominium* leant itself well to Hayek's own analysis that threats to liberty should be thought of almost entirely with reference to the government, the position he had developed as a result of his epistemic economics.

There are, however, moments in Hayek's work when private power is revealed as a threat to liberty and economic coordination. This is clearest in his writings on the trade unions. Influenced by Dicey, Hayek singled out the 1906 Trades Disputes Act as creating a situation in which unions were granted 'extra-legal' privileges, allowing them to coerce individuals into joining and excluding them from professions if they did not; the famous 'closed shop' (Hayek, 1960a, p. 268). Most importantly, it relieved trade unions of liability for damages caused to an employer during a dispute. Hayek argued that this placed unions outside the law. As such, they were the only group he consistently regarded as posing a threat to freedom other than the government. The introduction of the 1906 Act by Asquith's New Liberal government was a key moment in the ascendancy of Hayek's 'false' liberalism, allowing unions to prosecute their calls for social justice by employing the threat of 'extra-legal' force. In fact, the Act had simply resolved the ambiguous and changing legal position of trade unions over the second half of the 19th century and had only sought to reconfirm the legal position of the unions as expressed in legislation from the 1870s which certain courts had in the interim sought to overrule.[16] Nonetheless, what we have here is an admission on Hayek's part that private forms of power, or *dominium*, do pose a problem for the epistemic functioning of the market. That Hayek chose to limit his identification of *dominium* to the unions was his own political choice.

In the earlier part of his career, under the influence of ordoliberal theory which we shall explore in greater detail in the next chapter, Hayek displayed some sensitivity to the epistemic obstacles presented by another form of private power, monopoly. Although reflections on monopoly largely ceased to feature in his work after the Second World War, he retained a belief that a lack of choice could jeopardise market freedom. This resulted in a recognition of the possibility of *dominium* arising in other circumstances. 'A monopolist could exercise true coercion' he accepted,

> if he were, say, the owner of a spring in an oasis. Let us say that other persons settled there on the assumption that water would always be available at a reasonable price and then found, perhaps because a second spring dried up, that they had no choice but to do whatever the owner of the spring demanded of them if they were to survive: here would be a clear case of coercion. One could conceive of a few other instances where a monopolist might control an essential commodity on which people were completely dependent.
>
> (Hayek, 1960a, p. 136)

Furthermore, Hayek also later accepted that under conditions of monopsony or oligopsony – where there is only one employer or a severely limited number of employers – those in charge of existing firms are empowered to act tyrannically if they please. 'It may be true' he wrote 'that, in the last century in communities with only a single factory or mine, the local manager could exercise almost dictatorial power over the workers' (Hayek, 1984b, p. 41). This is true both with regard to the terms of employment and the treatment of those employed within the workplace. Hayek, nonetheless, believed that increased mobility and competition had brought an end to such abuses. This is in keeping with Robert Taylor's (2017) thesis that republicans have traditionally viewed liberal political economy as being consonant with liberty conceived as non-domination so long as there are exit routes available in instances of arbitrary rule. Although the option of exit may be preferable to its absence, it hardly renders those who continue to labour under the dictatorship free.

Furthermore, it does not solve the epistemic problems associated with arbitrary power that Hayek identifies.

The critical point is this: if we accept, as Hayek here clearly does, that *dominium* can exist even when stable and universal rules structure the economy and individuals act within a legally framed marketplace, then establishing its existence and its extent becomes an empirical task. It is not theoretically excluded. What constitutes *dominium* becomes a valid point of political discussion, and thus a whole range of rights and services may legitimately be called for to counter threats to liberty. This is the point at which we can prise open Hayek's ideological closures. That he chose to restrict his potential sources of *dominium* to instances of monopsony and oligopsony and to the power of the trade unions does not mean those who make use of his economic and philosophical insights must also do so.

We can go even further and posit that Hayek's unwillingness to address the problem of *dominium*, or insist on the absence of arbitrary power down to the level of the individual in the private firm, frustrates the full potentialities of a conception of the economy in epistemic terms. In general, firms function as islands of tyranny where both the price mechanism and the rule of law are absent. This, Hayek tells us elsewhere in relation to state planning, has deleterious effects on the use of knowledge. A fuller realisation of epistemic efficiency therefore requires measures be taken to counter such arbitrary private power, just as they should be taken to counter arbitrary public power.

The best use of knowledge in society demands that we insist on non-domination not in market relations alone, but across economic relations more broadly conceived, in the realm of production, especially in the private firm. In its absence, individuals are robbed of their ability to make full use of their knowledge and must instead simply submit to commands. What this might look like in an actually existing economy requires more work and a full consideration is beyond the scope of this book. However, at minimum it must involve the following three elements: first, something similar to the rule of law within the workplace and some avenue of redress so that those who govern, the managers and owners, cannot exercise unchecked arbitrary power over the governed, their employees; second, if liberty conceived as non-domination is appropriate to Hayekian epistemic economics, then we should also seek to incorporate fundamental aspects of the republican tradition it underpins into a vision of modern political economy. Going back as far as Aristotle, private property has been viewed as a prerequisite to liberty. It is therefore desirable, from a republican and epistemic perspective, for economic actors to have a stake in the enterprises within which they work – some level of worker ownership. This will undergird their free status, acting as a barrier to the epistemically inefficient abuse of arbitrary power by owners and managers, complimenting the regime of stable and universal rules within the firm; third, just as republicans insist that the highest offices of state have their capacity for arbitrary power, or *imperium*, limited by the processes of election, so the potential for *dominium* must be similarly limited by the practice of workplace democracy. A reform of ownership and economic governance offers the best possibility of ending the tyranny that resides in the firm, establishing a regime of liberty and achieving optimum epistemic efficiency.

We thus arrive at a surprising intellectual destination. Hayek's republicanism, when taken at face value, has the effect of frustrating attempts to redistribute ownership and power in society, reliant as those efforts are on the state, and is therefore significantly less progressive than the work of the neo-republicans. Yet it is also true that neo-republicanism has been comfortable with a generally liberal form of political economy (Dagger, 2006; Pettit, 2006). I have argued here, however, that by breaking the self-imposed limits of Hayek's conception of liberty and pursuing the implications of his epistemic insights down to the level of the individual in the firm, applying the republican concept of liberty not only to all market actors but to all economic participants, we arrive at a far more radical vision of future political economy.

We must develop Hayek's concept of liberty to its full and proper extent, paying proper attention to *dominium* as well as *imperium*, if it is to effectively do the job he wishes it to do; namely provide the bedrock conditions for the effective epistemic functioning of the economy as a whole, not just the market. Yet the integration of this more comprehensive development into his theory radically alters the type of political economy that emerges when we take his epistemic insights seriously. Rather than resulting in the type of liberal economy that has prevailed over the modern period, with its massive concentrations of arbitrary power and the entrenchment of enormous inequality, it points instead to the need for alternative, more equitable, models of ownership, a turn towards rules rather than commands in the firm, and at least some element of workplace democracy. The result would be a historic rebalancing of power.

Conclusion

In this chapter I have argued that in order to support his claim that true liberalism was concerned above all with market freedom, Hayek turned towards the republican political tradition and to the conception of liberty as non-domination. The genealogy of true individualism he constructed saw him locate its origins in republican Rome. With the rise and fall of the empire this was lost, to be rediscovered after the translation of classical texts in the 16th century. The understanding of liberty encountered in these texts infused subsequent struggles against state authority throughout the Atlantic world. Hayek incorporated this concept of liberty into his epistemic economics according to which individual economic plans must be secured against potential arbitrary interference. This further distinguishes his work from 19th century classical liberalism and its insistence that liberty requires the less demanding condition of non-interference. Like the early modern and Whig authors among whom he located the birth of modern liberalism, Hayek applied non-domination in a partial manner, in line with his epistemic economics. The overwhelming threat to individual liberty and hence to the use of knowledge in society emanated, he maintained, from the state. Hence, as in the Whig tradition on which he drew, his focus was almost exclusively upon the danger of *imperium*.

I closed the chapter by examining the issue that is at the core of this book: the limits to Hayek's insistence on liberty. These correlate with the limits of his epistemic economics examined at the close of Chapter 2. Finally, I sought to prise open the ideological closures that Hayek imposed on both his epistemic economics and his application of non-domination. When we do so we arrive at a radically different vision of what is required for freedom and the fullest use of knowledge in society.

Notes

1 This was despite the best efforts of some liberal intellectuals, such as Lord Acton, Alexis de Tocqueville and Benjamin Constant (here the British/Continental dichotomy is undermined again) to keep the flame of true liberalism burning.

2 Hayek may have arrived at this somewhat surprising argument through conversations with his colleague on the Committee for Social thought at the University of Chicago, John Nef (1932), an authority on the history of the British coal industry.

3 Hayek suggests Butterfield eventually recanted and accepted the benefits of Whig History. This is far from proven.

4 It is surely no coincidence that Butterfield's slim volume on Whig history had received far more attention when it was republished in 1950 than it had on its initial appearance in 1930. The republication was a result of the success of his bestselling 1949 volume *Christianity and History* (Butterfield, 1979). It should be noted the work, at least initially, had a lesser impact in the United States.

5 As we have seen, only at a superficial level did Hayek's own history resemble this.

6 Although Hayek also notes the role of 'the Italians of the early renaissance', Skinner places greater emphasis on the role of the Italian city-states and, in particular, Machiavelli's *Discorsi*, in re-energising the tradition and contributing to its re-emergence across Europe. Also, although Hayek had noted the influence of Livy, he overlooked the way in which it was Machiavelli who transmitted Livy's understanding of *libertas* as the ability 'to stand upright by means of one's own strength without depending on the will of anyone else'. See Skinner (1998, p. 46), Hayek, (1960a, p. 4).

7 For many of these authors a crucial advantage of commercial society was that it also helped to secure the freedom and security of the state. A wealthy nation was one that could defend itself and assert its interests.

8 This stands in stark contrast to authors such as Pocock and supporters of the neo-Athenian school of republicanism for whom commerce was a source of corruption in the republican tradition (Pocock, 1975, pp. 506–552)

9 Hayek himself makes reference to Trenchard and Gordon's Cato's Letters in 'The Denationalisation of Money'. See Chapter 4 section 8. See also Ian Higgins (2005).

10 Eugenio Biagini (2003) has also argued that the writings of many 19th century liberal authors were also imbued with 'neo-Roman' values, though those associated with the more civic and participatory aspect of neo-Romanism.

11 Hayek had been invited by the Bank of Egypt to deliver the lectures. See Hayek (1955). There was also an anecdote Hayek was fond of regarding his trip to Rome: 'In his *Autobiography*, Mill describes how the conception for his book *On Liberty* came to him walking up the steps of the capitol at Rome. When I repeated this on the appropriate day a hundred years later, no inspiration, however, came to me. And as I later noticed, it was indeed not to be expected, since Mill had fibbed: The letters show that the idea of writing such a book had come to him before he reached Rome. Nevertheless, shortly

after the conclusion of our journey, I had before me a clear plan for a book on liberty arranged round the Cairo lectures.' See Hayek, (1994, p. 116)

12 Hayek had spoken of 'arbitrary power' and 'arbitrary government' in *The Road to Serfdom* but not as part of an attempt to define liberty itself.

13 Hayek also identified both positive and negative liberty. Like Berlin, he regarded his own concept in negative terms. This does not invalidate the distinction between Hayek and Berlin being made here, however. The republican concept has also been understood in negative terms by its defenders. See Quentin Skinner (1998) *Liberty Before Liberalism* (Cambridge, 1998), 82–4. However, Skinner (2002, p. 262) has gone on to argue that the republican concept should be understood as a third concept, albeit still a negative one.

14 Ian Carter (2003) has observed that Hayek's basic conditions for liberty bear a similarity with those laid down by Pettit and Skinner. Ewige Kacenelenbogen (2009) has drawn attention to the fact that both Hayek and Pettit share a mistrust of overly ambitious and intrusive government. She has also argued that both adopt a position of 'epistemological modesty' which consists both in the timidity of the theorists about their political prescriptions, and in the theorists' awareness of the "natural" limits of individual knowledge when writing about social development and institutional design. MacGilvray (2011) also identifies Hayek's use of republican thinking, but believes this is only occasional and tactical.

15 In this context the Court Whigs, under Walpole, were chief corruptors, and were opposed by a shifting coalition of Country Whigs and Tories led by Bolingbroke. See Skinner (1974)

16 Most significant in this respect was the Taff Vale ruling of 1901 (Tomlinson, 1994, pp. 27, 44–45).

Works cited

Arendt, H. 1958. *The Human Condition*. Chicago: University of Chicago Press.

Berlin, I. 1969. 'Two Concepts of Liberty' in Isaiah Berlin (Ed.), *Four Essays on Liberty* (pp. 118–172). Oxford: Oxford University Press.

Biagini, E.F. 2003. 'Neo-roman Liberalism: "Republican" Values and British Liberalism, ca. 1860–1875', *History of European Ideas* 29, pp. 55–72.

Brugger, B. 1999. *Republican Theory in Political Thought: Virtuous or Virtual?* New York: Macmillan.

Burke, E. 1992. 'An Appeal from the New Whigs to the Old' in Daniel Ritchie (Ed.), *Further Reflections on the Revolution in France*. Indianapolis: Liberty Fund.

Butterfield, H. 1931. *The Whig Interpretation of History*. London: G. Bell.

Butterfield, H. 1979. *Writings on Christianity and History*. Oxford: Oxford University Press.

Carter, I. 2003. 'Positive and Negative Liberty' in Edward N. Zalta (Ed.), *The Stanford Encyclopedia of Philosophy*. Accessed at https://plato.stanford.edu/archives/sum2018/entries/liberty-positive-negative/

Casassas, D. 2013. 'Adam Smith's Republican Moment: Lessons for Today's Emancipatory Thought', *Economic Thought* 2:2, pp. 1–19.

Constant, B. 1819. 'The Liberty of Ancients Compared with that of Moderns'. Accessed at https://oll.libertyfund.org/titles/2251

Dagger, R. 1997. *Civic Virtues: Rights, Citizenship, and Republican Liberalism*. Oxford: Oxford University Press.

Dagger, R. 2006. 'Neo-republicanism and the Civic Economy', *Politics, Philosophy and Economics* 5:2, pp. 51–73.

Gourevitch, A. 2013. 'Labor Republicanism and the Transformation of Work', *Political Theory* 41:4, pp. 591–617.

Hayek, F.A. 1953a. The Decline of the Rule of Law', *The Freeman,* 20 April, pp. 518–520.

Hayek, F.A. 1955. *The Political Ideal of the Rule of Law*. Cairo: National Bank of Egypt.

Hayek, F.A. 1956. 'Freedom and the Rule of Law', BBC Broadcast. Friedrich A. von Hayek papers, Box no. 107, Folder no. 29. Hoover Institution Archives.

Hayek, F.A. 1960a. *The Constitution of Liberty*. Chicago: University of Chicago Press.

Hayek, F.A. 1960b. 'New Nations and the Problem of Power', *The Listener*, November, pp. 819–821.

Hayek, F.A 1967f. 'History and Politics' [1954] in Friedrich Hayek (Ed.), *Studies in Philosophy, Politics and Economics* (pp. 201–21). London: Routledge & Kegan Paul.

Hayek, F.A. 1982b. 'The Mirage of Social Justice' [1976] in *Law, Legislation and Liberty: A New Statement of the Liberal Principles of Justice and Political Economy* [3 Volume edition]. London: Routledge Kegan Paul.

Hayek, F.A. 1982d. 'The Political Order of a Free People' [1979] in *Law, Legislation and Liberty: A New Statement of the Liberal Principles of Justice and Political Economy* [3 Volume edition]. London: Routledge Kegan Paul.

Hayek, F.A. 1984b. 'The Distortion of Relative Prices by Monopoly in the Labour Market' in *Hobart Paper 87: Unemployment and the Unions* (pp. 13–64). London: Routledge & Kegan Paul.

Hayek, F.A. 1994. *Hayek on Hayek: An Autobiographical Dialogue*. Stephen Kresge and Leif Warner (Eds.). Chicago: University of Chicago Press.

Hayek, F.A. 2001. *The Road to Serfdom*. London: Routledge.

Higgins, I. 2005. 'Remarks on Cato's Letters' in David Womersley (Ed.), *Cultures of Whiggism* (pp. 127–148). Newark, DE: University of Delaware Press.

Honohan, I. 2002. *Civic Republicanism*. London: Routledge.

Honohan, I. and Jennings, J. (Eds.) 2006. *Republicanism in Theory and Practice*. London: Routledge.

Irving, S. 2017. 'Hayek's Neo-Roman Liberalism', *European Journal of Political Theory* (advance online).

Kacenelenbogen, E. 2009. 'Epistemological Modesty within Contemporary Political Thought: A Link Between Hayek's Neoliberalism and Pettit's Republicanism', *European Journal of Political Theory* 8:4, pp. 449–471.

Kalyvas, A. and Katznelson, I. 2008. *Liberal Beginnings: Making a Republic for the Moderns*. Cambridge: Cambridge University Press.

Kriegel, B. 1995. *The State and the Rule of Law*. Princeton: Princeton University Press.

Laborde, C. 2008. *Critical Republicanism: The Hijab Controversy and Political Philosophy*. Oxford: Oxford University Press.

Lovett, F. 2010. *A General Theory of Domination and Justice*. Oxford: Oxford University Press.

MacGilvray, E. 2011. *The Invention of Market Freedom*. Cambridge: Cambridge University Press.

Maynor, J. 2003. *Republicanism in the Modern World*. Cambridge: Cambridge University Press.

Nef, J. 1932. *The Rise of the British Coal Industry*. London: Frank Cass and Company.

Pettit, P. 1997. *Republicanism: A Theory of freedom and Government*. Oxford: Oxford University Press.

Pettit, P. 2002. 'Keeping Republicanism Simple: On a Difference with Quentin Skinner', *Political Theory* 30:3, pp. 339–356.

Pettit, P. 2006. 'Freedom in the Market', *Politics, Philosophy & Economics* 5:2, pp. 131–149.

Pocock, J.G.A. 1975. *The Machiavellian Moment: Florentine Political Thought and the Atlantic Republican Tradition*. Princeton: Princeton University Press.

Ramgotra, M. 2014. 'Conservative Roots of Republicanism', *Theoria: A Journal of Social and Political Theory* 61:139, pp. 22–49.

Robbins, L. 1961. 'Hayek on Liberty', *Economica* 28, pp. 66–81.

Sidney, A. 1996. *Discourses Concerning Government*. T.G. West (Ed.). Indianapolis: Liberty Fund.

Skinner, Q. 1974. 'The Principles and Practice of Opposition: The Case of Bolingbroke versus Walpole' in Neil McKendrick (Ed.), *Historical Perspectives: Studies in English Thought and Society in Honour of J. H. Plumb* (pp. 93–128). London: Europe Publications.

Skinner, Q. 1993. 'The Republican Ideal of Political Liberty' in Gisela Bock, Maurizio Viroli and Quentin Skinner (Eds.), *Machiavelli and Republicanism* (pp. 293–302). Cambridge: Cambridge University Press.

Skinner, Q. 1998. *Liberty Before Liberalism*. Cambridge: Cambridge University Press.

Skinner, Q. 2002. 'A Third Concept of Liberty', *Proceedings of the British Academy* 117, pp. 237–268.

Skinner, Q. 2006. 'Rethinking Political Liberty', *History Workshop Journal* 61, pp. 156–170.

Skinner, Q. 2008a. *Hobbes and Republican Liberty*. Cambridge: Cambridge University Press.

Skinner, Q. 2008b. 'Freedom as the Absence of Arbitrary Power' in Cécile Laborde and John Maynor (Eds.), *Republicanism and Political Theory* (pp. 83–101). Hoboken, NJ: Blackwell-Wiley.

Skinner, Q. 2008c. 'A Genealogy of the Modern State', *Proceedings of the British Academy* 162, pp. 325–370.

Sunstein, C. 1988. 'Beyond the Republican Revival', *Yale Law Journal* 97, pp. 1539–1589.

Taylor, R. 2017. *Exit Left Markets and Mobility in Republican Thought*. Oxford: Oxford University Press.

Tomlinson, J. 1994. *Government and the Enterprise Since 1900*. Oxford: Oxford University Press.

5   The danger of 'unlimited' democracy

It was the manner in which modern democratic systems functioned, Hayek argued, that provided the motive force for the expansion of arbitrary government. The critical issue was the absence of effective limits on what electorates could demand and on what politicians felt able to promise them. Encouraged by democratic mandates, parliaments no longer confined themselves to law-making but had, he argued, taken to directing an increasingly wide area of social life. Such an 'omnipotent sovereign parliament, not confined to laying down general rules, means that we have an arbitrary government', he wrote. Not only was it arbitrary, but its power was unlimited, especially in the British context where the doctrine of parliamentary sovereignty was supreme. This 'unlimited government' was the very essence of *imperium*.

Hayek had, of course, been warning of the threat that unlimited government posed both to individual liberty and epistemic efficiency since the 1930s. According to his political thought, such a government would always constitute a threat to market freedom whatever the century. In the 20th century, however, the danger of unlimited government was made all the more difficult to identify and address because it went by the name of 'democracy', which was regarded as having an essential moral value. Yet for Hayek, the democratic system had out run itself. It had succumbed to a simple majoritarianism which was, he argued, entirely at odds with its original principles when the term had also encompassed an appreciation that the power of democratic legislatures must be limited by the effective functioning of a mixed constitution. The ideal of the mixed constitution had been an intrinsic element of republicanism since its formulation by Polybius. It was precisely this, Hayek believed, that had been abandoned in the modern context of mass democracy.

Forsaking the older tradition of the mixed constitution had meant taking the first major strides along the road to serfdom. What Hayek advocated in response was a form of democracy with its remit radically curtailed. For him, 'unlimited democracy' was as absolutist in its pretensions as had been the monarchies of early modern Europe 'and once it is generally accepted that majority decisions can merely indicate ends and that the pursuit of them is to be left to the discretion of the administrators, it will soon be believed also that almost any means to achieve those ends are legitimate' (Hayek, 1960a, p. 116).

Hayek then wanted to return democracy to what he believed was its prior limited form, just as he wished to return liberalism to its prior 'true' state. In advancing this vision, he claimed to be defending democracy. This, however, leaves us again with something of a historical puzzle. When and where did democracy, properly practiced, exist? We can infer that he regarded the years prior to mass democracy, the advent of which resulted in injuriously activist legislatures, as constituting its best embodiment; perhaps it was even in the classical republics of Rome or Athens that this superior form of limited democracy had existed. These examples, for various reasons, can hardly be regarded as democratic in the modern sense. Just as Hayek had claimed that 'liberalism' was not actually what people had come to believe it was, he was also claiming that 'democracy' should also be interpreted differently. What he presented us with was a highly procedural vision of democracy understood primarily as an effective, peaceful, means of changing government, 'of counting heads in order to save breaking them' (Hayek, 1948d, p. 271). This though is a version of democracy shorn of all its powers to actually effect any significant economic or social change, because to do so, Hayek warned, contained totalitarian potential.

Unlimited democracy and the total state

Despite his unease with democracy as practiced in the 20th century, such was the mystique attached to the word that Hayek only began writing of 'unlimited democracy' rather than simply 'unlimited government' in the 1970s. Nonetheless, his analysis of the supposed pathology of 'unlimited democracy' is present from his first analysis of the rise of Nazism in Germany. For Hayek, politicians had appealed to the German electorate after the First World War with the promise that planning and economic intervention could improve their lives. When this failed, that electorate, now beguiled by planning, turned to the yet more radical plans of Hitler.

The Road to Serfdom provides the best context in which to explore the complexities of Hayek's attitude towards democracy. Although he drew upon a long European liberal tradition in the book, one of its central ambitions is to persuade the reader that liberalism is essentially British and planning, whether of a socialistic or nationalistic hue, is essentially European, and particularly German. It is therefore a remarkable peculiarity of the book that its analysis of the British political scene is almost entirely informed by German political and economic theory and, specifically, by an analysis of the weaknesses and decline of the German Weimar Republic.

The critical influence on Hayek's analysis – one which informed all his subsequent writing on the relationship between democracy and liberalism – was the work of Carl Schmitt (Cristi, 1998; Scheuerman, 1999). Hayek mentions Schmitt on four, consistently negative, occasions in *The Road to Serfdom*. This is hardly surprising given that the text is an anti-Nazi work and Hayek regarded Schmitt as 'the leading Nazi theoretician of totalitarianism' who had cleared the way of many of the theoretical and legal obstacles to the Nazi's assumption of power. (Hayek, 2001, p. 192). Yet Hayek was an attentive reader of Schmitt and, as Perry Anderson (1992) noted, 'he was never far from Hayek's mind', being cited in all his major works.

Schmitt (2015) held that the evolution of government proceeds 'in three dialectic stages: from the absolute state of the seventeenth and eighteenth centuries through the neutral state of the liberal nineteenth century to the totalitarian state in which state and society are identical'. (Hayek, 2001, 182). Although Hayek sought to avert the 'totalitarian' end point of this schema, he nonetheless concurred that what had undermined the liberal neutral state he sought to resuscitate was the blurring of the binary between the economic and political spheres that had existed during the 19th century. As Renato Cristi (1984, p. 523) observed, in many respects Hayek's logic provides the mirror image of Schmitt's own work, only departing from it in the final instance by offering a defence of a liberal order rather than the 'decisionism' of Schmitt's dictator.

In order to understand how Schmitt, an avowed enemy of liberalism, could have influenced Hayek, one of its greatest champions, we need to appreciate their differing interpretations of the term. For Schmitt, liberalism was essentially a politico-cultural phenomenon. Somewhat like Berlin, he viewed it as a doctrine of pluralism. Its appropriate political institutions were parliamentary, the purpose of which was to allow a plurality of opinions to be aired, with agreement reached via reasoned discussion. Schmitt, however, did not regard this form of government as appropriate for modern Germany. For him, democracy, which he presented in primarily plebiscitarian terms, was antithetical to political liberalism as 'democracy demands an identity between civil society and the state, and its pressures from below have the effect of weakening the state as an autonomous political entity' thus undermining its neutrality and its ability to stand aside from the market. Liberal government had been unable to preserve 'economic freedom' because of the demands of a new mass electorate. Worse still, it had been unable to maintain social order. For Schmitt (2007 pp. 22–26), famously, the essence of the political is the distinction between friend and enemy. The expansion in the number of political actors, beyond the aristocratic and business interests who had previously overseen government, had inevitably entailed the emergence of a heterogeneous form of politics with those in parliament no longer sharing broadly the same class interests. This had resulted, Schmitt argued, in the clear locus of power that had existed in the liberal state being lost, replaced by confusion and conflict.[1] Consequently, a proliferation of the friend/enemy distinction within German society had occurred, when it should properly be based upon the opposition of the German nation to external competitors.

Despite all Schmitt's emphasis on order, and his desire to frame his critique as one of scale and numbers, heterogeneity and homogeneity, the order he hoped to preserve was one that served the material interests of the German elites. The 'neutral' liberal state had really been a state that served the interests of the landed aristocracy and, increasingly, big capital. Although Schmitt (1999) rarely addressed economic issues directly, he was nonetheless clear that the economic result of opening the political process up to a mass electorate was the rise of 'an economic state, a cultural state, a welfare state, a social security state, a provider state'.[2] To illustrate the extent to which politics and economics had become enmeshed, Schmitt liked to cite the statistic that by 1928, the state had control of 53 per cent of Germany's gross national income (Balakrishnan, 2000, p. 50). This was what he described as the unlimited 'quantitative total state', a state without any prescribed limit, that threatened to 'seize hold of all domains of public life, and not only immediately financial and economic affairs' (Balakrishnan, 2000, p. 50). Its endurance would inevitably terminate the 'self-regulating mechanism of a free economy and a free market' (Meierhenrich, 2017, p. 193). Yet given the new identity between state and society there was no way back from the total state. What was necessary was to impose order upon it, to establish not a 'quantitative', but a 'qualitative total state' within which the decisionist leader could set down the fundamentals of the economic order, without question and without the confusion associated with the democratic competition for government power. Although he, like Hayek, rejected a class analysis, it is clear that this new centre would be expected to exercise power in the interests of capital. The result, in distinction to the Weimar republic within which workers had been able to assert their interests in parliament, would be the creation of a single industrial/political elite group.[3]

For Hayek, liberalism was, as we have seen, an essentially economic phenomenon. Like many 19th century liberals before him, he worried about the effects of democracy on economic freedom and private property. Schmitt's critique of 'liberalism' and of how mass democracy could disturb the existing economic and social order therefore held a particular appeal, even if Hayek initially rejected his anti-parliamentary conclusions. Crucially, the quantitative total state described by Schmitt corresponds to Hayek's description of an 'unlimited democracy'. In 'Freedom and The Economic System', his analysis already echoed Schmitt's when he argued that 'the increasing discredit into which democratic government has fallen is because it has been burdened with tasks for which it is not suited is a fact of the greatest importance' (Hayek, 1997c, p. 205). In chapter five of *The Road to Serfdom* Hayek provided a remarkably Schmittian account of the threat posed by democracy to market freedom. The expansion of government power to areas of the economy where it is unable to exercise decisive influence and becomes instead the object of interest group competition results in confusion as,

> neither the people nor its representatives need therefore be able to agree on any particular plan. The inability of democratic assemblies to carry out what seems to be a clear mandate of the people will inevitably cause dissatisfaction with democratic institutions. Parliaments come to be regarded as ineffective 'talking shops', unable or incompetent to carry out the tasks for which they have been chosen.
>
> (Hayek, 2001, p. 65)

As interventionism proliferates, the public sector grows in size. The result is that 'once the communal sector, in which the state controls all the means, exceeds a certain proportion of the whole,' Hayek (2001, p. 73) wrote, 'the effects of its actions dominate the whole system', putting an end, just as Schmitt had warned, to free competition. Schmitt's influence is further confirmed when Hayek employs the former's favourite statistic to support his own argument:

> Where, as was, for example, true in Germany as early as 1928, the central and local authorities directly control the use of more than half the national income (according to an official German estimate then 53 per cent) they control indirectly almost the whole economic life of the nation.
>
> (Hayek, 2001, p. 64)

After the war, Hayek would continue to draw, at a distance, on Schmitt. Although previously he had employed Schmitt's analyses to support his arguments against economic planning, in the years after 1945 both men shared a similar critical position in their assessment of the post-war *Sozialstaat*, and William Scheuerman (1997) has shown how Hayek's long-running criticism of 'social justice' again drew significantly on Schmitt's analysis of the 'total' provider state. In *The Constitution of Liberty* he cited both Schmitt's *Constitutional Theory* and *The Guardian of the Constitution* as offering the 'most learned and perceptive' account of how unlimited democracies undermine the liberal order (Hayek, 1960a, p. 485).

It was in the multivolume *Law, Legislation and Liberty*, with its extended treatment of the dangers of unlimited democracy, that Schmitt's influence comes most strongly to the fore, and is where the reader is told that 'the weakness of the government of an omnipotent democracy was very clearly seen by the extraordinary German student of politics, Carl Schmitt, who in the 1920s probably understood the character of the developing form of government better than most people' (Hayek, 1982d, pp. 194–195). Central to this book was the distinction between 'law' which is general, impersonal, and essentially negative in character, and 'legislation' which has a specific object, relates to identifiable groups, and is positive. For Hayek, only government conducted within the confines of the former was consistent with a free society. Government in which the latter took precedence amounted to little more than government according to authoritarian directive. Here again, the influence of Schmitt, who had in 1932 made a similar distinction between 'legality' and 'legitimacy' as a result of his debates with the legal positivist Hans Kelsen, is pronounced. Kelsen had argued that law could be improved upon by government in order to meet the needs of society, Schmitt (2004) had insisted that legislation (*Gesetz*) did not automatically enjoy the same status as a law (*Rechts*) which was embedded in social practice and generally recognised as legitimate. He regarded legal positivism as merely a justification for the political interventionism and disorder he opposed. This is, essentially, the analysis Hayek adopted and developed for application to the post-war political order across his three volumes.

Despite Hayek's debt to Schmitt in diagnosing the dangers of unlimited democracy, there remain acute differences between them regarding the appropriate remedy and over what a healthy society might look like. A number of authors have argued that Schmitt adhered to a liberal, even *laissez-faire* economic outlook (Bonefeld, 2016; Cristi, 1998; Scheuerman, 1999). Ishay Landa (2010, pp. 166–171) has even gone so far as to argue that its defence was the fundamental purpose Schmitt's entire body of work. Although it is true that Schmitt hoped to defend the private property of elites, this did not equate to a defence of economic liberalism. In contrast to Hayek and earlier classical liberals, he hoped to strengthen the state relative to the individual. Furthermore, he believed, because of the rise of the quantitative social state, that the binary between state and individual had been eroded in a manner it would not be possible to reverse, whereas such a reversal was precisely Hayek's political project.

One of the rare occasions on which Schmitt (1933) addressed issues of political economy directly was in a speech entitled 'A Strong State and a Healthy Economy', which he gave to the *Lagnamverein*, the association of industrialists, on 23 November 1932. Despite his denunciation of the economic intervention associated with the quantitative total state, Schmitt remained clear that the strict demarcation between politics and economy belonged to the past, and that an active economic policy would also be a feature of the qualitative total state. He did not envisage an end to economic intervention. Instead, with an active economic policy no longer the object of political contest, it could be rationalised. Schmitt envisioned three economic spheres: a nationalised sector consisting of major services; a traditional private sector and a corporatist, monopoly-based, third sector in the 'commanding heights' of the economy (Cristi, 1998, p. 33). 'State power also means' wrote Schmitt:

> today in an entirely different sense from earlier, simultaneously power over national economic income, and the national economy itself . . . out of this there develops the necessity of a great, long-term plan . . . I am in complete agreement with Hans Freyer that it is not the planners who should rule, but the rulers who should plan.
>
> (Balakrishnan, 2000, p. 51)[4]

In line with the new reality of the identity between state and civil society, a new form of politics would be required. Although wistful for the liberal neutrality of the past, when government could be conducted by means of 'reasonable' discussion, he had already decided as early as 1923 in *The Crisis of Parliamentary Democracy* that the Rubicon had been crossed (Schmitt, 1988). What was required was a 'decisionist' leader who could impose harmony by re-creating a clear locus of power. This was the basis on which Schmitt expected dictatorial rule to function. In the 1920s Schmitt envisioned this role being played by the *Reichspräesident*, the constitutional president of the republic. This somewhat ambiguous office remained an element of the Weimer Constitution largely as the residue of the influence of Max Weber (1994) and the emphasis he placed upon the importance of charismatic leadership as a means of offsetting the modern and socially enervating effects of bureaucratisation. The ability of the *Reichspräesident* to declare emergency powers and put measures to the people via plebiscites were the mechanisms that Schmitt felt would allow the holder of that office to fulfil that role. Indeed, Schmitt presented plebiscitary democracy as true democracy. However, such was the inability of the electorate to engage in disinterested debate, most decisions would have to be taken by a decisionist leader dispensing with constitutional restraints through the enactment of emergency powers. This was the only way in which the disorder of parliamentary democracy might be brought to an end and the interests of German elites protected. Following Hitler's appointment as Chancellor in January 1933, however, and as Nazi *machtergreifung* unfolded, he came to regard Hitler, not the aged president Hindenburg, as most likely to restore order. In May 1933 Schmitt joined the Nazi Party.[5]

Like Schmitt, Hayek (2001, p. 71) recognised that a logical consequence of unlimited democracy was a new authoritarian settlement. 'Hitler did not have to destroy democracy' he warned his readers in *The Road to Serfdom*, 'he merely took advantage of the decay of democracy and at the critical moment obtained the support of many to whom, though they detested Hitler, he yet seemed the only man strong enough to get things done'. Yet it was precisely because Hayek rejected Schmitt's corporatist economic vision that his constitutional solution was also unacceptable. From the very beginning, Hayek dismissed the Nazi political and economic model that Schmitt had outlined. Moreover, any apparent difference between Nazism and socialism, argued Hayek (1933), was merely superficial:

> The persecution of the Marxists, and of democrats in general, tends to obscure the fundamental fact that National 'Socialism' is a genuine socialist movement, whose leading ideas are the final fruit of the anti-liberal tendencies which have been steadily gaining ground in Germany since the later part of the Bismarckian era, and which led the majority of the German intelligentsia first to 'socialism of the chair' and later to Marxism in its social-democratic or communist form.

One of the reasons Nazism had proved so successful, Hayek believed, was that 'many capitalists are themselves strongly influenced by socialistic ideas and have not sufficient belief in capitalism to defend it with a clear conscience'. Nonetheless, he warned that 'the German entrepreneur class have manifested almost incredible short-sightedness in allying themselves with a movement of whose strong anti-capitalistic tendencies there should never have been any doubt' (Hayek, 1933). Hayek recognised, however, that this was not the socialism of the proletariat but,

> middle-class socialism, and that it is, in consequence, inclined to favour the small artisan and shop keeper and to set the limit up to which it recognizes private property somewhat higher than does communism. In the first instance, it will probably nominally recognise private property in general.

But private initiative will probably be hedged about with restrictions on competition so that little freedom will remain.

With the benefit of hindsight, Hayek's portrayal of Nazi political economy appears to be inaccurate. Although the party may have drawn significant support from the middle class, it governed decisively in favour of German 'big business'. Thomas Piketty (2014) has shown that German capital share of the economy rose consistently following Hitler's coming to power and was far in excess of that held by capital in the United States under President Franklin Delano Roosevelt's New Deal. Similarly, Adam Tooze (2006) has demonstrated the steep increase in the rate of return on German capital in the years of Nazi rule until 1940. And although Hayek tells us the term 'welfare state' is German in origin, *Wohlfahrtstaat*, the same may be said for the term 'privatisation' or *Reprivatisierung* (Bel, 2006). This was the policy by which 'the Nazi regime transferred public ownership to the private sector. In doing so, they went against the mainstream trends in western capitalistic countries, none of which systematically reprivatized firms during the 1930s' Bel (2010, p. 34). Privatisation was actively pursued by the Nazi Party essentially to buy the support of German industry. None of this, of course, conforms to Hayek's conception of market freedom as non-domination any more than a middle-class or working-class socialism would. Furthermore, it does not contradict Hayek's position that Nazism was based upon a deeply interventionist economic policy. Yet it was not 'middle class' socialism of the sort that might arise out of electoral competition. It was not the demands of voters and the promises of politicians, but the influence of vested interests in a period of re-armament that drove the process.

The Road to Serfdom can be read as an early work in the field of public choice, with its chapter-long analysis of 'why the worst get on top' in a socialised system. According to this logic, placing such decisionist power in the hands of a dictator could only lead to ruin. Furthermore, for Hayek Schmitt's economic vision was economically irrational, for all the reasons he had set out over the 1930s. It would still be the case that 'the best the dictator could do . . . would be to imitate as closely as possible what would happen under free competition' (Hayek, 1991, p. 26). And it would be a poor imitation. Although Schmitt may have regarded his dictatorial version of the strong state as essential for a healthy economy, Hayek argued that any attempt to shape the overall economic order or establish national priorities was bound to lead to greater government action and a reduction in the market freedom he prized. Instead, quite unlike Schmitt, Hayek wished to turn the clock back to a time when parliament's economic role remained limited.

A self-limiting democracy

The Road to Serfdom attempted to sketch a way in which parliamentary democracy might be reconciled with economic liberalism.[6] In doing so it drew upon the work of a group of economists referred to as the Freiberg or ordoliberal school. Freiberg was the University at which Walter Eucken, the father of the movement, and Franz Böhm would establish the journal *Ordo* in 1948, but the tenets of ordoliberalism were already in place, having been developed over the previous two decades by theorists such as Wilhelm Röpke, Alexander Rüstow, Leonard Miksch, Alfred Müller Armack and of course Böhm and Eucken (Ptak, 2009).

It was in responding to the challenge of Schmitt's decisionist political economy that Hayek's thought takes on an ordoliberal hue in *The Road to Serfdom* (Irving, 2018). The ordoliberals agreed with Schmitt that liberalism had been undermined by the economic interventionism of the social democratic state. Like Schmitt, they ascribed the breakdown of the Weimar Republic to the redistributive and interventionist nature of its government. Like him, they too wanted a strong state to set things right. They rejected *laissez-faire* as outdated and the leading ordoliberals were equally as dismissive of the viability of parliamentary democracy as Schmitt. Eucken (1932, p. 312), like Schmitt, had written of parliamentary democracy as posing a threat to liberal order arguing that 'the chaotic force of the masses' had transformed the liberal state into a redistributive, social democratic state. 'Great dangers have arisen' he wrote, to the practice of orderly government, 'as the result of its involvement in the economy'. The only way in which it was possible to restore order was for government to free itself 'from the influence of the masses' and 'once again distance itself in one way or another from the economic process'.

Similarly, Röpke argued that mass parties had been allowed to 'abuse the rules of liberal-parliamentarianism' and the result had been the 'totalitarian [welfare] state'. In order to achieve the necessary reforms, an authoritarian leader would be required to head a 'democratic dictatorship' in keeping with Schmitt's plebiscitary model. Rüstow, drawing on both Schmitt and Max Weber, also called for a form of authoritarian plebiscitarian democracy 'in which the masses are led by an enchanting elite that governs with an ethics of responsibility and provides charismatic underpinning to a disenchanted world of economic value and domination by abstract rules and ordering regulations' (Bonefeld, 2016). Authoritarianism, then, was at the heart of the ordoliberal project.

Despite this, the model of dictatorship and the associated conception of political economy the ordoliberals espoused differed from that which Schmitt had outlined in 1932. What they would not countenance, at least in theory, was a decisionist leader imbued with the ability to interfere at will in the economic sphere. Having witnessed the breakdown of the Weimar state, their chief concern was *ordnungspolitik* or a 'politics of order' that would entrench the rule of law (Bonefeld, 2006). One consistent element within ordoliberal theory was its insistence on a clear 'legal and institutional framework' within which economic policy must be pursued. This was intended to limit the discretionary power of government – dictatorial or democratic. It was, wrote Röpke (1942, p. 6) 'the only alternative to *laissez-faire* and totalitarianism, which we have to offer'. In contrast to the decisionism of Schmitt, their model was designed to prevent arbitrary intervention. That key difference is drawn out by a comparison of the title of Schmitt's 1932 address to the *Lagnamverein*, 'A Strong State and a Healthy Economy', with that of a lecture delivered by Rüstow to the same gathering entitled the 'Free Economy and the Strong State'. Despite the common concern for 'strength', Schmitt had imagined the dictator serving as a good doctor, overseeing the economic health of the social body, intervening when necessary. In contrast, for the ordoliberals the proscription of discretionary political power from the economy offered the only means of inoculating 'economic life from political infection' (Röpke, 2009, p. 108).

There were of course a range of positions held within the ordoliberal school and Ralph Ptak (2009) has argued that although certain members, notably Miksch and Müller Armack, hoped their work would be instructive to the Nazi state, others such as Wilhelm Röpke and Rüstow found themselves unable to continue their work under the regime. The coherence of the School's rejection of dictatorial economic intervention is also questionable. At one end of the spectrum was Eucken who held a classically inflected outlook and was relatively keen to limit the role of government; at the other was Rüstow for whom the state must pursue a policy of *Vitalpolitik* and work to create the ethical conditions of self-reliance in society, thus countering the ethic of state dependency that he associated with socialism. This, however, involved a range of policies, such as the creation of small towns and promotion of family industry, that would inevitably have required the type of radically interventionist policy supposedly anathema to the ordoliberals. Such measures could therefore only be justified on the grounds that they would be part of a foundational reorganisation of society after which government could be conducted in a properly restrained manner. Given the amount of state power necessary to meet these ends it is hardly surprising that we find Rüstow more enthusiastic than others regarding the benefits of dictatorship. What is more, it cannot be imagined that such schemes could be made to conform to Hayek's epistemic economics or his view of the state as posing an active danger to economic freedom (Irving, 2018). This lack of definition regarding the proper dimensions of the legal 'framework', within a group for whom that concept was a core concern, was a serious problem for the coherence of the movement, and it was one Hayek shared, particularly during this period of his career when the ordoliberal influence on his work was at its greatest. Despite this, what Hayek found in ordoliberalism was a device which, he believed, offered a means of averting the totalitarian end point of Schmitt's evolutionary schema. Hayek hoped that democratically elected governments in Britain might recognise the value of the legal framework and limit themselves accordingly. With such a framework in place, it might be possible to resuscitate the market freedom that had prevailed in the previous century.

Hayek warned that to allow politics to determine the allocation of economic output in post-war Britain would be disastrous. Instead, the only way to improve society was once more to embrace free competition. 'We should not' he argued, 'by short sighted attempts to cure poverty by a redistribution instead of by an increase in our income, so depress large classes as to turn them into determined enemies of the existing political order', as to do so would be to repeat the mistakes that had been made in Germany. 'It should never be forgotten' he continued 'that the one decisive factor in the rise of totalitarianism on the Continent, which is yet absent in this country, is the existence of a large recently dispossessed middle class'. There should, he argued, be a recognition that 'our hopes of avoiding the fate which threatens must indeed to a large extent rest on the prospect that we can resume rapid economic progress' (Hayek, 2001, p. 144).[7] In order to entrench such a rejection of redistribution a new framework of law would be required which was active in shaping the best environment for competition but which did not seek to intrude upon competition itself.

As we have seen in Chapter 3, *The Road to Serfdom* begins with a clear rejection of *laissez-faire* in a manner consistent with the writing of the ordoliberals (Hayek, 2001, p. 18). In this, Hayek was reiterating a position he had arrived at in the 1930s when he had argued that 'to say that partial planning of the kind we are alluding to is irrational is, however, not equivalent to saying that the only form of capitalism which can be rationally advocated is that of complete *laissez-faire* in the old sense'. In a further dismissal of one of the central tenets of 19th century liberalism he wrote:

> It is important not to confuse opposition against this kind of planning with a dogmatic *laissez-faire* attitude. The liberal argument is in favour of making the best possible use of the forces of competition as a means of co-ordinating human efforts, not an argument for leaving things just as they are. It is based on the conviction that where effective competition can be created, it is a better way of guiding individual efforts than any other. It does not deny, but even emphasises, that, in order that competition should work beneficially, a carefully thought-out legal framework is required, and that neither the existing nor the past legal rules are free from grave defects. Nor does it deny that where it is impossible to create the conditions necessary to make competition effective, we must resort to other methods of guiding economic activity.
>
> (Hayek, 2001, p. 37)

It was still possible, Hayek argued, to limit democracy within a parliamentary context, so long as 'government in all its actions is bound by fixed and announced beforehand-rules'. It is the price of democracy, he continued, 'that the possibilities of conscious control are restricted to the fields where true agreement exists' (Hayek, 2001, p. 73). The reason the legal framework must be applied, he argued, was that without it, the dictatorship Schmitt welcomed became likely.

A hard proposal for the dimensions of such a framework is, however, absent from Hayek's thought. Hayek (2001, p. 124, 1960a, p. 285) accepted that there is a legitimate role for government in providing basic levels of social welfare, writing 'nor is the preservation of competition incompatible with an extensive system of social services–so long as the organisation of these services is not designed in such a way as to make competition ineffective over wide fields' (Hayek, 2001, p. 39). Given that much of Hayek's analysis was based on the Schmittian position that the political battle over securing the proceeds of welfare had resulted in the demise of Weimar, this statement indicates a problematic indeterminacy about the proper nature of the legal framework and its relationship to democracy within Hayek's work.

Once there is an acceptance that the state must do certain things, and in a democracy these things must ultimately be subject to political debate, there can be no definitive way of stipulating exactly what the limits to government action should be. A framework may be expansive, allowing a wide range of activities to take place within its bounds only seeking to enforce things such as criminal and property law. This would look something like the minimal state advocated by Robert Nozick (1974). Alternatively, frameworks may be tight prohibiting a large number of productive or market practices. Whilst not prescriptive, as in a planned economy, this may result in at least a direction of the economy by means of proscription. Hayek sat in neither of these camps but, as Andrew Gamble (1996, pp. 49, 109–111) has noted, by allowing a measure of government economic action, albeit with regard to welfare, he opened his philosophy to criticism from those on the right, such as Murray Rothbard whose own position was at least consistent in forbidding state activity, as well as from those on the left, who have argued that his general desire to restrict government was politically motivated and intellectually unsupported by his theory. Despite the ostensible dualities of his rhetoric, Hayek's thought left him exposed on centre ground.

In his early response to the book, Keynes identified the indeterminacy regarding the framework and the proper relationship between government and economy that it contains. He had read *The Road to Serfdom* on his way to the Bretton Woods negotiations in America. Keynes (2012g) was as opposed to the sort of central planning it described as Hayek was, and wrote, 'in my opinion it is a grand book [. . .] Morally and philosophically I find myself in agreement with virtually the whole of it: and not only in agreement with it, but in deeply moved agreement.' However, he recognised the fault line that lay within it:

> I come finally to what is really my only serious criticism of the book. You admit here and there that it is a question of knowing where to draw the line. You agree that the line has to be drawn somewhere [between free-enterprise and planning], and that the logical extreme is not possible. But you give us no guidance whatever as to where to draw it.

Keynes was more of a technocrat than Hayek, for him the expert economist and civil servant could know best. In a democratic society, however, there is a strong argument to be made that the shape and extent of the framework must be a subject of political debate. Indeed, Hayek (1997b) had even seemed to suggest as much himself in an early version of 'Freedom and the Economic System', having written that government action may be appropriate 'because a clear object desired by an overwhelming majority can only be achieved if a small dissenting minority is coerced.' Clearly, however, this earlier position went against the entire argument of the *Road to Serfdom* and all his subsequent arguments against majoritarianism. Ultimately, Hayek was never able to provide a satisfactory answer to the question of 'where to draw the line?'

Arbitrary power and ungovernability

The Road to Serfdom was primarily intended for an English readership. It is, therefore, a fundamental shortcoming of Hayek's approach that the concept of an enduring legal framework with 'fixed' rules was, and remains, singularly unsuited to the British constitution. Indeed, the constitutional fundament of parliamentary sovereignty can be regarded as the acme of unlimited democracy. Despite, or perhaps because of, the high esteem in which he held the British political tradition, this core aspect of it was to cause Hayek increasing frustration as the decades progressed. Rather than act with restraint, within the bounds of a framework of general rules, in the three decades after the war Hayek believed that the government of the country accelerated down the path of intervention, driven by the unlimited nature of democracy.

In the years after 1960, with his republican conception of liberty as non-domination serving as a guide to his writing, Hayek developed his previous warnings about unlimited government in market republican terms. When reflecting on the prerequisites necessary for the government of a liberal state that would serve to preclude unlimited democracy, Hayek invoked the words of the English republican James Harrington who in *Oceana* had written that for liberty to exist what was needed was 'the empire of laws and not of men'. The great danger was that Parliament was now unlimited in its ambitions and Hayek warned that an 'almighty Parliament means the death of the freedom of the individual'. It was time the British understood that political license did not equate to liberty, which was, of course, to be understood in market terms. Confusion regarding what freedom should mean, believed Hayek, had produced a situation in which 'a free constitution no longer means the freedom of the individual but a licence to the majority in Parliament to act as arbitrarily as it please', and he continued, 'we can either have a free Parliament or a free people' (Hayek, 1982d, p. 102). What was generally taken for freedom, political liberties, in fact resulted in nothing more than *imperium*.

That arbitrary power now operated under the banner of democracy particularly concerned Hayek, as this had legitimated its exercise in the public mind. Although parliaments might have acted as a break on the exercise of royal power prior to the age of mass democracy,

> In its present unlimited form democracy has today largely lost the capacity of serving as a protection against arbitrary power. It has ceased to be a safe-guard of personal liberty, a restraint on the abuse of governmental power which it was hoped it would prove to be when it was naively believed

that, when all power was made subject to democratic control, all the other restraints on governmental power could be dispensed with. It has, on the contrary, become the main cause of a progressive and accelerating increase of the power and weight of the administrative machine.

(Hayek, 1982d, p. 138)

Hayek was not the only person on the political right alarmed at the use of parliamentary powers. Lord Hailsham (1978) also warned of the dangers of a new form of 'elective dictatorship'. Such figures warned that the combination of arbitrary power, industrial unrest and a steep rise in inflation during the early 1970s had produced a crisis of ungovernability, which is not entirely congruent with their simultaneous warnings of dictatorship.[8] It begins to make sense, however, when considered in light of Schmitt's analysis of democratic overreach, and certainly his influence on many of the ideas of what came to be known as the 'new right' was significant.

Industrial unrest had indeed become the 'leitmotif' of British politics by the time of the Conservative Edward Heath's premiership, 1970–74. His introduction of the 1971 Industrial Relations Act was resisted fiercely by the unions and at least ten million days were lost to strike action in every year of his premiership, with a state of emergency being declared five times in less than four years (Pitchford, 2011). The fact that many industries were nationalised further enabled unions to directly influence the government. Water, iron and steel, public transport, electricity, car manufacture and many other areas of the economy were administered by government bodies deriving their authority from Parliament (Cohen, 1973) and the period saw the apogee of the 'mixed economy' that Hayek (1935a) had described some 40 years earlier as 'interventionist chaos'.

In February 1974, Heath called a general election in the face of wage demands made by the mining unions. The question he posed to the country was 'Who governs?' arguing that Parliament must not be forced to bow to union pressure. In the campaign, the Conservative manifesto argued that inflationary demands made by the unions could 'destroy not just our standard of living, but all our hopes for the future' (Conservative Party, 1974a). The result was a hung Parliament with Labour as the largest party. Harold Wilson, Labour Prime Minister for a second time, called another election in October of the same year. This time the language from the Conservatives was even more incendiary warning that 'inflation at its present rate threatens not only the standard of living of everybody in the country, but also the survival of our free and democratic institutions' (Conservative Party, 1974b). The result, however, was an increase in the Labour vote, giving the party an overall majority of one seat. On the right, alarm peaked, *The Spectator* claiming that 'Britannia's dream of apocalypse' was about to come true; *The Banker* worried that unless the situation was arrested rapidly the last chance would have been lost 'for the parliamentary system to cope with Britain's economic problems' (Tomlinson, 2012).[9] Peter Jay wrote a series in *The Times* suggesting that British democracy might not survive a further period of industrial unrest. It was a journalistic trend that became known as 'doomwatch' (Vinen, 2010, pp. 76–77).

Hayek (1978c, p. 107) shared the sense of impending doom, admitting that, despite his previous ordoliberal-influenced optimism regarding the ability of democratically elected governments to limit their actions he had

> belatedly come to agree with Josef Schumpeter who 30 years ago argued that there was an irreconcilable conflict between democracy and capitalism-except that it is not democracy as such but particular forms of democratic organisation, now regarded as the only forms of democracy, which will produce a progressive expansion of governmental control of economic life even if the majority of the people wish to preserve a market economy.

In keeping with the alarmist rhetoric of his new allies on the British right who warned of ungovernability and social breakdown, by the mid-1970s, Hayek (1982d, p. 134) was ready to state that the days of 'unlimited democracy are numbered'. What remained to be seen was whether this would result in the sort of fascist decisionism that Schmitt had advocated forty years earlier or whether free market liberals could, in alliance with conservatives, devise alternative arrangements. In order to end the chaos, what was necessary, Hayek insisted, was a 'basic alteration in the structure of democratic government' – the adoption of a 'different form' of electoral politics that preserves what is 'valuable in democracy while discarding its "objectionable features"' (Hayek, 1982a, pp. xi–xiii). The experience of unlimited government had radicalised Hayek's thought to such a degree that he was now ready to advocate a constitutional revolution.

Conclusion

The defining characteristic of modern democracy was its unlimited nature, Hayek believed. This posed a major problem for his epistemic economics which maintained that market actors must be able to formulate plans safe in the knowledge that they will not be subject to the arbitrary interference of government and he defined the basic features of unlimited democracy in *The Road to Serfdom*. In this chapter, I have shown how Carl Schmitt's analysis of the total state was the critical theoretical influence on Hayek's thinking in this regard. Nonetheless, he steadfastly rejected the decisionist outcome of Schmitt's thought and the interventionist and corporatist form of political economy associated with it. Although Schmitt was happy to embrace a new totalitarian era, Hayek wished to turn back the clock to a lost age of liberal governance.

It is then surprising the he turned to another group of German theorists, in their way equally as supportive of dictatorship as Schmitt, for a device that might avert the totalitarian endpoint of the Schmittian developmental schema that Hayek otherwise endorsed. In *The Road to Serfdom*, Hayek advocated applying the model of the self-limiting legal framework, not in the context of dictatorship as his German colleagues had, but in that of British parliamentary democracy. As we saw in the chapter three, his book was received with some confusion by its English readership, even among those otherwise favourable to his work. The application of German political theory to the English political scene was problematic, not least because the concept of a restrictive legal framework was so out of step with the British constitution and the doctrine of parliamentary sovereignty.

Over the subsequent decades, as the practice of unlimited democracy only seemed to intensify, Hayek became increasingly disillusioned regarding the ability of the executive in Parliament to limit its own powers. Following his adoption of the republican concept of liberty, Hayek framed the issue explicitly in terms of arbitrary government power. What, in this book, I refer to as *imperium*. It only gradually became apparent to Hayek, because of his experience of the political and economic developments of the 1960s and '70s, that limiting *imperium* would, at least in the British context, require revolutionary constitutional change.

Notes

1 This view is echoed in the work of economic historian Knut Borchardt (1991) for whom the increasingly active role taken by Weimar governments in wage bargaining between employers and unions resulted in the alienation of capital and a willingness to accept the radical alternative of the Nazi Party.
2 This is reflected in the remarkably sparse treatment of economic issues in the recent *Oxford Handbook of Carl Schmitt* (Meierhenrich and Simons, 2017).
3 Article 7 of the Weimar Constitution outlined that the new republic was entitled to pass legislation pertaining to the welfare of its citizens and Article 51 states that 'the economy must be organised based on the principles of justice with the goal of achieving life in dignity for everyone'. What exactly this meant was open to interpretation, but that government had responsibilities across these areas was explicit (Stolleis, 2013).
4 Freyer was a conservative German sociologist and philosopher. See Oron (1958).
5 It is true that in the years after Hitler's seizure of power, Schmitt moved towards advocating a 'concrete order' in which decisionism could function in a less arbitrary manner. The fact remains, however, that both the political and economic order would remain focussed on a single individual.
6 As such it is not correct to argue, as Keith Tribe (2009, p. 72) has, that Hayek's response to Schmitt was simply rhetorical.
7 This is reminiscent of Foucault's (2008, p. 144) statement that for ordoliberals there 'can only be one true and fundamental social policy: economic growth'.
8 The early 1970s were also the bloodiest period of the conflict in Northern Ireland.
9 On the right, there were also widespread fears of subversion by communists, 'the enemy within', during the period.

Works cited

Anderson, P. 1992. 'The Intransigent Right: Michael Oakeshott, Leo Strauss, Carl Schmitt, Friedrich von Hayek', *London Review of Books*, 24 September.

Balakrishnan, G. 2000. *The Enemy: An Intellectual Portrait of Carl Schmitt*. London: Verso.

Bel, G. 2006. 'The Coining of "Privatization" and Germany's National Socialist Party', *Journal of Economic Perspectives* 20:3, pp. 187–194.

Bel, G. 2010. 'Against the Mainstream: Nazi privatization in 1930s Germany', *Economic History Review* 63:1, pp. 34–55.

Bonefeld, W. 2006. 'Freedom and the Strong State: Democracy and Dictatorship', *Critique* 34:3, pp. 237–252.

Bonefeld, W. 2016. 'Authoritarian Liberalism: From Schmitt via Ordoliberalism to the Euro', *Critical Sociology* 43:4–5, pp. 747–761.

Borchardt, K. 1991. *Perspectives on Modern German Economic History and Policy.* Peter Lambert (Trans.). Cambridge: Cambridge University Press.

Cohen, R.K. 1973. *British Nationalisation, 1945–1973.* London: Palgrave Macmillan.

Conservative Party. 1974a. 'Firm Action for a Fair Britain'. Accessed at www.conservative manifesto.com/1974/feb/february-1974-conservative-manifesto.shtml

Conservative Party. 1974b. 'Putting Britain First: A National Policy'. Accessed at www.con servativemanifesto.com/1974/oct/october-1974-conservative-manifesto.shtml

Cristi, F.R. 1984. 'Hayek and Scmhitt on the Rule of Law', *Canadian Journal of Political Science / Revue canadienne de science politique* 17:3, pp. 521–535.

Cristi, R. 1998. *Carl Schmitt and Authoritarian Liberalism: Strong State, Free Economy.* Cardiff: University of Wales.

Cristi, R. 2014. 'Decisionism', *The Encyclopaedia of Political Thought,* pp. 831–833. Accessed at http://onlinelibrary.wiley.com/doi/10.1002/9781118474396.wbept0244/references

Eucken, W. 1932. 'Staatliche Strukturwandlungen und die Krisis des Kapitalismus', *Weltwirtschaftliches Archiv* 36, pp. 297–321.

Foucault, M. 2008. *The Birth of Biopolitics, Lectures at the College de France 1978–1979.* M. Senellart (Ed.). London: Routledge.

Gamble, A. 1996. *Hayek: The Iron Cage of Liberty.* Cambridge: Polity Press.

Hailsham, Q.H. 1978. *The Dilemma of Democracy.* London: Collins.

Hayek, F.A. 1933. 'Nazi Socialism'. Friedrich A. von Hayek papers, Box no. 105, Folder no. 10. Hoover Institution Archives.

Hayek, F.A. 1935a. 'The Nature and History of the Problem' in Friedrich Hayek (Ed.), *Collectivist Economic Planning* (pp. 1–40). London: Routledge & Kegan Paul.

Hayek, F.A. 1948d. The Economic Conditions of Interstate Federalism', in Friedrich Hayek (Ed.), *Individualism and Economic Order* (pp. 225–272). Chicago: University of Chicago Press.

Hayek, F.A. 1960a. *The Constitution of Liberty.* Chicago: University of Chicago Press.

Hayek, F.A. 1978c. 'Economic Freedom and Representative Government' [1973] in Friedrich Hayek (Ed.), *New Studies in Philosophy, Politics, Economics, and the History of Ideas* (pp. 105–118). London: Routledge & Kegan Paul.

Hayek, F.A. 1978f. 'The Campaign Against Keynesian Inflation' [a collection of articles from 1974/75/75/76] in Friedrich Hayek (Ed.), *New Studies in Philosophy, Politics, Economics and the History of Ideas* (pp. 191–231). London: Routledge & Kegan Paul.

Hayek, F.A. 1982a. 'Introduction' [1982] in *Law, Legislation and Liberty: A New Statement of the Liberal Principles of Justice and Political Economy* [3 Volume edition]. London: Routledge Kegan Paul.

Hayek, F.A. 1982b. 'Rules and Order' [1973] in *Law, Legislation and Liberty: A New Statement of the Liberal Principles of Justice and Political Economy* [3 Volume edition]. London: Routledge Kegan Paul.

Hayek, F.A. 1982d. 'The Political Order of a Free People' [1979] in *Law, Legislation and Liberty: A New Statement of the Liberal Principles of Justice and Political Economy* [3 Volume edition]. London: Routledge Kegan Paul.

Hayek, F.A. 1991. 'The Trend of Economic Thinking' [1933] in W.W. Bartley III and Stephen Kresge (Eds.), *The Trend of Economic Thinking: The Collected Works of FA Hayek, Vol. 3* (pp. 13–30). Chicago: University of Chicago Press.

Hayek, F.A. 1997b. 'Freedom and the Economic System' [1938] in Bruce Caldwell (Ed.), *Socialism and War: The Collected Works of FA Hayek, Vol. 10* (pp. 189–212). Chicago: University of Chicago Press.

Hayek, F.A. 1997c. 'Freedom and the Economic System [1939] in Bruce Caldwell (Ed.), *Socialism and War: The Collected Works of FA Hayek, Vol. 10* (pp. 213–220). Chicago: University of Chicago Press.

Hayek, F.A. 2001. *The Road to Serfdom*. London: Routledge.

Irving, S. 2018. 'Limiting Democracy and Framing the Economy: Hayek, Schmitt and Ordoliberalism', *History of European Ideas* 44:1, pp. 113–127.

Keynes, J.M. 2012g 'Letter to Hayek' [1944] in in Elizabeth Johnson and Donald Moggridge (Eds.), *The Collected Works Writings of John Maynard Keynes, Vol. 27* (online) (pp. 385–388). London: MacMillan.

Landa, I. 2010. *The Apprentice's Sorcerer: The Liberal Tradition and Fascism*. Boston: Brill Press.

Meierhenrich, J. 2017. 'Fearing the Disorder of Things' in Meierhenrich and Simon (Eds.), *The Oxford Handbook of Carl Schmitt*. Oxford: Oxford University Press (online).

Meierhenrich, J. and Simons, O. (Eds.) 2017. *The Oxford Handbook of Carl Schmitt*. Oxford: Oxford University Press (online).

Nozick, R. 1974. *Anarchy State and Utopia*. Oxford: Basic Books.

Oron, J.H. 1958. 'Gottfried Feder Calls Hitler to Order: An Unpublished Letter on Nazi Party Affairs', *The Journal of Modern History* 30:4, pp. 358–362.

Piketty, T. 2014. *Capital in the Twenty-First Century*. Cambridge, MA: The Belknap Press of Harvard University Press.

Pitchford, M. 2011. *The Conservative Party and the Extreme Right 1945–1975*. Manchester: Manchester University Press.

Ptak, R. 2009. 'Neoliberalism in Germany: Revisiting the Ordoliberal Foundations of the Social Market Economy' in Philip Mirowski and Dieter Plehwe (Eds.), *The Road from Mont Pelerin: The Making of the Neoliberal Thought Collective* (pp. 98–138). Cambridge, MA: Harvard University Press.

Röpke, W. 1942. *International Economic Disintegration*. London: William. Hodge.

Röpke, W. 2009. *The Social Crisis of Our Time*. New Brunswick, NJ: Transaction.

Scheuerman, W.E. 1997. 'The Unholy Alliance of Carl Schmitt and Friedrich Hayek', *Constellations* 4:2, pp. 172–188.

Scheuerman, W.E. 1999. *Carl Schmitt: The End of Law (20th Century Political Thinkers)*. Lanham, MA: Rowman and Littlefield.

Schmitt, C. 1933. 'Starker Staat und gesunde Wirtschaft. Ein Vortrag vor Wirtschaftsführern' [A Strong State and a Healthy Economy: A Lecture for Business Leaders], *Volk und Reich Politische Monatshefte*, pp. 81–94.

Schmitt, C. 1988. *The Crisis of Parliamentary Democracy*. Cambridge, MA: Harvard University Press.

Schmitt, C. 1999. 'The Way to the Total State' in Simona Draghici (Ed. and Trans.), *Four Articles, 1931–1938* (pp. 1–18). Washington, DC: Plutarch Press.

Schmitt, C. 2004. *Legality and Legitimacy*. Durham, NC: Duke University Press.

Schmitt, C. 2007. *The Concept of the Political*. G. Schwab (Trans.). Chicago: University of Chicago Press, 2007.

Schmitt, C. 2015. *The Guardian of the Constitution. Hans Kelsen and Carl Schmitt on the Limits of Constitutional Law*. L. Vinx (Trans.). Cambridge: University of Cambridge Press.

Stolleis, M. 2013. *Origins of the German Welfare State: Social Policy in Germany to 1945*. Berlin: Springer.

Tomlinson, J. 2012. 'Thatcher, Monetarism and the Politics of Inflation' in Ben Jackson and Robert Saunders (Eds.), *Making Thatcher's Britain* (pp. 62–77). Cambridge: Cambridge University Press.

Tooze, A. 2006. *The Wages of Destruction: The Making and Breaking of the Nazi Economy*. London: Allen Lane.

Tribe, K. 2009. 'Liberalism and Neoliberalism in Britain, 1930–1980' in Philip Mirowski and Dieter Plehwe (Eds.), *The Road From Mont Pelerin: The Making of the Neoliberal Thought Collective* (pp. 68–97). Cambridge, MA: Harvard University Press.

Vinen, R. 2010. *Thatcher's Britain: The Politics and Social Upheaval of the Thatcher Era*. London: Simon & Schuster UK.

Weber, M. 1994. 'The President of the Reich' in Peter Lassman and Ronald Spiers (Eds.), *Political Writings* (pp. 304–309). Cambridge: University of Cambridge Press.

6 Inflation and social justice

By the period of the so called 'post-war consensus', Hayek (1967g, p. 220) reflected that the threat of 'hot socialism' had receded, writing in 1956 that 'future historians will probably regard the period from the revolution of 1848 to about 1948 as the century of European socialism.'[1] Yet the drive for socialism had been replaced with something equally as pernicious to his mind, the pursuit of 'social justice'. For Hayek (Hayek, 1978b), the concept was nothing more than a 'mirage', 'social' was a 'weasel word' that could be used by those who wanted to enforce a particular pattern of distribution that conformed to their own moral vision, with market freedom as the first casualty. Yet not only did social justice legitimise redistribution, it also, he argued, engendered a new morality, inculcating dependence on the state. Furthermore, growing expectations of the state inevitably led to the proliferation of government agencies and thus expanded the potential for the exercise of arbitrary power by the new bureaucrats who staffed them.

Fundamental to social justice was the post-war commitment, common across the western world, to maintain full employment. Never again, politicians insisted, would society return to the boom and bust economy of the pre-war era or the unemployment that had accompanied it. That commitment was made alongside a further promise, in Britain, to create and maintain a welfare state that would educate, house, cure and care for the society, and its children, that had won the war, from cradle to grave. What this vision of a 'New Jerusalem' needed was a way of subjecting the economy to the power of the state. Although planning had held immediate appeal in the years after the war, especially on the left of the Labour Party, it was to be that other old enemy of Hayek's, Keynesian counter cyclical policy, that was to become the primary means by which the ends of social justice and full employment were to be met.[2]

The fuel for this process, according to Hayek, was inflation. It was the ability of governments to expand the money supply that enabled political parties to make profligate promises regarding welfare in the pursuit of votes. Such promises were frequently the result of trade union pressure. The more prevalent the appeal of social justice, the more militant union leaders were likely to be, Hayek believed. The apparent weakness of governments under conditions of unlimited democracy meant they were always likely to succumb. For Hayek, this sort of arbitrary government only compromised market freedom and disturbed the conditions necessary for the epistemic efficiency.

Hayek's political response to the loose money policies of governments was, in the years prior to the mid-1970s, similar in form to that he offered in response to the issue of unlimited democracy. He counselled self-imposed restraint. The central bank, which in the British case had been nationalised since 1946, should look to restrain rather than excite further any unwarranted credit expansion being facilitated by private banks. Yet, just as the experience of the 1960s and '70s led him to conclude that governments could not be relied upon to impose a self-limiting legal framework, that same experience ultimately led him to conclude that simply urging restraint with regard to government oversight of the monetary framework was also hopeless.

Full employment and the new morality

Although Hayek had been a prominent participant in debates over the role of money during the 1930s, after the war and the ascendency of Keynesianism, he retreated from them (Hayek, 1978f).[3] One reason for this is general disappearance of debates about inflation from political discourse. The Bretton Woods agreement, as part of a bundle of other arrangements, resulted in a period of unprecedented economic growth in the thirty years after the war. As Gamble writes, 'exchange rates were fixed and progress towards reduction of tariffs through successive rounds of negotiation through GATT were endorsed. The IMF and the World Bank were confirmed as the principle international agencies charged with policing and lubricating the system' (Gamble, 1996, p. 17). For Hayek, however, all of this was enabled by a long inflationary boom which would eventually require a major correction. In place of a gold standard, currencies were pegged to the dollar, which was theoretically convertible to gold. In addition, governments were required to keep the value of their currency to within 1 per cent of an agreed exchange rate. In practice, he argued, this gave governments far too much scope to pursue inflationary policies. The general acceptance of Keynesian approaches put pressure on surplus countries to expand their money supply, rather than requiring deficit countries to contract, in order to maintain the agreed rates (Hayek, 1978f, p. 201). Yet despite Hayek's and others' occasional warnings, inflation remained low exhibiting no particular trend between the early 1950s and late '60s. Hilde Behrend, in her research during the period, found that over a third of the population had 'no clear view of what the word meant' (Tomlinson, 2012, p. 754). During what Hayek himself admitted was 'a unique 25 year period of great prosperity', combined with relatively low inflation, the audience for jeremiads was small.[4] Given this, it is perhaps of little surprise that work on the subject was a secondary concern, even for him.

The second reason for Hayek's lack of writing on the matter was that so dominant was Keynesianism, he admitted that 'when even some of the colleagues I most respected supported the wholly Keynesian Bretton Woods agreement,

I largely withdrew from the debate, since to proclaim my dissent from the near unanimous view of the orthodox phalanx would merely have deprived me of a hearing on matters about which I was more concerned at the time' (Hayek, 1978f, p. 219). As we have seen, by this he meant his attempt to decontest the liberal tradition and develop a conception of liberty appropriate to his epistemic economics. By the mid-1970s, however, inflation would become the most significant economic and electoral issue, providing the nexus upon which all other debates converged, resulting in Hayek's re-entry into the debate.

In the winter of 1961–2, at the age of 62, Hayek received the offer of a professorship, with favourable terms of retirement, from the University of Freiburg.[5] Soon after arriving he began to draft his three-volume work, *Law, Legislation and Liberty*. The impetus for embarking on what proved to be a long and major undertaking, so soon after completing what had been intended as the comprehensive statement of his thought, was the increasing hold that the concept of 'social justice' appeared to have over the popular and political imagination. Hayek came to regard it as a 'Trojan horse' and a new means by which socialists could pursue their rationalistic and organising aims, given that their previous methods of economic planning had, he maintained, been largely discredited (Vanberg, 2013).

As early as 1956, Hayek (1967g, p. 224) recognised that 'six years of socialist government in England have not produced anything resembling a totalitarian state'. Nonetheless, he went on:

> those who argue that this has disproved the thesis of *The Road to Serfdom* have really missed one of its main points: that the most important change which extensive government control produces is a psychological change, an alteration in the character of the people.

Fundamental to this change in character was the rise of a new morality he associated with social justice, a morality that looked to the state rather than the self for security and cultivated dependence. This, of course, was the very antithesis of freedom understood in republican terms. Hayek developed the theme further the following year when he wrote of how this new way of thinking:

> differed fundamentally from the traditionally accepted tenets of morality and justice, which, on principle, expect a man to give due consideration only to those consequences of his actions which in normal circumstances would be readily apparent to him; from this it easily followed that a man came to regard it as desirable that he should be instructed as to what he should or could do in any given case by someone endowed with greater knowledge and judgment than himself. This whole conception of social conduct is most closely linked, therefore, with a desire for a comprehensive blueprint of the social scene as a whole and a code of social conduct based upon it in accordance with a uniform and orderly plan.
>
> (1967h, p. 240)

This article 'What is "Social"?-What Does it Mean?', had been prompted by a break with his intellectual allies in the German ordoliberal School who had deemed it 'appropriate and desirable to qualify the term 'free market economy' by calling it 'social market economy'. Hayek (1967h, p. 238) complained 'that even the constitution of the Federal German Republic, instead of adhering to the clear and traditional conception of a *Rechtsstaat*, used the new and ambiguous phrase 'a social *Rechtsstaat*'. Yet, he added, 'I doubt very much whether anyone could really explain what the addition of this adjectival frill is supposed to denote.' Of all the members of the School, it was Eucken who Hayek had held in the greatest esteem and with whom he had the closest relationship and they resumed contact after the end of the Second World War (Goldschmidt and Hesse, 2013). Victor Vanberg (2013) has accurately observed that the concept of *Ordnungspolitik* seems to find expression in Hayek's work during the period of the 1930s and '40s when he was in regular contact with Eucken. After Eucken's death in 1950, the influence of the ordoliberal perspective on Hayek's work seemed to wane. Such was Hayek's deep mistrust of government, informed by his thinking about liberty and fed by his dislike of policies in pursuit of social justice, that even after his move to Freiberg, the spiritual home of ordoliberalism, he could no longer accept the more positive role the School assigned to the state. Although, in the context of rejecting the still discredited *laissez-faire* he might admit government had a role to play, it was an increasingly limited one. A related issue is Hayek's changed views on monopolies and anti-trust legislation. It is noticeable how in the period of *The Road to Serfdom*, (2001, p. 203) he proposed measures to counter the growth of monopolies in keeping with an ordoliberal perspective. As the ordoliberal influence declined, however, although recognising that monopolies may pose a threat to liberty, he became increasingly wary of measures to counter them as his distrust of active government grew. Hayek (1992, pp. 188–189) would later remark that because of Eucken's death 'the *Ordo* circle never matured into a major movement' instead it exhibited 'a restrained liberalism' and that although at one time 'Eucken and his circle embodied the Great German liberal tradition' it 'had unfortunately become defunct. Hayek's break with ordoliberalism would accompany his loss of faith in the possibility of a self-imposed limiting legal framework in the face what he perceived as inflation-fuelled unlimited democracy.

Law, Legislation and Liberty grew out of a desire on Hayek's (1982a, p. xvi) part to demonstrate that 'social justice' is in effect 'a universally used expression which to many people embodies a quasi-religious belief that has no content whatever and serves merely to insinuate that we ought to consent to a demand of some particular group'.[6] If socialism had been an influence in 'all parties' before and during the Second World War, now that same influence was exercised by social justice. Central to the dynamics of its pursuit were the trade unions. It was the unions, argued Hayek (1982b, p. 142) who first

> succeeded in clothing their demands with the aura of legitimacy (and in being allowed to use coercion for their enforcement) by representing them

as a requirement of 'social justice'. . . . It is now simply those who are numerically strong, or can readily be organised to withhold essential services, who gain in the process of political bargaining which governs legislation in contemporary democracy.

At the core of the belief in social justice was the commitment to full employment. Alongside greater public expenditure and an expansion of public services, this was the critical driver of inflation, argued Hayek. In *The Constitution of liberty* he had warned that the provision of such things as healthcare and old age pensions would have the effect of encouraging government to expand the money supply in order to meet growing demand, thus creating inflation (Hayek, 1960a, pp. 295–305). By the 1970s, in an era of increased trade union militancy, this seemed like a secondary problem to their wage demands:

> With regard to the trade union demands, particular trade unions can achieve only a relative improvement of the wages of their members, at the price of reducing the general productivity of labour and thus the general level of real wages, combined with the necessity in which they can place a government that controls the quantity of money to inflate, this system is rapidly destroying the economic order. Trades unions can now put governments in a position in which the only choice they have is to inflate or to be blamed for the unemployment which is caused by the wage policy of the trades unions (especially their policy of keeping relations between wages of different unions constant). This position must before long destroy the whole market order, probably through the price controls which accelerating inflation will force governments to impose.
>
> (Hayek, 1982d, p. 144)

Despite singling out the role of the trade unions in causing inflation, ultimate responsibility lay not with them, but with the government. In this, Hayek agreed with the foremost proponent of the need to restrict the money supply to counter inflation, Milton Friedman (1956) whose 'monetarist' doctrine was to become influential in policy making circles. Union wage demands only had inflationary effects in the context of the commitment to full employment. As Hayek (1960a, p. 280) had written;

> the effect of union action will depend on the principles governing monetary policy. What with the doctrines that are now widely accepted and the policies accordingly expected from the monetary authorities, there can be little doubt that current union policies must lead to continuous and progressive inflation. The chief reason for this is that the dominant 'full-employment' doctrines explicitly relieve the unions of the responsibility for any unemployment and place the duty of preserving full employment on the monetary and fiscal authorities. . . . If labour insists on a level of money wages too high to allow of full employment, the supply of money

must be so increased as to raise prices to a level where the real value of the prevailing money wages is no longer greater than the productivity of the workers seeking employment.

Thus, by increasing the money supply the actual value of money fell and it became possible to sustain full employment. This was not, however, a sustainable situation Hayek warned. Although such inflationary policies may maintain high employment in the short term, they merely postponed, and even exacerbated, the reckoning that must come, causing much greater unemployment later on (Hayek, 1982d, p. 59).

The politics of deflation

It was something of an error, and indeed a regret, of Hayek's that his critique of Keynesianism and the inflation he associated with it was dispersed across a range of publications (Hayek, 1994, p. 128). However, in 1972 the Institute of Economic Affairs published selections from a collection of articles which drew together Hayek's critique. This collection, *A Tiger by the Tail*, came at a fortuitous moment (Hayek, 1972). In 1967 the Labour government had been forced to devalue the pound. It had inherited a significant budget deficit of around £800 million and this, combined with a slowdown in exports, made devaluation the only alternative to borrowing from abroad to finance the deficit. The hope was that such a move would also boost Britain's flagging exports. The only discernible consequence of note was a steep increase in inflation (Cairncross and Eichengreen, 1983).

This was compounded when, in the winter of 1971/72, The United States severed the link between gold and the dollar, signalling the end of the Bretton Woods arrangements. With such restraints removed, national governments were free to pursue policies of monetary expansion unhindered by that previous, albeit somewhat lax, discipline. The rising rate of inflation was accelerated still further by the 1973 oil crisis. As Jim Tomlinson (2014, p. 752) has outlined, 'inflation rose further to an average 7.6 per cent between 1970 and 1972. From 1973 to 1975 there was another major acceleration, with the average rate rising to 16.4 per cent per annum. By 1975, it hit its all-time high of 27 per cent.' As the collection's editor Sudha Shenoy later commented 'Keynes's unassailability died between the first and second editions' of the collection, published in 1972 and 1978 respectively (Shenoy, 2003) as a result of the low growth and inflation that together gripped western economies.

The recent relative success of the collection, combined with the apparent confirmation of all Hayek's warnings, may well have caught the attention of the awarding committee for the Nobel Memorial Prize in Economic Science. In December 1974, the prize was shared by Hayek and Gunnar Myrdal, the Swedish social democratic economist. Its award to the 75-year-old Hayek, a man who had not written in an applied manner in the field for over a quarter of a century, testifies to the great extent to which the profession was in ferment as the 'Keynesian consensus' split in the face of new economic realities.[7] From 1974 onwards, free market economists, albeit from the neo-classical Chicago School rather than those of the Austrian variety, would increasingly come to dominate the winners list (Laidler, 2013, pp. 71–73).[8] In his acceptance speech, 'The Pretence of Knowledge', Hayek (1978a) argued that the policies pursued over the previous twenty-five years were the product of the sort of rationalism, or scientism, that he had identified during his wartime 'abuse of reason' project. Although the formulas that underpinned Keynesianism made sense to a scientific mind, the truth was that the economy was constituted not by the aggregates upon which those formulas were based, but by millions of micro relationships for which there was no possible formulaic expression.

One major inconsistency in Hayek's writing on money does arise during this period. It is inconsistent not only with his earlier work when, in the 1930s, he had argued for Britain remaining on the gold standard despite the economic crisis, but also with his subsequent writings in which he wished away the existence of macroeconomic policy entirely. At this point in the 1970s, Hayek was ready to accept that the deflationary dangers of a downturn could be catastrophic and had indeed played a major role in turning the economic crash of 1929 into a depression. 'I have to confess' he admitted,

> I did then believe that a short process of deflation might break that rigidity of money wages. . . . If I were today responsible for the monetary policy of a country I would certainly endeavour to prevent a threatening actual deflation, that is an absolute decrease of the stream of incomes, with all suitable means, and would announce that I intend to do.
>
> (Hayek, 1978f, pp. 206–207)

It is a striking admission for someone who had argued for a vision of the market as ultimately self-correcting. His long-time friend Gottfried Harberler (1986, p. 422) had earlier warned of the dangers of a secondary deflation following an initial downturn. Although the first may have a corrective quality, the second had none. It seems to be this second phase to which Hayek was referring. He did recognise 'that 40 years ago I argued differently and that I have since altered my opinion' but not, he maintained, 'about the theoretical explanation of the events but about the practical possibility of removing the obstacles to the functioning of the system in a particular way' (Hayek, 1978f, p. 206). Thus, to his mind he was not renouncing his basic view of the market, he was simply recasting his advice in terms of what he considered politically pragmatic. This bears some resemblance to Hayek's comments to Wilhelm Röpke in 1930 that monetary expansion should be avoided in Germany, as was then being considered by the Braun Committee on which Röpke sat, 'unless the political situation is so serious that continuing unemployment would lead to a political revolution' (Hayek, 1978f, p. 211). Under the threat of a major depression, Hayek had been, and remained, ready to countenance monetary expansion in order to counter the sort of secondary deflation that Harberler had earlier warned of. What this makes clear is that even for him, decisions about monetary policy were ultimately subject to political considerations and he was willing to compromise his position *in extremis*.

If Hayek had discovered pragmatism, it was of a strange kind, one that involved asking how far the existing economic and political system could be pushed before it broke entirely. A restriction of the money supply of the sort Hayek advocated by the early 1970s would have required something like the deflationary policies introduced by Britain in 1922 or, more dramatically, a reform of the currency of the sort carried out by Germany in 1923 with all of the social consequences that entailed for employment and welfare spending (Gamble, 1996). In 1975 Hayek appeared on NBC's 'Meet the Press'. One of the interviewers pressed him to say what level of unemployment he felt willing to tolerate should governments follow his advice and reduce the money supply in order to combat inflation. Hayek argued that a significant monetary contraction would have the desired effects in a rapid fashion: unemployment might rise steeply, but it would not last long. As such he could not exclude a 'temporary rise to thirteen, fourteen per cent' unemployment, 'or something like that'. When pressed as to whether 'the social fabric' of the country could tolerate such a rate, Hayek (1975) responded 'for a few months certainly'. This, of course, involved the assumption that the economy would then correct itself. Yet such confidence hardly accords with his recent admission that expansionary policies may indeed be required in extreme circumstances.

If monetary policy must ultimately be subject to political considerations, as Hayek acknowledged, instigating a rise in unemployment was a political decision Hayek clearly endorsed. A salutary impact of a sharp increase in unemployment, one he was eager to draw to viewers' attention, was its potential to seriously weaken the power of the trade unions. For him the situation was clear: a significant increase in unemployment was not only unavoidable, it was desirable. With this achieved, 'the primary aim' he wrote, 'must again become the stability of the value of money and the currency authorities must again be effectively protected against that political pressure which today forces them so often to take measures which are politically advantageous in the short run but harmful in the long run' (Hayek, 1978f, p. 207).

Similar debates regarding the maximum level of unemployment society could withstand were also being had in Britain, particularly within the Conservative Party. When Edward Heath called the General Election in February 1974 many within the party felt his campaign had asked the wrong question of electorate: the critical issue was not 'who governs?' but 'how do we govern?' Among hardliners, the conviction was growing that the only way to bring the unions to heel and curtail inflation was to take Hayek's advice and radically limit the money supply. One of the first figures to be impressed by Hayek was Enoch Powell, a figure who wielded huge influence in the party during the 1960s and continued to do so even after his expulsion by Heath for his infamous 'rivers of blood' speech on the basis that it amounted to an incitement to racial hatred. Powell's influence over many Conservatives had not, however, been based on his anti-immigrant stance but on his steadfast opposition to all forms of government intervention in the economy. Increasingly he argued that the sole economic duty of government lay in the control of the money supply (Vinen, 2010, pp. 50–51). In a speech at Chippenham the month after the 'rivers of blood' speech, he echoed Hayek's insistence that 'inflation with all its attendant evils, comes about for one reason and one reason only: the Government causes it' (Powell, 1968).[9]

Despite Powell's enduring hold over many Conservatives, his absence from the party removed any possibility of him wielding direct influence over policy. The mantle of chief monetarist had passed to Keith Joseph, the leading critic in the party of the Heathites who had, like Powell before him, been influenced by Hayek (Denham and Garnett, 2001). In 1974 he established the Centre for Policy Studies which, along with the Institute for Economic Affairs that Hayek had encouraged Anthony Fisher to found twenty years earlier, sought to advance free market ideas. In a speech at Preston in September 1974 entitled 'Inflation is Caused By Governments' he made his position clear: 'inflation is threatening to destroy our society. It is threatening to destroy not just the relative prosperity to which most of us have become accustomed ... but it will lead to catastrophe ... and to the end of freedom' (Joseph, 1974a). The speech took aim at Keynesianism and insisted that ultimately it was government that posed a threat to economic order through its monetary policies. Hayek wrote to Joseph to congratulate him on the speech to which Joseph (1974b) admiringly replied that he was 'only far too gratified' by Hayek's 'blessing'. In 1975 the monetarist wing of the party received a major boost when Margaret Thatcher was elected to the leadership of the party after Heath's second general election defeat.[10]

Thatcher appointed Joseph as the head of policy and research and, when in power, as first Secretary of State for Industry, and then as Secretary of State for Education. He remained one of her closest advisors throughout the early period of her leadership.[11] Like Hayek, he felt that a sharp reduction in the money supply would produce a severe but short increase in unemployment and that this was favourable to a prolonged period at a lower level. Such a shock would quickly produce a change in the behaviour of economic actors and, crucially, break the power of the trade unions (Tomlinson, 2012, pp. 69–72). There were others in the party who would become known derisively as the 'wets' who counselled caution. Shortly after her election, during a meeting on future economic policy, Thatcher was confronted by colleagues urging a cautious approach to treatment of the money supply. In what may well be an apocryphal recounting, she is reputed to have held up a copy of *The Constitution of Liberty* and exclaimed 'This is what we believe!' (Cockett, 1994, p. 174)[12] Within a month of her second election win in July 1983, Joseph (1974b) wrote to Hayek insisting 'It is you ... who have done more than any other to animate and educate the counter-attack on socialism'.

Social justice and market republicanism

Trade union influence, the pursuit of social justice, and the resultant inflation were all a product, Hayek argued, of the unlimited nature of democracy. In *The*

Constitution of Liberty, Hayek (1960a, p. 133) had argued for the need to limit government's discretionary oversight of the monetary framework. 'On balance' he wrote 'probably some mechanical rule which aims at what is desirable in the long run and ties the hands of authority in its short-term decisions is likely to produce a better monetary policy than principles which give to the authorities more power and discretion.' However, he advised such a measure be taken not because inflation in itself posed a threat to his newly adopted republican concept of liberty, but because it served to frustrate economic coordination over time as conceived within his epistemic economics. 'It should perhaps be explicitly stated' Hayek continued, 'that the case against discretion in monetary policy is not quite the same as that against discretion in the use of the coercive powers of government.' In marked contrast to his later writing on the subject he maintained that 'even if the control of money is in the hands of a monopoly its exercise does not necessarily involve coercion of private individuals'. Instead, 'the argument against discretion in monetary policy rests on the view that monetary policy and its effects should be as predictable as possible'.

There was, however, a clear insistence on Hayek's part that the pursuit of social justice facilitated by inflation did pose a definite threat to individual liberty. This was primarily because it ran contrary to the principle of *isonomia* or equality before the law that liberty demanded. Hayek (1960a, pp. 234–235) traced the ideal of social justice to the demands for distributive justice that emerged with the growth of democracy following the French revolution. 'As is becoming clear in ever increasing fields of welfare policy' he wrote, an insistence on this distributive social justice required that,

> an authority instructed to achieve particular results for the individuals must be given essentially arbitrary powers . . . full equality for most cannot but mean the equal submission of the great masses under the command of some elite who manages their affairs. While an equality of rights under a limited government is possible and an essential condition of individual freedom, a claim for equality of material position can be met only by a government with totalitarian powers.
>
> (Hayek, 1982c, p. 83)

It was precisely the arbitrary nature of the powers that the pursuit of social justice apparently required that rendered it inimical to his conception of liberty as non-domination. Compounding this, it also inculcated an ethic of dependency that would engrain reliance on the *imperium* associated with the welfare state. If *dominium* had been a greater fixture in Hayek's thought, he may have viewed the pursuit of social justice as a means of combatting the abuses that can result from concentrations of arbitrary private power. In its absence, however, he viewed it simply a vehicle for *imperium*.

Even in 1960, Hayek had advised that all those who 'wish to stop the drift toward increasing government control should concentrate their efforts on monetary policy' as 'there is perhaps nothing more disheartening than the fact that there are still so many intelligent and informed people who in most other respects will defend freedom and yet are induced by the immediate benefits of an expansionist policy to support what, in the long run, must destroy the foundations of a free society' (Hayek, 1960a, pp. 138–139.) Yet here he was still taking the long view and remained of the opinion, echoing his work in the 1930s, that the only way to prevent such destruction was the establishment of 'rules versus authorities in monetary policy' (Hayek, 1960a, p. 334).

By the 1970s, however, Hayek had become radicalised. His realisation that the parliamentary system would not adopt a self-limiting framework also meant that he lost faith in its ability to combat inflation and call off the pursuit of social justice. Rather than view the issue of inflation as being at a remove from matters of liberty, he began to warn that arbitrary government control of money, with all its inflationary consequences,

> is a power which at present is the most serious threat not only to a work-ing international economy but also to personal freedom; and it will remain a threat so long as governments have the physical power to enforce such controls. It is to be hoped that people will gradually recognise this threat to their personal freedom and that they will make the complete prohibition of such measures an entrenched constitutional provision.
>
> (Hayek, 1999h, p. 222)

Hayek was no longer convinced of the value of advising restraint. Instead, alongside his plans for limiting democracy, he began to devise ways of remov-ing control of money from the government entirely.

Conclusion

Although Hayek had largely retreated from the debate over the monetary framework in the thirty years after the Second World War, he held to a tech-nical view of inflation as a threat to economic coordination, but not itself a threat to individual liberty. Over the subsequent decade and a half, however, his thought was radicalised by a decade of increasingly 'unlimited' democracy and the progressive pursuit of social justice. By the mid-1970s, his criticisms of Keynesian techniques seemed to have been confirmed. As the inflationary crisis of the 1970s worsened, he would once again enter the fray. This time, however, rather than regard issues of money as a primarily technical matter, he would view them from the perspective of his market republicanism and through the prism of liberty conceived as non-domination.

For Hayek, it had been the decline in the appeal of planning that had prompted those on the left to embrace the monetary 'license' provided by Keynesianism in order to pursue the replacement creed of social justice. In the vanguard, because of the manner in which the material interest of their members could be linked to it, were the trade unions. For him, however, social justice was simply a Trojan horse that allowed sectional interests and their allies among the political classes to impose a particular pattern of distribution on society according to both their ideals and interests. The consequences for the economy, he warned, were stark and a reckoning was inevitable. As the inflationary crisis of the 1970s worsened, Hayek and his political allies on the right advocated a radical retrenchment that would drive up unemployment, break the unions and necessitate abandoning the pursuit of social justice. Yet by the middle of that decade, unlike his political allies, who still sought to assert their socio-economic plans using existing powers and institutions, Hayek had begun to devise new, libertarian schemes that would conclusively terminate monetary *imperium*.

Notes

1 The existence of a consensus has been hotly debated by political theorists and historians (Pimlott et al., 1989).
2 Keynes in fact died in 1946, but the policy applications of his theory, in the British context, would be worked through by Nicholas Kaldor, a former colleague of Hayek, among many others.
3 Hayek goes on to suggest, however, that the British economists in particular supported the agreement because they felt it would be in the best interests of Britain rather than providing a 'satisfactory monetary order'.
4 There were exceptions to this particularly in the Conservative Party. For example, 1958 saw the resignation of the Chancellor of the Exchequer, Peter Thorneycroft, along with ministers Enoch Powell and Nigel Birch. They disagreed with Macmillan's increased government spending plans. Thorneycroft later became a strong supporter of monetarism under Margaret Thatcher. See Tomlinson (2014, p. 63).
5 Ordinarily Hayek's age would have disqualified him from such an offer. Special arrangements had to be made by the Dean of the University with the Prime Minister of Baden-Wurttemberg. Both were keen to counter the growing influence of Social Democracy in the state and felt Hayek would prove a useful intellectual ally (Vanberg, 2013).
6 For contemporaneous reviews see Salkever (1981); Altham (1982); Schaefer (1980).
7 Hayek himself had been sceptical about the establishment of the prize and felt that if anything it should be awarded for recent work. This opinion was delivered after his award, however, and at the time he was very happy to receive it. See Ebenstein (2001, p. 262)
8 For example, Milton Friedman, 1976; George Stigler, 1982; Gary Becker, 1992. After Friedman's award Gunnar Myrdal called for the prize to be abolished.
9 Powell was a member of Hayek's Mont Pèlerin Society (MPS) and had been impressed by *The Constitution of Liberty*. He had, however, become angry with Hayek after he had revealed, somewhat indiscreetly, in an interview with *The Daily Telegraph* that he considered Powell to suffer from 'emotional instability'. This was because of Powell's refusal to observe a minute's silence, called at the MPS, for the Israeli Olympic athletes murdered in 1972 on the basis that it would be wrong to mark one set of murders in the midst of what he considered an 'epidemic' of political violence. Hayek apologised and Powell accepted. Nonetheless, he would resign from the MPS in 1980, dismissing it as a 'Hayek adulation Society, with a minor niche for Freidman'. Powell expressly disliked Hayek's 'Teutonic habit of telling the English, whom he does not in the least understand, how to set about governing themselves' (Stapleton, 2001, p. 179). Powell's statement regarding the MPS as an adulation society is probably misleading. By 1980 Hayek's involvement was diminishing while Friedman's influence was ascendant as was that of its more economistic American members. See Angus Burgin (2012).

10 Thatcher was viewed, however, as a moderate on the economy, falling somewhere between staunch advocates of monetarism and the Heathites, during her election campaign.

11 Jospeh was regarded as a likely future leader of the party but, in an echo of Powell's earlier extremism, excluded himself from consideration as a result of controversial comments made regarding the 'human stock' of the nation in October 1974. His relationship with Thatcher was extremely close 'England's greatest man' was how Thatcher herself chose to describe him – or, when the Prime Minister happened to see her Secretary of State for Education scurrying through the streets, 'a darling man'. It was an affection reciprocated by Joseph: 'I beam at the very sight of her'. At Joseph's memorial service Thatcher said, 'Keith should have become Prime Minister. . . . So many of us felt that was his destiny' (Clarke, 2001).

12 Thatcher claimed to have been inspired by *The Road to Serfdom* at University though how familiar she was with Hayek's work is in fact far from clear (Campbell, 2007, p. 60).

Works cited

Altham, J.E.J. 1982. 'The Political Order of a Free People', *Philosophy* 57, pp. 274–278.

Burgin, A. 2012. *The Great Persuasion: Reinventing Free Markets Since the Depression*. Cambridge, MA: Harvard University Press.

Cairncross, A. and Eichengreen, B. 1983. *Sterling in Decline: The Devaluations of 1931, 1949 and 1967*. Oxford: Basil Blackwell.

Campbell, J. 2007. *Margaret Thatcher, Vol. 1: The Grocer's Daughter*. London: Vintage Books.

Clarke, P. 2001. 'The Antagoniser's Agoniser', *London Review of Books,* 19 July.

Cockett, R. 1994. *Thinking the Unthinkable: Think Tanks and the Economic Counter Revolution, 1931–1983*. London: Fontana Press.

Denham, A. and Garnett, M. 2001. *Keith Joseph*. Abingdon: Routledge.

Ebenstein, A. 2001. *Friedrich Hayek: A Biography*. New York: Palgrave, St Martin's Press.

Friedman, M. 1956. 'The Quantity Theory of Money – A Restatement' in M. Friedman (Ed.), *Studies in the Quantity Theory of Money* (pp. 3–21). Chicago: University of Chicago Press.

Gamble, A. 1996. *Hayek: The Iron Cage of Liberty*. Cambridge: Polity Press.

Goldschmidt, N. and Hesse, J.O. 2013. 'Hayek, Eucken and the Road to Serfdom' in Robert Leeson (Ed.), *Hayek: A Collaborative Biography, Part 1 Influences from Mises to Bartley* (pp. 123–145). London: Palgrave Macmillan.

Harberler, G. 1986. 'Reflections on Hayek's Business Cycle Theory', *Cato Journal* 6:2, pp. 422–435.

Hayek, F.A. 1960a. *The Constitution of Liberty*. Chicago: University of Chicago Press.

Hayek, F.A. 1967g. 'The Road to Serfdom after Twelve Years' [1956] in Friedrich Hayek (Ed.), *Studies in Philosophy, Politics and Economics* (pp. 216–228). London: Routledge & Kegan Paul.

Hayek, F.A. 1967h. 'What Is "Social"? What Does It Mean?' [1957] in Friedrich Hayek (Ed.), *Studies in Philosophy, Politics and Economics* (pp. 237–247). London: Routledge & Kegan Paul.

Hayek, F.A. 1972. *A Tiger By the Tail*. Sudha Shenoy (Ed.). London: Institute of Economic Affairs.

Hayek, F.A. 1975. 'Meet the Press' interview with NBC, 22 June. Accessed at https://mises.org/library/hayek-meets-press-1975

Hayek, F.A. 1978a. 'The Pretence of Knowledge' [1974] in Friedrich Hayek (Ed.), *New Studies in Philosophy, Politics, Economics and the History of Ideas* (pp. 23–34). London: Routledge & Kegan Paul.

Hayek, F.A. 1978b. 'The Atavism of Social Justice' [1976] in Friedrich Hayek (Ed.), *New Studies in Philosophy, Politics, Economics and the History of Ideas* (pp. 57–70). London: Routledge & Kegan Paul.

Hayek, F.A. 1978f. 'The Campaign Against Keynesian Inflation' [a collection of articles from 1974/75/75/76] in Friedrich Hayek (Ed.), *New Studies in Philosophy, Politics, Economics and the History of Ideas* (pp. 191–231). London: Routledge & Kegan Paul.

Hayek, F.A. 1982a. 'Introduction' [1982] in *Law, Legislation and Liberty: A New Statement of the Liberal Principles of Justice and Political Economy* [3 Volume edition]. London: Routledge Kegan Paul.

Hayek, F.A. 1982b. 'Rules and Order' [1973] in *Law, Legislation and Liberty: A New Statement of the Liberal Principles of Justice and Political Economy* [3 Volume edition]. London: Routledge Kegan Paul.

Hayek, F.A. 1982c. 'The Mirage of Social Justice' [1976] in *Law, Legislation and Liberty: A New Statement of the Liberal Principles of Justice and Political Economy* [3 Volume edition]. London: Routledge Kegan Paul.

Hayek, F.A. 1982d. 'The Political Order of a Free People' [1979] in *Law, Legislation and Liberty: A New Statement of the Liberal Principles of Justice and Political Economy* [3 Volume edition]. London: Routledge Kegan Paul.

Hayek, F.A. 1992. 'Ludwig von Mises' [composed of several essays 1951/73/78] in Friedrich Hayek (Ed.), *The Fortunes of Liberalism: The Collected Works of F.A. Hayek, Vol. 4* (ed.), Peter Klein (pp. 126–159). Chicago: University of Chicago Press.

Hayek, F.A. 1994. *Hayek on Hayek: An Autobiographical Dialogue*. Stephen Kresge and Leif Warner (Eds.). Chicago: University of Chicago Press.

Hayek, F.A. 1999h. 'The Denationalisation of Money' [1976] in Stephen Kresge (Ed.), *Good Money Part Two: The Collected Works of F.A. Hayek, Vol. 6* (pp. 128–229). Chicago: University of Chicago Press.

Hayek, F.A. 2001. *The Road to Serfdom*. London: Routledge.

Joseph, K. 1974a. 'Inflation Is Caused by Governments' Speech at Preston, 5 September 1974. Accessed at www.margaretthatcher.org/document/110607

Joseph, K. 1974b. Letter to Friedrich Hayek. Friedrich A. von Hayek papers, Box no. 29, Folder no. 43, Hoover Institution Archives.

Laidler, D. 2013. 'The 1974 Hayek-Myrdal Nobel Prize' in Robert Leeson (Ed.), *Hayek: A Collaborative Biography, Part 1 Influences from to Bartley* (pp. 71–73). London: Palgrave Macmillan.

Pimlott, B., Kavanagh, D. and Morris, P. 1989. 'Is the Post-War Consensus a Myth?' *Contemporary Record* 2:6, pp. 12–15.

Powell, E. 1968. Speech at Chippenham, 11 May. Accessed at www.enochpowell.net/fr-46.html

Salkever, S.G. 1981. 'Review of Law, legislation and Liberty, Vol. 3', *The Journal of Politics* 43:1, pp. 234–236.

Schaefer, D.L. 1980. 'Review of Law, Legislation and Liberty, Vol. 3', *The American Political Science Review* 74:1, pp. 165–166.

Shenoy, S. 2003. Interview with Mises Daily. Accessed at http://mises.org/library/global-perspective

Stapleton, J. 2001. *Political Intellectuals and Public Identities in Britain Since 1850*. Manchester: Manchester University Press.

Tomlinson, J. 2012. 'Thatcher, Monetarism and the Politics of Inflation' in Ben Jackson and Robert Saunders (Eds.), *Making Thatcher's Britain* (pp. 62–77). Cambridge: Cambridge University Press.

Tomlinson, J. 2014. 'British Government and Popular Understanding of Inflation in the Mid-1970s', *The Economic History Review* 67:3, pp. 750–768.

Vanberg, V. 2013. 'Hayek in Freiburg' in Robert Leeson (Ed.), *Hayek: A Collaborative Biography, Part 1 Influences from Mises to Bartley* (pp. 93–122). London: London: Palgrave Macmillan.

Vinen, R. 2010. *Thatcher's Britain: The Politics and Social Upheaval of the Thatcher Era*. London: Simon & Schuster UK.

7 A market republican constitution

In this and the following chapter, I will examine what Hayek referred to as his 'intellectual emergency equipment': the 'Model Constitution' and his plan for the 'Denationalisation of Money'. He arrived at these radical schemes because he had lost faith in the ability of the political system to limit its legislative and monetary excesses. 'Development towards a totalitarian state is made inevitable' Hayek (1982a, p. xx). wrote, 'by certain deeply entrenched defects of construction of the generally accepted type of "democratic" government' and Britain was now at 'an impasse from which political leaders will offer to extricate us by desperate means' of the type Schmitt had outlined forty years previously. Although the urgency with which he called for the implementation of his equipment varied in response to broader political developments, it is clear that they were not merely an intellectual diversion. He regarded both pieces as concrete proposals, the adoption of which was eminently necessary to save Britain, and elsewhere, from 'the nightmare of increasingly totalitarian powers'. The situation had become desperate, the moment when 'the breakdown of the existing institutions becomes unmistakable' was at hand. In 1977, he stated clearly that 'my proposal is not, as I would wish merely a sort of standby arrangement of which I could say we must work it out intellectually to have it ready when the present system completely collapses' (Hayek, 1999i) because the point of collapse was imminent.[1] Such was his disillusionment with the existing political system that even when political allies came to power in Britain and the United States, Hayek (1982a, p. xx) remained convinced they would not be able to resist the pressure to adopt 'unlimited' methods. He thus continued to regard his equipment as offering 'a possible escape from the fate which threatens us.' Hayek's emergency equipment is not, therefore, a belated aberration in his body of work. Instead, it provides us with a concrete description of the institutions and form of government appropriate to Hayekian political economy: it demands our attention.

With his advice that government should impose a self-limiting framework to restrict its legislative reach having gone unheeded, Hayek's Model Constitution was intended to provide a constitutional fix that would recreate the framework at a meta legal level. It would confer on an Upper House of Parliament the ability to establish the bounds within which the daily business of government, conducted by the Lower House, must operate. Hayek regarded this first piece of intellectual emergency equipment as one of the two major inventions of his career, along with the second piece – his scheme for the denationalisation of money. He crafted these two inventions very much with his one 'discovery' – the epistemic conception of the economy presented in 'Economics and Knowledge' – very much in mind. Together, they were designed to help establish a new form of political economy that would result in the 'dethronement of politics' and allow the epistemic process of market coordination to proceed unmolested. Having established the market republican nature of Hayek's theory, we can now identify these two pieces of intellectual emergency equipment as the pillars of an economically liberal market republic.

Despite Hayek's hopes, during the 1940s and '50s, that governments might yet recognise the need for a legal framework, he had in fact already begun to experiment with ideas for a European federation that might serve to limit the economic interventions of government. The rationale was simple: federation members would not tolerate a fellow member intervening to promote or protect their own economies. The rules of the federation would, therefore, forbid it. In 'The Economic Conditions of Interstate Federalism' Hayek argued that 'planning, or central direction of economic activity, presupposes the existence of common ideals and common values; and the degree to which planning can be carried on is limited to the extent to which agreement on such a common scale of values can be obtained or enforced.' It was therefore rational to assume that in a federation of many nations, such agreement would be extremely difficult to achieve and this in itself could be relied upon to put an end to large-scale planning because 'although, in the national state, the submission to the will of a majority will be facilitated by the myth of nationality, it must be clear that people will be reluctant to submit to any interference in their daily affairs when the majority which directs the government is composed of people of different nationalities and different traditions' (Hayek, 1948a, p. 264). In the absence of a single cultural identity, the sort of solidarity that underpins economic interventions or wealth transfers in favour of a particular group would, Hayek believed, not exist.

In conceiving of this model, it is entirely possible that Hayek was influenced by the way in which the Austro-Hungarian Empire, into which he had been born, had functioned (Slobodian, 2018). As an economically liberal, yet essentially undemocratic, empire it had overseen a regime of free trade and non-intervention across central Europe, and its very heterogeneity had tended to preclude direct economic intervention to the benefit of one group for fear of antagonising another. Others have suggested that Hayek's paper has served as a guiding document for the development of the European Union, at least since the mid-1980s. According to Streek (2015), following the decline of the broadly Keynesian outlook of European Community over the 1980s, the union was reconceived along ordoliberal lines as a disciplinary apparatus for the enforcement of competition and the promotion of free market liberalism. Whatever the accuracy of this analysis, in the years after the war the European project commanded surprisingly little of Hayek's attention and one could hardly contend, at least in its initial decades, that it was a model of Hayekian political economy. To his mind, it had instead been captured, like the rest of the west, by the 'Keynesian phalanx'. Accordingly, Hayek's attentions turned, at least ostensibly, to the developing world.

Origins of the model constitution

Although it would take the experience of the 1960s and '70s for Hayek to recommend its implementation in the 'mature' western democracies, the Model Constitution had in fact made its first appearance in his work as early as 1960, in a radio broadcast on the BBC's Third Programme entitled 'New Nations and the Problem of Power' (Hayek, 1960b, pp. 819–821). In it, Hayek reflected on the constitutional order appropriate for those nations that were gaining their independence as a result of decolonisation. What is striking about the broadcast, however, is that, although nominally directed at 'the problem of power' in 'new nations', he was in fact discussing a pathology he located in the British constitution, namely the unlimited power of Parliament. His talk involved privileging the distinction drawn by Schmitt, the theorist he had previously condemned, between *Rechts* and *Gesetz*, over the doctrine of parliamentary sovereignty, one of the great achievements of Whiggism, which was of course the political tradition with which he wished to be associated.

It is significant that Hayek's new constitutional scheme emerged in the book in which he also outlined his republican conception of liberty and presented in greatest detail his intellectual history. The ideas expressed in the broadcast had grown out of what had been only a footnote in his recent work, *The Constitution of Liberty*, where he reflected that the business of government had become confused with the business of law-making when the House of Lords acquiesced in allowing the Commons to exercise power in the absence of general restraining principles or laws. The problem of 'unlimited democracy' had been facilitated, Hayek argued, by the confusion between law-making and administration. 'It is interesting to speculate' he wrote,

> what the development would have been if at the time when the House of Commons successfully claimed the exclusive control over expenditure and thereby in effect the control of administration, the House of Lords had succeeded in achieving exclusive power of laying down general laws, including the principles on which the private individual could be taxed. A division of competence of the two legislative chambers on this principle has never been tried but may be well worth consideration.
>
> (Hayek, 1960a, p. 488)

Had the Commons not claimed these powers, 'the result, would have been the development of . . . two assemblies with different tasks . . . [one – "a legislative assembly in the true sense"] developing the general laws of the country . . . [the other – "an executive assembly"] directing the administration'. In the modern context, 'if you look at the Acts of Parliament', he complained, 'you will find that 90 per cent are not laws but are administrative orders decided by a democratic body . . . and called for that reason a law. I think we ought to call them Acts of Parliament and not laws' (Hayek, 1960b, pp. 819–820). This was a more nuanced point than his previous warnings of 'unlimited democracy', and it was a constitutional confusion that the 'dogmatic democrats' were able to take advantage of. Hayek's reflections, then were framed with reference to issues of 17th century England, certainly not those facing the newly independent countries of the developing world. The talk was informed by his republican understanding of liberty and his intellectual history of English liberalism; at least one of these discourses we might imagine the 'new' states would have been eager to abandon.

The suggestions that Hayek (1960b, p. 820) put forward for new nations were intended to separate law-making and government administration in the developing world and, as such, act as a brake on those who wished to use the powers of government to structure the economy and redistribute wealth. What new nations required, he argued, was for 'the functions of government' to be 'definitely curtailed'. By doing so the reach of democracy could be limited. Establishing two distinct houses of Parliament would achieve this: 'I am proposing to have two different bodies' said Hayek, 'one dealing with current administration, and one with the gradual amendment of the permanent framework of the law': an administrative and a legislative assembly. Confusingly, Hayek called the general law-making body a 'Legislative Assembly' despite his distinction between law proper and legislation.

In addition, he suggested 'a rather high age limit' be set for eligibility for election to the legislative assembly and on the basis of a term of fifteen years, in order to 'give greater permanence' and 'much greater stability in every sense' (Hayek, 1960b, p. 820). Also contained in his proposal was a far greater role for the judiciary and the legal profession. A Supreme Court would be required to adjudicate on matters where the functions of the two houses might come into conflict. He also reflected that 'it is a great pity that in fact lawyers no longer regard themselves as competent to suggest what the law might be'. Instead, in another echo of Weimar disputes, he argued that under the influence of legal positivism, they had put themselves at the disposal of politics and 'listen to what the politicians want' rather than seeking to restrain them (Hayek, 1960b, p. 821). Law, for Hayek, was something to be interpreted by an expert elite, rather than decided upon by the people and their representatives.

The fact that Hayek was willing to put forward such a radical scheme may seem surprising given that his recent book had given such weight to the importance of culturally evolved institutions, like those emphasised by Hume and Smith. Hayek was not insensible to the charge and observed that he laid himself 'open to the . . . objection of being inconsistent . . . I have been arguing that constitutions in the old Whig tradition ought to grow and not be made; and to suggest any completely new constitutional system is somewhat absurd.'

However, he was able to justify doing just this on the grounds that in the 'new democracies' institutions had not been allowed to evolve as they had in the west and as such a devised scheme would be required. Moreover, certain groups in such countries held the 'rightly sound fear that without any traditional political morals the newly elected bodies may exceed their reasonable powers'. Whilst Hayek (Hayek, 1960b, p. 820) remained vague regarding who those groups were, it is clear he was referring to owners of property and capital. In many of the 'new nations' this inevitably meant the small minority of European settlers among whom private property was concentrated.

Despite this apparently global turn in his thinking, that Hayek somewhat incongruously based his analysis on the British experience strongly suggests that what would be good for the new nations would be equally good for the old. In 1960, however, he resisted that conclusion. He remained keen to stress that his scheme was designed only with 'new nations' in mind and that 'large-scale constitutional reform' was not a 'possible or a likely development in this country'. Perhaps he was aware of the political infeasibility of such ideas in Britain, where 'today most people would think it is probably irrelevant' to suggest 'large scale constitutional reform'. He did not, however, state that it was undesirable. Nonetheless, it seemed that Hayek was still willing to believe, as he had in the 1940s, that Parliament might come to recognise the importance of refraining from taking an active role in the economy and would begin to limit itself to the creation of general laws. Hayek's problem was that few seemed to be taking his warnings of the dangers of unlimited government sufficiently seriously.

More challenging for the consistency of Hayek's body of work, is that if we pursue the implications of his analysis, described above, it undermines his thesis that cultural evolution had brought about the rules-based order required for market freedom. Once again, the problems Hayek runs into are historical in nature. The pre-eminence of the Commons, the very thing that set the confusion of law and administration in motion and led to the growth of unlimited government, had been asserted since the deposition of James II at the end of the 17th century, an event Hayek otherwise regarded as a great Whig victory Hayek (1960a, p. 169). And yet, despite this, it was the subsequent centuries that witnessed the 'rediscovery' of economic and market freedom. The confusion he identifies can hardly then be said to have impeded Britain's economic growth. On the contrary, it appears more that unlimited government was a prerequisite to the emergence of economic liberalism. Power was exercised energetically to extend the reach of the market with Acts of Parliament employed to do away with the last vestiges of pre-liberal moral economy. The enclosure of common land was accelerated, trade unions were outlawed, and older forms of welfare that were reckoned to distort wages, such as the Speenhamland system, were abolished (Polanyi, 2001). Moreover, this muscular extension of market relations can be said to prefigure the way in which 'unlimited' parliamentary power would once again be used to promote market liberalism during the 1980s and '90s, despite Hayek's abiding fears of unlimited government.

The model constitution

In the 'emergency' situation of the 1970s, Hayek at last felt able to recommend his constitutional design not only to new nations, but to Britain itself.[2] In fact, the model was especially suited to the particular challenge of parliamentary sovereignty, for the simple reason that it had, despite all the talk of new nations, been designed with this in mind.[3] Hayek (1982d, p. 31) had also been thinking of Britain when he wrote that 'to leave the law in the hands of elective governors is like leaving 'the cat in charge of the cream jug – there soon won't be any, at least no law in the sense in which it limits the discretionary powers of government'. Those subject to Parliament in the 18th century were aware of the danger Hayek described, he argued, in a way that those of the 20th were not. Returning again to the 'defect in the construction of our supposedly constitutional democracies' he wrote, that 'we have in fact again got that unlimited power which the eighteenth-century Whigs represented as "so wild and monstrous a thing that however natural it be to desire it, it is as natural to oppose it"'. From Hayek's perspective, the tragedy was that their opposition had not resulted in an irreversible limitation of such arbitrary rule.

The threat to freedom represented by the confusion of law-making and administration was further compounded by the expansion of government functions, usually as a result of the pursuit of social justice. Here, Hayek was not only arguing that bureaucracy was an inefficient way of running the economy as Mises (2007) had. He was rather arguing, in a manner that echoed much contemporaneous public choice literature, that there had emerged an,

> exceedingly wasteful apparatus of para-government . . . consisting of trade associations, trades unions and professional organizations, designed primarily to divert as much as possible of the stream of governmental favour to their members. It has come to be regarded as obviously necessary and unavoidable yet has arisen only in response to (or partly as defence against being disadvantaged in) the increasing necessity of an all-mighty majority government maintaining its majority by buying the support of particular small groups.
>
> (Hayek, 1982d, p. 13)

'Administrative agencies' he wrote, had become 'capable of issuing binding orders' thus undermining the rule of law yet further. Moreover, the 'para-government' could not be properly subject to parliamentary scrutiny as representatives, constrained by lack of time and expertise, and moved by the need to please, could at best give only 'general directions' (Hayek, 1982d, p. 144). This arbitrariness was embodied in an unaccountable bureaucracy, which he had also come to regard as constituting another major threat to market freedom understood in republican terms.

In 'A Model Constitution', chapter seventeen of volume three of *Law, Legislation and Liberty*, Hayek set out his recommendations for rectifying the confusion between law-making and administration that he felt plagued the British constitution. The suggestions made would have been familiar to those who had tuned in to the Third Programme in 1960. The first thing to note is that, once again, Hayek was aware of the charge that, for a theorist who had stressed the importance of evolutionary institutions to propose such a novel conception seemed self-contradictory. In response, he quoted Hume, whose own evolutionary thought he held in the highest regard, with a passage taken from his 'The Idea of a Perfect Commonwealth':

> In all cases it must be advantageous to know what is the most perfect in the kind, that we may be able to bring any real constitution or form of government as near it as possible, by such gentle alterations and innovations as may not give too great a disturbance to society.
>
> (Hayek, 1982d, p. 105)

However, this does not absolve Hayek of the charge of incoherence. His plan is not gentle, and its implementation would cause no small disturbance. Nor could it be realised by gradual reform. In proposing a Model Constitution, not as some abstract ideal but as a piece of emergency equipment, he transcends Hume's limiting criterion. He is in fact proposing something revolutionary. It remains inconsistent to criticise socialists and nationalists as constructivists, to denounce the French Revolution for its Cartesianism, and to censure an entire tradition within western political thought, encompassing figures as diverse as Hobbes and Jefferson, for its contractarianism, only to then devise a 'Model Constitution' because evolved institutions are not performing according to a certain political pattern.

As in his 1960 broadcast, Hayek envisioned an Upper House named the Legislative Assembly which lay down the general laws which the Lower House, the Governmental Assembly would have to conform to when passing legislation on specific issues and dealing with the administrative business of government:

> The one important difference between the position of such a representative Governmental Assembly and the existing parliamentary bodies would of course be that in all that it decided it would be bound by the rules of just conduct laid down by the Legislative Assembly, and that, in particular, it could not issue any orders to private citizens which did not follow directly and necessarily from the rules laid down by the latter. Within the limits of these rules the government would, however, be complete master in organising the apparatus of government and deciding about the use of material and personal resources entrusted to the government.
>
> (Hayek, 1982d, p. 119)

Importantly, the volume of government activity and the amount of money raised from taxation would still be in the hands of the Government Assembly. But the nature of government activity permitted under the law and the manner in which taxes are raised would be specified and limited by the more general rules set down by the Legislative Assembly. This was then a constitutional means of establishing a legal framework with the intention of 'dethroning politics'.

Fundamental to Hayek's Model Constitution was his conception of liberty as non-domination, with the concept of a protected domain, free of arbitrary power, central.[4] He wrote:

> The basic clause of such a constitution would have to state that in normal times, and apart from certain clearly defined emergency situations, men could be restrained from doing what they wished, or coerced to do particular things, only in accordance with the recognised rules of just conduct designed to define and protect the individual domain of each; and that the accepted set of rules of this kind could be deliberately altered only by what we shall call the Legislative Assembly. . . . Such a clause would by itself achieve all and more than the traditional Bills of Rights were meant to secure; and it would therefore make any separate enumeration of a list of special protected fundamental rights unnecessary.
>
> (Hayek, 1982d, pp. 108–110)

The key question here, remains, what is to be the scale and nature of this domain? Donald Hamowy (1961), a sympathetic reader, had earlier criticised Hayek's conception of the rule of law on the grounds that just because a law was known and general did not necessarily make it compatible with liberty. For example, 'legislation prescribing the enslavement of each male citizen for a period of two years, such enslavement to fall during the period of his prime (say, between the ages of 18 and 36)' would be compatible with that criterion. Hayek provided the unsatisfactory response that only coercion to prevent worse coercion should be permitted and that such coercion should not be regarded as inimical to liberty (Raz, 1983). How agreement on what constituted such coercion might be reached was not explained. Circumstances may still arise in which a given community regards a period of enslavement as reasonable in order to prevent greater coercion. Indeed, the prevailing culture of social justice Hayek dismissed is, in his eyes, a potential step on the road to just such an endorsement. There is nothing to stop his Legislative Assembly being characterised by a similar concern for social justice, or indeed, full blown socialism. It is simply not the case that it would make 'all socialist measures for redistribution impossible' (Hayek, 1982d, p. 150). All it must do, on Hayek's terms, is make laws that are both known and universal. On these terms, all sorts of legal regimes are imaginable.

Hayek (1982d, pp. 113–118) built in other mechanisms for curtailing unlimited democracy. One of these was a change in the franchise. The Legislative Assembly was to be composed of those members of society who have distinguished themselves in other fields, in 'the ordinary business of life' and should not be chosen in the same manner as those sitting in the government assembly. Candidates should, moreover, only become eligible for election when they reach the age of 45 and their terms should last no longer than 15 years. Only their peers, those also aged 45, should be able to vote. This means therefore that taking part in elections to the Upper House becomes a once in a lifetime event:

> The result would be a legislative assembly of men and women between their 45th and 60th years, one-fifteenth of whom would be replaced every year. The whole would thus mirror that part of the population which had already gained experience and had had an opportunity to make their reputation, but who would still be in their best years.
>
> (Hayek, 1982d, p. 113).

Keen, as usual, to draw classical associations Hayek wrote that,

> Something like this was attempted by the ancient Athenians when they allowed only the *nomothetae*, a distinct body, to change the fundamental *nomos* ... the term *nomothetae* was revived in a somewhat similar context in seventeenth century England and again by J.S. Mill, it will be convenient occasionally to use it as a name for that purely legislative body.
>
> (Hayek, 1982d, pp. 111–112)

He also hoped that 'the formation of clubs of contemporaries' from a relatively early age would both engender greater sociability between classes as well as help to educate and identify eventual candidates for election. When he wrote that 'they would also provide a regular channel for the expression of dissent of those not yet represented in a Legislative Assembly' his language was revealing. This was to be law-making by an elite, free of the need to seek re-election. Law was not to be the will of the people, but the will of the *nomothetae*, who could only be tenuously influenced by extra-parliamentary means.

A constitution of oligarchy

Hayek had shown himself willing to radically alter the terms of the franchise for the Legislative Assembly, but he also applied similar logic to the Lower House, the Governmental Assembly. He had no commitment to the type of universal adult suffrage that characterised contemporary democracies. Political freedoms do not constitute a bedrock element of his concept of liberty. As Hayek (1960a, pp. 13–14) wrote, 'it can scarcely be contended that the inhabitants of the District of Columbia, or resident aliens in the United States, or persons too young to be entitled to vote do not enjoy full personal liberty because they do not share in political liberty'. For him, the period of greatest liberty, vaguely identified as some time in Victorian England, or perhaps even the era of republican Rome, predated the modern era of mass democracy. Democratic processes should be regarded as good only in procedural terms; as the most effective means of changing a government when it becomes unpopular. As we have seen, however, Hayek had come to regard unlimited democracy as posing a threat to market freedom. Consequently, he proposed further changes to the franchise. 'That civil servants, old age pensioners, the unemployed, etc.', wrote Hayek (1982d, p. 120),

> should have a vote on how they should be paid out of the pocket of the rest, and their vote be solicited by a promise of a rise in their pay, is hardly a reasonable arrangement. Nor would it seem reasonable that, in addition to formulating projects for action, the government employees should also have a say on whether their projects should be adopted or not, or that those who are subject to orders by the Governmental Assembly should have a part in deciding what these orders ought to be.

Under such arrangements, as a university professor in receipt of government money, Hayek would have been disenfranchising himself. Such individuals, were their wages to be paid by government for their entire careers, would then in effect only have the opportunity to vote once in their lifetimes, in their 45th year, for the Upper House. Moreover, he had earlier expressed his concern that the structure of the modern economy, in which most individuals are salaried employees rather than independent business people, itself posed a threat to liberty as it did not educate them in the importance of private property and instead cultivated a collectivist mindset, 'They are thus relieved of some of the responsibilities of economic life', he wrote, and,

> Where this class predominates, the conception of social justice becomes largely adjusted to its needs. This applies not only to legislation but also to institutions and business practices. Taxation comes to be based on a conception of income which is essentially that of the employee. The paternalistic provisions of the social services are tailored almost exclusively to his requirements. Even the standards and techniques of consumers' credit are primarily adjusted to them. And all that concerns the possession and employment of capital as part of making one's living comes to be treated as the special interest of a small privileged group which can justly be discriminated against.
>
> (Hayek, 1960a, p. 123)

Indeed, one of the greatest dangers in a democracy, he argued, comes from the fact that the majority of the electorate is not composed of truly independent individuals but instead of the comfortably employed. Such individuals,

> regard as unnecessary many exercises of freedom which are essential to the independent if he is to perform his functions, and they hold views of deserts and appropriate remuneration entirely different from his. Freedom is thus seriously threatened today by the tendency of the employed majority to impose upon the rest their standards and views of life. It may indeed prove to be the most difficult task of all to persuade the employed masses

that in the general interest of their society, and therefore in their own long-term interest, they should preserve such conditions as to enable a few to reach positions which to them appear unattainable or not worth the effort and risk.

(Hayek, 1960a, p. 120)

Hayek was concerned about the market freedom of the entrepreneurial minority to such an extent that he was willing, as we have seen, to restrict both the franchise and the powers of government. On the basis of his thinking then, it is logically sound to advocate the removal of the vote from anyone in receipt of a salary of any kind. Indeed, as Gamble (1996, p. 94) writes, 'the political system he most admires, that of nineteenth century England, had a property franchise and a gender franchise' and 'Hayek states that a political system that restricts the vote to persons over forty, income earners, heads of households, or literate persons is as much a democracy as one which confers the vote on all adults at eighteen'. On the basis of Hayek's logic, and his insistence that laws need only to be known and general, it therefore becomes possible to disenfranchise any number of groups for any number of reasons. In such circumstances, however, the formal procedural value Hayek attaches to electoral democracy, and its useful quality of allowing the peaceable expressions of widespread disapproval and approval, also becomes meaningless, as so many would be excluded from the process.

Like his 1960 broadcast, *Law, Legislation and Liberty* reserved a critical role for a constitutional court. Again, the court would decide which issues fall within the purview of which House when it was not clear whether a matter related to government or to law-making, as 'one could not assign different tasks to the two assemblies, unless one had a third body deciding, in each particular instance, whose function it was' (Hayek, 1960b, p. 120). The role of judges in society generally was also to be crucial, as it was to be the function of the judge to interpret cases in such a way that allowed the legal framework to evolve. In line with Hayek's high regard for common law, it would be at the bench, rather than in the Upper House, that the majority of law would come into being. This would place great power in the hands of the judiciary. Indeed, Richard Bellamy (1994, p. 423) has gone so far as to suggest that, for Hayek, an ideal society would be one governed solely by judges and that Hayek's retains democratic procedures only to 'prevent the legal profession itself from becoming a monopoly of particular interests'.

Some consideration of Hayek's own epistemological theory, however, suggests that he overestimated the abilities of this judicial elite. Theodore Burczak has argued that rule by judges would be ineffective because it would not be possible for that elite group to acquire all the knowledge appropriate to good law-making any more than it would a dictator or, for that matter, an economic planner. 'Hayek's mistaken rejection of democracy as a constitutive component of freedom' writes Burczak (2014), 'is the result of his overestimation of the epistemological abilities of judges.' The same criticism, though in a weaker form because of the retention of an elective element, can be levelled at Hayek's Legislative Assembly.

John Gray (1984, p. 7) has argued that Hayek sought to devise a common law *Rechtsstaat* and looks to establish a *tertium quid* between the work of Hume and Kant by emphasising the interpretive function of judges whilst limiting the scope of interpretation by the need for rules to be universal and stable. Given the expanded role of government in modern society, however, it becomes increasingly difficult to think in terms of the binary of general rules and directives in the way Hayek did (Bellamy, 1994). Under modern conditions of expansive government responsibilities new measures are always likely to be justifiable as necessary either on universalist Kantian grounds or alternatively as the product of an evolutionary legal order, or indeed both. Those seeking the implementation of a rule may adopt various strategies. There is, therefore, no reason to assume that judges would be able to satisfactorily resolve cases when there were disputes about remit between the Upper and Lower Houses.

At times, Hayek (1953a, p. 518) was willing to admit the actual nature of the constitutional arrangements he advocated. and he noted that 'Thucydides speaks without hesitation of an "isonomic oligarchy," and later we find *isonomia* used by Plato quite deliberately in contrast to, rather than in vindication of, democracy.' Having illustrated the centrality of the rule of law in Hayek's market republicanism and the elitist nature of his intellectual emergency equipment, we can conclude that isonomic oligarchy is a settlement he was happy to endorse. As Bellamy (1994, p. 435) has observed, what Hayek desired above all was 'a return to an idealised version of the notable politics of the late eighteenth and early nineteenth centuries, in which a few basic rules are set out by members of a public-spirited elites'. This Whiggish idealisation was, however, informed by older classical ideas and we can regard the ultimate goal of Hayek's emergency equipment as the establishment of an oligarchic market republic.

Despite holding that the legislative assembly would limit the scope of government power rather than the extent, his is really a vision of a society where the market is the appropriate sphere of individual action and agency, not the political arena. It is a vision of a market society overseen by judges where government activity is peripheral and the preserve of an elite. To portray the system, as Hayek does, as one of legal equality ignores all actual inequalities in power, and the consequent capacity to interpret and shape the law that entails.

Nevertheless, the Model Constitution does clearly issue from Hayek's market republicanism. It was designed to insulate market relations from the arbitrary power of government. Inevitably, that also meant limiting democracy. It is not, however, entirely clear that the scheme achieves the goal of limiting arbitrary public power. Although Hayek spent his career warning of the dangers of arbitrary public power, his Model Constitution magnifies the potential for just such *imperium*. It places huge, largely unchecked, power in the hands of a governing and judicial elite, leaving the people with very little means of redress. It removes what Philip Pettit has described as the 'tracking' function that democracy performs. Furthermore, there is little to prevent those in government, or indeed within the judiciary, from shaping and intervening in market and economic relations in a manner Hayek regarded as deeply injurious to market freedom.

The common theme throughout Hayek's 'Model Constitution' is faith in a judicial elite and a governing class which he assumes will, under his new system, be liberal. This is remarkable given that he viewed a large part of his intellectual mission to warn against the danger of government by 'experts'. However, those were experts of a leftist stripe. In his idealised system his idealised elite would govern in a manner sensitive to an idealised market. However, that he should imagine his elite would govern in such a way ignores a whole series of public choice warnings about the nature of government. (Farrant and McPhail, 2014)[5] Again this is remarkable given that *The Road to Serfdom* can be seen, as Peter Boettke and Edward Lopez (2002) have argued, as a forerunner of the public choice literature.[6] Hayek finds himself in strange, almost Fabian, company if he imagines that virtue and expertise, rather than public accountability, will produce good law-making.

Conclusion

In this chapter I have shown that far from being an isolated curiosity in his work, Hayek's Model Constitution is a product of some of his core concerns. It should be understood as an outline of the constitutional arrangements necessary to preserve market freedom viewed through a market republican lens. This was to be achieved via the limiting of democracy and the dethronement of politics. Although Hayek's interest in novel quasi constitutional arrangements, in the form of interstate federalism, as a means of curtailing the powers of democratically elected governments dates back to the 1940s, the initial appearance of the first piece of intellectual equipment can be traced back to 1960. The distinction between law and legislation, which he took from Schmitt, assumed greater prominence in Hayek's thought over the next decade as it offered an avenue into thinking about how the legislative excess he associated with unlimited government might be curbed. In order to achieve this, a clear demarcation between law and legislation must be drawn. Although he had lost faith in the prospect of Parliament adopting a self-imposed framework, it remained possible that a constitutional fix could be found. This would involve the establishment of a massively empowered senatorial Upper House which would be able to impose a legally restrictive framework to bound the daily conduct of government, all to be overseen by a judicial elite.

Initially, Hayek viewed this design as providing a means of protecting property and preserving liberal economy in the developing world. However, the pathology the Model Constitution was designed to cure was in fact located in its most concentrated form in the British body politic. It is not then surprising that, as a result of his radicalisation during the 1960s and '70s, Hayek recommended just such a constitutional revolution for Britain as well.

Although it was never a claim Hayek himself made, having established the centrality of his conception of liberty as non-domination, and the market republican nature of his thought in his work post 1960, I suggest that it makes sense to regard the Model Constitution as the first pillar of an economically liberal market republic (crowned or otherwise) within which epistemically conceived market processes would be free to play out. The Model Constitution was not simply an intellectual distraction. Although it may have proved a folly, it was not intended as such, but was regarded by Hayek as a viable long-term solution to unlimited democracy and the inflationary pursuit of social justice. I have also argued that, contrary to Hayek's intentions, rather than limit the individual's exposure to *imperium* the Model Constitution would in fact enhance it.

Notes

1 Inconsistently, Hayek refers to it in *Law, Legislation and Liberty* as 'standby' equipment.
2 Hayek had restated his plan, with the minor variation of specifying forty as the appropriate voting age for the Upper House, in a 1967 piece, 'The Constitution of A Liberal State'. There, however, the tone is abstract rather than urgent.
3 Hayek (1982d, pp. 29–31) noted that the doctrine of the sovereignty of parliament, with the accrual of administrative as well as rule making powers it entailed, was one of the key concerns of the American revolutionaries but that despite this 'American attempts to meet this difficulty' set out the Constitution 'have provided only a limited protection.'
4 This was also a move away from Hayek's (1960a, p. 216) earlier support for a Bill of Rights.
5 Andrew Farrant and Edward McPhail make this point with reference to Hayek's apparent faith in certain dictators, which will be addressed in Chapter 9. However, the criticism can be applied to his constitutional scheme more broadly.
6 For public choice arguments on the danger of bureaucracy and an unaccountable public sector see Gordon Tullock (2005).

Works cited

Bellamy, R. 1994. '"Dethroning Politics": Liberalism, Constitutionalism and Democracy in the Thought of F. A. Hayek', *Journal of Political Science* 24:4, pp. 419–441.
Boettke, P.J. and Lopez, E.J. 2002. 'Austrian Economics and Public Choice', *The Review of Austrian Economics* 15:2/3, pp. 111–119.
Burczak, T. 2014. 'Dictating Liberty', *Review of Political Economy* 26:3, pp. 368–371.
Farrant, A. and McPhail, E. 2014. 'Can a Dictator Turn a Constitution into a Can-opener? F.A. Hayek and the Alchemy of Transitional Dictatorship in Chile', *Review of Political Economy* 26:3, pp. 331–348.
Gamble, A. 1996. *Hayek: The Iron Cage of Liberty*. Cambridge: Polity Press.
Gray, J. 1984. *Hayek on Liberty*. Oxford: Oxford University Press.
Hamowy, R. 1961. 'Hayek's Concept of Freedom: A Critique', *New Individualist Review* 1:1, pp. 28–31.
Hayek, F.A. 1948a. 'Individualism: True and False' [1945] in Friedrich Hayek (Ed.), *Individualism and Economic Order* (pp. 1–33). Chicago: University of Chicago Press.
Hayek, F.A. 1953a. 'The Decline of the Rule of Law', *The Freeman*, 20 April, pp. 518–520.
Hayek, F.A. 1953b. 'The Case Against Progressive Income Taxes', *The Freeman*, 28 December, pp. 229–232.
Hayek, F.A. 1960a. *The Constitution of Liberty*. Chicago: University of Chicago Press.
Hayek, F.A. 1960b. 'New Nations and the Problem of Power', *The Listener* (London), November, pp. 819–821.

Hayek, F.A. 1982a. 'Introduction' [1982] in *Law, Legislation and Liberty: A New Statement of the Liberal Principles of Justice and Political Economy* [3 Volume edition]. London: Routledge Kegan Paul.

Hayek, F.A. 1982b. 'Rules and Order' [1973] in *Law, Legislation and Liberty: A New Statement of the Liberal Principles of Justice and Political Economy* [3 Volume edition]. London: Routledge Kegan Paul.

Hayek, F.A. 1982d. 'The Political Order of a Free People' [1979] in *Law, Legislation and Liberty: A New Statement of the Liberal Principles of Justice and Political Economy* [3 Volume edition]. London: Routledge Kegan Paul.

Hayek, F.A. 1999i. 'Towards a Free Market Monetary System' [1977] in Stephen Kresge (Ed.), *Good Money Part Two: The Collected Works of F.A. Hayek, Vol. 6* (pp. 230–237). Chicago: University of Chicago Press.

Mises, L. 2007. *Bureaucracy*. B. Greaves (Ed.). Indianapolis: Liberty Fund.

Polanyi, K. 2001. *The Great Transformation: The Political and Economic Origins of Our Time*. Boston: Beacon Press.

Raz, J. 1983. *The Authority of Law: Essays on Law and Morality*. Oxford: Oxford University Press.

Slobodian, Q. 2018. *Globalists: The End of Empire and the Birth of Neoliberalism*. Cambridge, MA: Harvard University Press.

Streek, W. 2015. 'Heller, Schmitt and the Euro', *European Law Journal* 21:3, pp. 361–370.

Tullock, G. 2005. *Bureaucracy: The Selected Works of Gordon Tullock, Vol. 6*. C.K. Rowley (Ed.). Indianapolis: Liberty Fund.

8   Market republican money

The second pillar of Hayek's intellectual emergency equipment was his scheme for the denationalisation of money. Although the Model Constitution would limit the arbitrary power of government with regard to legislation, his money scheme was designed to terminate arbitrary control of the monetary framework. Like his Model Constitution, Hayek's plan for denationalising money originated in the *Constitution of Liberty* (White, 1999). It grew from the kernel of the question 'should we not rely on the spontaneous forces of the market to supply whatever is needed for a satisfactory medium of exchange as we do in most other respects?' (Hayek, 1960a, p. 324). In that work, Hayek answered in the negative, but the thought clearly persisted. He came to view the scheme as one of the chief means of attaining a form of government founded on *The Constitution of Liberty*'s core contribution, the conception of liberty as non-domination.

Having experienced the inflationary crisis of the 1970s, Hayek no longer cautioned restraint. The threat to market freedom had become too acute: government must lose its monopoly of the issue of money. This second piece of intellectual emergency equipment was designed to be implemented alongside the first and both were, in his mind, mutually reinforcing. 'The sort of monetary system I propose' he reflected 'may be possible only under a limited government such as we do not have, and a limitation of government may require that it be deprived of the monopoly of issuing money. Indeed, the latter should necessarily follow from the former' (Hayek, 1999h, p. 186). Hayek's eventual position on money reveals both a shift and a basic consistency in his work. It certainly involved a move from advocating fixed exchange rates, tied to a gold standard, to supporting free-floating ones. His fundamental aim, however, remained the same: that government should be deprived of the ability to 'control' money. Yet his thought took a libertarian turn when he advocated that, in effect, government money should cease to exist.

The denationalisation of money

In *The Constitution of Liberty* there is a definite ambivalence born of the distinction between the role a central bank could ideally play in calming excitement and restraining expansions of credit issuing from private banks, and the reality of how central banks operated under conditions of unlimited democracy. Hayek had believed that

> a monetary policy independent of financial policy is possible so long as government expenditure constitutes a comparatively small part of all payments and so long as the government debt (and particularly its short-term debt) constitutes only a small part of all credit instruments.

However, he continued that

> today this condition no longer exists. In consequence, an effective monetary policy can be conducted only in co-ordination with the financial policy of government. Co-ordination in this respect, however, inevitably means that whatever nominally independent monetary authorities still exist have in fact to adjust their policy to that of the government. The latter, whether we like it or not, thus necessarily becomes the determining factor
>
> (Hayek, 1960a, p. 327)

What this amounted to was that even a responsible and restrained central bank policy, one whose purpose was to maintain the total money stream, would under real-world conditions be forced to fall in line with the political priorities of the day.

During the 1940s, influenced by the ordoliberal theory of the state taking an active role in maintaining the appropriate institutional framework, Hayek regarded central banking, with oversight of interest rates and hence influence over the level of inflation, as one of the appropriate roles government must fulfil to maintain the necessary conditions for stability and competition. During the 1950s, however, this certainty seemed to wane. In his 1960 work he wrote that,

> Compared with the preceding century . . . governments have assumed a much more active part in controlling money, and this has been as much a cause as a consequence of instability. It is only natural, therefore, that some people should feel it would be better if governments were deprived of their control over monetary policy.
>
> (Hayek, 1960, p. 324)

However, he concluded 'it is important to be clear at the outset that this is not only politically impracticable today but would probably be undesirable if it were possible'. Nonetheless, as Lawrence White has observed, he went on to reflect that although central banks and national monies may be necessary, it may be possible to subject them to competition, and that 'one of the most effective measures for protecting the freedom of the individual might indeed be to have constitutions prohibiting all peacetime restrictions on transactions in any kind of money or the precious metals'. It is evident that it was Hayek's newly developed conception of liberty as non-domination that was pushing him to think of the role of money not simply in technical terms, but in terms of its relationship with individual liberty. It is this link between liberty and money that would, in the context of an inflationary crisis, lead him to his radical conclusions.

At the 1975 Geneva Gold and Monetary Conference in Lausanne, Hayek (1999g) renounced his support for central banking and instead advocated competition between national currencies within any territorial jurisdiction. Always keen to place his work in the longer Whig/liberal tradition, in his lecture 'Choice in Currency' he framed the central problem facing the monetary system as that posed earlier in Trenchard and Gordon's *Cato's Letters*. 'I have just read in an English Whig tract more than 250 years old: "Who would establish a bank in an arbitrary country, or trust his money constantly there?"' he wrote, with 'arbitrary', denoting a country in which government is not restrained by law.[1] Hayek argued that permitting the use of any national currency within the territory of another would introduce competition into the currency system, with individuals favouring the currencies of states that maintained polices of 'sound money' and kept their currencies stable. Those who did not would find their currency becoming increasingly worthless. By such a means, Hayek argued, governments would be dissuaded from expansionary monetary policies if they wished their currencies to remain in use. By introducing competition, the territorial monopoly of a single government over money would be broken. 'I have no objection to governments issuing money', he wrote,

> but I believe their claim to a *monopoly*, or their power to *limit* the kinds of money in which contracts may be concluded within their territory, or to determine the *rates* at which monies can be exchanged, to be wholly harmful. At this moment it seems that the best thing we could wish governments to do is for, say, all the members of the European Economic Community, or, better still, all the governments of the Atlantic Community, to bind themselves mutually not to place any restrictions on the free use within their territories of one another's – or any other – currencies, including their purchase and sale at any price the parties decide upon, or on their use as accounting units in which to keep books.
>
> (Hayek, 1999g, p. 121)

The introduction of competition would also be better than the establishment of a monetary union across Europe in the manner that had begun to be proposed. Competition, and not 'a utopian European Monetary Unit, seems to me now both the practicable and the desirable arrangement to aim at' offered Hayek (1999g, pp. 121–125). 'The upshot' of the system he proposed,

> would probably be that the currencies of those countries trusted to pursue a responsible monetary policy would tend to displace gradually those of a less reliable character. The reputation of financial righteousness would become a jealously guarded asset of all issuers of money, since they would

know that even the slightest deviation from the path of honesty would reduce the demand for their product.

The great benefit of the scheme would be that it would end the influence of macro economists over politicians. 'You may feel' he wrote,

> that my proposal amounts to no less than the abolition of monetary policy; and you would not be quite wrong. . . . It seems to me that if we could prevent governments from meddling with money, we would do more good than any government has ever done in this regard. And private enterprise would probably have done better than the best they have ever done.

Curiously, it is not clear that Hayek's proposals were as subversive as he believed them to be. Although he wrote of a government monopoly of money and opined that were his scheme to be put into action governments would likely seek to thwart it, he provided little evidence for either of these positions (Hayek, 1999i). Indeed, he readily admitted he was unsure of the legality, or otherwise, of his proposals. The claims about government monopoly of currency that he makes are somewhat undermined by his own acceptance, which he cites in order to support his argument for the viability of competition, that in many border regions more than one type of currency is regularly used, noting that there was nothing in the law to prevent parties from engaging in bilateral exchange in any medium they chose to do so.

All of this raises an important point. Although it might be possible to rectify faith in a currency where its continued existence is guaranteed, brands subject to competition frequently disappear never to return. What effect this might have in a world still composed of nation states is missing from the argument but, from our appreciation of his support for the gold standard and an end to monetary policy, we can conclude that Hayek was quite comfortable with states forever losing control over the circulation of money within their own borders. This, of course, has radical consequences for public spending. Crucially, there would be an in-built incentive for governments to reduce public spending in order to retain a high value for their own currency. Thanks to such an instrument of discipline as competition in money, the pursuit of social justice might thus be brought to an end.

In 1976 Hayek (1999j) went even further, pursuing the libertarian logic his turn of thought had taken to call for capitalist money for the capitalist system, insisting that capitalists must 'be allowed to provide themselves the money they need'. In doing so he hoped to strike at the heart of state power. In the pamphlet 'The Denationalisation of Money' Hayek (1999h) called not simply for a disciplining of governments but for the opening of a market in private as well as public currencies. If adopted, he believed, no longer would special interests, in the name of social justice or any other creed, be able to pressure governments through the ballot box to pursue inflationary policies in a manner that was inimical to market freedom.

In the piece, Hayek once again made use of historical argument to support his case. Attempts to debase the currency were the chief means by which rulers had for centuries sought to extend their power while undermining market freedom. Furthermore, so massive had the issue of inflation become that, although it had fallen from his focus for some decades, Hayek (1999h, pp. 237–148) could write that 'history is largely a history of inflation'. He had, however, been freed, he felt, from 'the mystique of legal tender', which was evident even in his reflections on money in *The Constitution of Liberty*. Again, the decline of the Roman republic is presented as a decisive moment in the assertion of *imperium* as 'the minting prerogative of the ruler was firmly established under the Roman emperors.' Over the following centuries 'as coinage spread, governments everywhere soon discovered that the exclusive right of coinage was a most important instrument of power as well as an attractive source of gain' and currency became crucial to absolutism and its unlimited government and 'when Jean Bodin developed the concept of sovereignty, he treated the right of coinage as one of the most important and essential parts of it'. So it was that 'the coins served, indeed, largely as the symbols of might, like the flag, through which the ruler asserted his sovereignty, and told his people who their master was, whose image the coins carried to the remotest parts of his realm.' What struck Hayek as remarkable was the endurance of *valor impositus*, the notion that it is government imprimatur, in some semi mystical sense, that confers value upon currency, and that he and everyone else had allowed themselves to remain under this delusion for over two thousand years.

Despite the significant length of the pamphlet, the essence of the scheme can be gained by the following quotations:

> Since readers will probably at once ask how such issues can come to be generally accepted as money, the best way to begin is probably to describe how I would proceed if I were in charge of, say, one of the major Swiss joint stock banks. Assuming it to be legally possible (which I have not examined), I would announce the issue of non-interest bearing certificates or notes, and the readiness to open current cheque accounts, in terms of a unit with a distinct registered trade name such as 'ducat'. The only legal obligation I would assume would be to redeem these notes and deposits on demand with, at the option of the holder, either 5 Swiss francs or 5 D-marks or 2 dollars per ducat. This redemption value would however be intended only as a floor below which the value of the unit could not fall because I would announce at the same time my intention to regulate the quantity of the ducats so as to keep their (precisely defined) purchasing power as nearly as possible constant. I would also explain to the public that I was fully aware I could hope to keep these ducats in circulation only if I fulfilled the expectation that their real value would be kept approximately constant.
>
> (Hayek, 1999h, p. 153)

Hayek's old idea of the commodity standard underpins the scheme as it is by keeping the value of the 'ducat' stable in relation to such a basket of commodities that confidence in a currency is maintained:

> And I would announce that I proposed from time to time to state the precise commodity equivalent in terms of which I intended to keep the value of the ducat constant, but that I reserved the right, after announcement, to alter the composition of the commodity standard as experience and the revealed preferences of the public suggested.
>
> (Hayek, 1999h, p. 153)

However, although the value of the unit would be kept in line with these goods, it would be non-redeemable for those commodities or for gold as

> Convertibility is a safeguard necessary to impose upon a monopolist, but unnecessary with competing suppliers who cannot maintain themselves in the business unless they provide money at least as advantageous to the user as anybody else.
>
> (Hayek, 1999h, p. 210)

Private currencies were to be purely fiat, their value maintained only by their performance in a competitive marketplace.

Although Hayek (1999h, p. 172) noted that people might wish to use a currency prone to depreciation for loans and appreciation for savings and similar transactions, he was confident that those currencies that could maintain stability would ultimately win out in the market, not least because of the accounting needs of businesses. He also believed that 'a thousand hounds' of a vigilant press would ensure that banks reported accurately on the value of their currency in relation to the commodity standard. In such a monetary system government monetary policy would be 'neither desirable nor possible' and national central banks would inevitably be abolished. Alongside his Model Constitution, Hayek (1999h, pp. 228–229) viewed his scheme as 'the one way in which we may still hope to stop the continuous progress of all government towards totalitarianism which already appears to many acute observers as inevitable'. Although he recognised that his scheme might be dismissed as utopian he countered that,

> We cannot, of course, hope for such a reform before the public understands what is at stake and what it has to gain. But those who think the whole proposal wholly impracticable and utopian should remember that 200 years ago in *The Wealth of Nations* Adam Smith wrote that 'to expect, indeed, that the freedom of trade should ever be entirely restored in Great Britain, is as absurd as to expect that an Oceana or Utopia should ever be established in it.' It took nearly 90 years from the publication of his work in 1776 until Great Britain became the first country to establish complete free trade in 1860.

Hayek (1999j) even had a secret name for 'The Future Unit of Value' which he refused to share as, after having taken legal advice found it was only possible to take out a trademark on an article in which a person or entity was dealing. As the scheme remained entirely an academic exercise, he was of course unable to register his term for the unit as a trademark. Instead, in public at least, he referred to the future unit as the 'solid'.

Reception and viability of the scheme

A fundamental criticism of Hayek's money scheme is that it dismisses the fact that central banks developed and endured because they perform socially desirable functions. As such, they cannot be regarded simply as the product of brute *imperium* as Hayek believed. For example, they serve as lenders of last resort and guarantee the deposits of savers. An early reviewer of Hayek's work noted that 'if one treats the government's role in money production as a social institution that has evolved as a "result of human action but not of design" then a more reserved attitude should be taken towards changing it' (Howard, 1977). In other words, in arguing that government money is the product of state force Hayek was too willing to dismiss its role in the evolution of the modern economy. A similar criticism has been made by Chandran Kaukathas (1989, pp. 218–225) when he writes of the instability between Hayek's Humean and Kantian elements.

Even Hayek admitted that, under his system, if a private currency collapsed then savers would lose all the cash they held in that currency. He assumed that they would have other assets. This is remarkable given his early Viennese experience of what currency depreciation could do to individuals and families. Yet, rather than consider the human element, what was most important for Hayek was that in a competitive system the loss of one currency would at least mean that 'the whole structure of long-term contracts would remain unaffected' (Hayek, 1999h, p. 225). However, he underestimated the political unacceptability of such a position along with the political and financial anarchy that the introduction of such new arrangements would involve. Central banks had developed over time in the evolutionary manner he usually prized in order to avoid such calamities and not simply as the instrument of dominating governments (Clapham, 1944; Wood, 2005).

The economist most closely associated with advocating a reduction in the money supply is not Hayek, but his one-time colleague at Chicago, Milton Friedman.[2] Both men held similar political views on the proper relationship between government and the market and Friedman would testify to Hayek's influence on him politically, although the two were never close socially or even professionally. Friedman's insistence that the volume of money should grow 'month by month, and indeed, so far as possible, day by day, at an annual rate of X per cent, where X is some number between 3 and 5' is known as the doctrine of monetarism. By such a method he too hoped to end the arbitrariness of prevailing monetary policy. Hayek, however, disapproved of Friedman's work in much the same way as he disapproved of Keynes's. Both were based on the macroeconomic aggregates Hayek found so objectionable. Although sympathetic to the desire to end government control over the increase in money, Hayek thought that setting a monetary target on the basis of a macroeconomic formula again overlooked the microeconomic complexities of the real economy. Moreover, to make publicly known the limit to the increase in money in any given period would, he warned, cause panic when that limit was approached. When interviewed he remarked,

> you know, one of the things I often have publicly said is that one of the things I most regret is not having returned to a criticism of Keynes's treatise, but it is as much true of not having criticised Milton's [Essays in] *Positive Economics*, which in a way is quite as dangerous a book.
>
> (Hayek, 1994, p. 128)

In recalling Walter Bagehot's reflections on free banking, Friedman and his collaborator Anna Schwarz argued that had government not established financial regulations and central banks then many private sources of money may have sprung up in a manner in keeping with Hayek's evolutionary perspective. However, it did and now it is government money that people turn to.[3]

Defenders of Hayek could point to his endorsement, albeit fleeting, of Karl Popper and William Warren Bartley's philosophy of 'critical rationalism'.[4] They opposed what they termed justificationism, the attempt to justify a stance with reference to a further anterior position, because of the manner in which it leads either to infinite regress or dogmatism. Unfortunately, they argued, such attempts at justification characterised all the major strains of western thought. Instead, they advocated a 'critical rationalist' approach which, as described by Rafe Champion (2013), 'holds all positions and propositions open to criticism'. As such 'it is possible to justify a preference for a particular position in the light of evidence and arguments produced to date, on the understanding that preferences change in the light of new evidence and arguments'. However, that preference must remain based upon universal moral standards and a respect for moral systems, forbidding positions that are radically transformative of an overall moral or social order. Champion has argued that this overcomes Kukathas's critique of instability in Hayek's work. As Hayek wrote,

> The proper conclusion from the considerations that I have advanced is by no means that we may confidently accept all the old and traditional values. Nor even that there are any values or moral principles which science may not occasionally question. The social scientist who endeavours to understand how society functions, and to discover where it can be improved, must claim the right to examine critically, and even to judge every single value of our society. The consequence of what I have said is merely that we can never at one and the same time question all of its values. Such absolute doubt could lead only to the destruction of our civilisation.
>
> (Champion, 2013, p. 220)

So, for Hayek, as for Popper, some institutions and rules could be changed so long as the whole social structure was not threatened. This line of thought can be traced back at least as far as Popper's (1945) endorsement of 'piecemeal social engineering', in *The Open Society and Its Enemies*. However, the radical and far-reaching nature of some of Hayek's 1970s proposals, with their consequences for the integral working of both politics and the economy is of such scale as to fall foul of Hayek's own limiting criterion. Just as his Model Constitution exceeds the bounds of what Hume thought acceptable in such designs, so his money scheme oversteps the bounds of Critical Rationalism.[5]

Despite the high regard with which his ideas were held within the Conservative Party, Hayek (1999h, p. 132) had been right to reflect on his money scheme that it was 'at present impracticable'. It was not only impracticable; it was also completely unhelpful to his political allies. What he had advocated was a diminution of state power of the sort that, once in government, Thatcher and those close to her had no desire to entertain. Much more amenable to the requirements of power were the ideas of Friedman who required no 'utopian' measures in order to bring inflation under control. It remained the case, however, that even his approach was not strictly adhered to, and other measures such as increasing the interest rate to reduce borrowing and decrease the money supply were not taken up. This was because they clashed with other elements of the Thatcherite agenda, particularly the longstanding Conservative vision of a 'home owning democracy', which required prospective home owners to have access to large loans, or mortgages, without interest rates becoming prohibitively expensive (Tomlinson, 2012, p. 740). With this in mind, we can perhaps appreciate Hayek's enduring mistrust of politicians, even those he admired, and hence his desire to end their control of the money supply.

That Friedmanite's macro aggregate-based monetarism should prove an amenable tool of government hardly surprised Hayek. Other Austrian economists would go further arguing that there was in essence 'no difference between Friedman and Keynes and that Monetarism does not differ in its fundamental approach from the other dominant branch of macroeconomics, that of Keynesianism' (O'Driscoll and Shenoy 1974). This analysis accords with that offered by Jim Bulpitt (1986) in an influential article in which he argued that monetarism should be understood as a technique of Thatcherite statecraft that was in essence not qualitatively different to Keynesianism.[6] Both assume government supervision of money, diverging only with regard to the matter of quantity. As Bulpitt noted, insisting on a reduction of the money supply in effect allowed the state to absent itself from disputes between 'interests', namely the unions and employers, in exactly the manner Hayek had hoped for but had been unable to imagine without his own emergency equipment. It also allowed the Conservatives to pursue policies aimed at reducing government debt.[7] In the longer term, although monetarism as a creed slipped from prominence it has remained the overriding priority of government to keep inflation low, rather than to secure full employment. (Howells, 2013). It is the international financial money markets that have imposed monetary discipline by virtue of 'the huge volume of mobile liquid capital and by the ever-increasing sophistication and integration of the financial circuit' (Gamble, 1994, p. 41). All of this was, of course, achieved without Hayek's utopian scheme.

Although he was opposed to the state monopoly of currency, Hayek over-looked the way in which competition could recreate the old problems of government monopoly on a far greater scale, with one currency potentially acquiring a virtual global monopoly. Benjamin Klein (1976, pp. 513–519) was the first to argue that 'I do not think that adoption of Hayek's . . . policy rec-ommendation of complete domestic freedom of choice in currency would significantly reduce the amount of monopoly power on currency issue cur-rently possessed by each individual European government.' The danger was that all would seek to hold the same, the strongest, currency. Although this may speed trade, it would undermine all the benefits of competition and magnify all the dangers of monopoly. Hayek had been sensitive to the danger of private monopoly during the 1930s, under the influence of the ordoliberals, however, his increasing estrangement from their movement had occasioned a decline in his concerns. He had instead come to believe that competition could always be trusted to yield beneficial outcomes. It was this mindset that gave rise to his money schemes. Hayek's antipathy towards public power and public institu-tions again obscured any market-based private threats to market freedom. This is reflected in his plan for currency competition, in that it fails to recognise that the existing system of national currency use prevents its monopolisation by any one currency. What is equally missing is any mechanism to offset this danger of monopoly were such a system of competition to be adopted. Therefore, Hayek's own proposals could, rather than ensure competition prevails, result in its destruction.

To transfer responsibility for the monetary system from government to banks would of course place enormous power in the hands of private institutions and the elite actors who populate them.[8] What we see again then is an example of his partial interpretation of the conception of freedom as non-domination. The focus is entirely on the danger to economic freedom posed by *imperium*, to the neglect of the threat posed by private power, or *dominium*. If the 1970s seemed to point to the failure of governments to maintain market order and refrain from arbitrary interference, more recent history suggests that markets, poorly regulated by political power, are at least as much of a danger.

Cryptocurrencies

With the victory of Friedmanite monetarism over Hayek's more radical scheme, it seemed that proposals for private currencies had been definitively relegated to the libertarian margins of debate. However, with the emergence of online cryp-tocurrencies, the once 'utopian' prospect of competition in money has become at least something of a reality, even if their use in the real economy remains minor, with national fiat monies still dominant. Although Hayek had assured his readers that record and reputation alone would define the worth of private currency units, the value of cryptocurrencies such as Bitcoin are underpinned by blockchain technology. My purpose here is not to dwell on the technicalities of cryptocurrencies, but to briefly reflect on their implications for liberty as non-domination. Nonetheless, some basic detail regarding their functioning is necessary.

As Bitcoin, founded in 2009, is the pre-eminent cryptocurrency it will be my focus. As Weber (2016, p. 7) outlines,

> bitcoin endeavours to be a virtual currency and payment system based on a computer code. In the words of Bitcoin.org, the software is a 'community-driven, free, open-source project'. It provides a platform that allows its users to produce what its proponents call money and to transmit payments anonymously among each other without using established intermediaries.

Unlike the bank issued currencies of Hayek's scheme, there is no board of governors responsible for the standing of the currency, and rather than being issued, each coin must be 'mined' employing computing power. Inspired by the gold standard, its pseudonymous founder Satoshi Nakomoto, set a finite number of coins at 21 million, which can also be held or used in fragments. In a similar, but more predictable, manner than gold – the value of which is subject to new and unexpected finds – the value of Bitcoin is therefore intrinsically tied to its scarcity.

The transaction ledger, the blockchain made manifest, is Nakamoto explains 'massively replicated and updated by a swarm of mutually distrustful parties running in a peer-to-peer network instead of being stored on one site only. To make this work, nodes pull transactions off of a peer-to-peer broadcast network, then compete for the opportunity to tack them on the end of the chain.' It is this that validates payments. 'To keep one party from dominating this process (and posting bad transactions)' he continues, 'competition is enforced by making the parties solve hard mathematical problems called >proofs of work<'. Those who succeed in validating the transaction by decoding the problems are rewarded with a certain number of new Bitcoins. This is the process of 'mining'. However, the amount awarded diminishes as the combined total of all existing Bitcoins reaches the upper limit of 21 million (Weber, 2016, p. 26). Therefore, over time, the business of mining becomes progressively more difficult requiring ever greater computing power and becoming increasingly expensive. An inbuilt function of the blockchain is therefore to exclude those who hold relatively little wealth from acquiring further wealth through the mining process, leaving the process open to those who can access large amounts of computing power. The environmental effects of the mining process are also becoming clear and it frequently uses more energy than smaller developed nations.

Key for our purposes is that advocates of these currencies view them, much as Hayek viewed his own scheme, as an effective way of securing individual freedom against the state. The most radical free market libertarian theorists of cryptocurrency look to a world beyond national governments where the state has been abolished, replaced by polities based on private law and 'pure' property rights: a world in which *imperium* has been forever vanquished. They view such currencies as central to their hopes. Bitcoin (BTC) appeals to libertarians for the following reasons:

> 1) cryptocurrencies reduce the monetary policy capabilities of the State because BTC's money supply is managed algorithmically by computer software, not by government-controlled central banks; (2) transactions are verified across a distributed P2P network, so there is no single authority in control; (3) it is the BTC miners, not Governments, who receive seignior-age, a term derived from Old French that literally means: 'the right of the lord to mint money'. It refers to the revenue earned by issuing the cur-rency, which can occur in many ways, but, at its most basic, it's the profit earned because there's a difference between the value of money and what it costs to have it produced and distributed; and (4) the cryptographic nature of BTC means that their ownership is difficult, if not impossible, to match to real people.
>
> (Huckle and White, 2016)

A further appeal of the blockchain technology on which Bitcoin is based is that it promotes competition in currencies, just as Hayek would have wished. Bit-coin is based on open source GitHub code which can be adopted and used by anyone wishing to create their own competitor cryptocurrency and a plethora of these, such as Ethereum and Ripple, have emerged.

It is important to note that Bitcoin claims to facilitate a form of 'non-political economy'. This is based on the fact that it bypasses both bank and state power. In reality, Bitcoin and other cryptocurrencies are no more 'neutral' than the gold standard that preceded and inspired them.

Power, as we have reflected, cannot be wished away. Just because power does not lie with the state, does not mean it ceases to exist. Conversely, state power frequently serves to counter the concentration, amplification and abuse of pri-vate power. Bitcoin is intended to degrade this countering power. Further-more, unaccountability is hard-wired into its very operation in the form of the anonymity it bestows upon users. The effect here then is, in terms of non-domination, to assault *imperium* while facilitating the growth of *dominium* in much the same way as Hayek's schemes.

We can think of this in terms of a higher and a lower order of threat. The first affects the functioning of public power in the context of currently existing systems of political economy. Blockchain technologies are purposively difficult to track. Over its short history, therefore, Bitcoin has been primarily used by those who wish to evade tax or engage in criminal or terrorist conspiracies. The former use is an in-built attraction of the scheme to libertarians who view taxation as theft. The clearest consequence of an increasingly widespread use of Bitcoin would be to reduce tax revenues. Even if states continued to insist on tax receipts in national monies, its general use would massively reduce the amount governments are able to spend in providing basic services such as education, healthcare and housing. The lack of such provision would constitute a historic challenge to personal liberty, as the lack of even basic provisions – of the type, we should remember, that Hayek himself regarded as entirely legitimate – would expose countless millions to the domination of private actors.

At the second, higher order we need to envisage the universalisation of cryptocurrencies. At present, the prospect of Bitcoin or any other cryptocurrency replacing national currencies seems remote. However, were this to happen, it would amount to imbuing Keynes's 'barbarous relic' with new power. Once again, just as under the gold standard, the government would be unable to spend beyond the amount of hard currency it held or could raise. Social justice is no longer generally a major consideration of government spending as it was when Hayek wrote. Yet state spending is still far in excess of what he would regard as responsible. Under a global cryptocurrency standard, therefore, a reduction in state size and spending of genuinely historic proportions would be required. Combined with its new inability to effectively collect tax revenues, because of crypto-enabled evasion, it is in fact unlikely that the state would survive in anything like its current form. This, of course, is the long-term goal of radical crypto partisans. However, with the state's demise we would witness the end of the protections it provides against the abuse of private power, however meagre they may often seem today. In their quest to terminate *imperium*, therefore, the cryptocurrency crusaders risk initiating a new age of unrestricted *dominium*.

Conclusion

In this chapter, I have examined Hayek's second piece of intellectual emergency equipment, his scheme for the denationalisation of money, intended to work alongside his Model Constitution. Up to 1960, Hayek had defended both central banks and redeemable currencies. The period of his radicalisation, when the twin menaces of unlimited democracy and social justice seemed to him to pose a threat to the survival of western civilisation, had caused him to lose faith in the ability of state authorities to maintain sound money policies, hence his turn to more radical solutions. After 1960, and his market republican turn, 'liberty' itself became the prism through which he addressed the problem of money and inflation. The purpose of his new and radical scheme was to terminate, arbitrary state control of money.

Despite Hayek's popularity among members of the Conservative Party, the nature of his emergency equipment did not lend itself to the exercise of government power, quite the reverse. Consequently, the Thatcher government adopted Friedmanite monetarism as the solution to inflation, albeit temporarily and incompletely. Friedman's technique served as an instrument of statecraft. Furthermore, the retrenchment it required provided an avenue for a more general withdrawal of government from direct involvement in the economy, serving as a prelude to a major programme of privatisation. Money, however, was not included. For some decades, this seemed to mark the end for the libertarian financial logic exhibited in the 'Denationalisation of Money'. It was, however, to re-emerge with the advent of cryptocurrencies. As with Hayek's earlier scheme, although potentially eliminating the possibility of *imperium*, the general use of such currencies would only promote that other element of the concept of non-domination, *dominium*.

Notes

1 For more on Cato's Letters written by a fellow traveller of Hayek's also involved with his collected works, see Ronald Hamowy (1990).
2 Friedman was also a member of Hayek's Mont Pèlerin Society.
3 They quote Bagehot: 'The whole rests on an instinctive confidence generated by use and years.... If some calamity swept it away, generations must elapse before at all the same trust would be placed in any other equivalent. A many-reserve system, if some miracle should put it down in Lombard Street, would seem monstrous there. Nobody would understand it or confide in it. Credit is a power which may grow but cannot be constructed.' For a comparison of the positions of Hayek and Friedman on such currencies see Luther (2013).
4 Bartley, having completed a biography of Popper also received the task of acting as Hayek's official biographer. He was also, as discussed in the introduction, Hayek's chief assistant for his final work, *The Fatal Conceit*, though it seems this was in fact as much Bartley's as it was Hayek's.
5 Stanley Fischer (1986) wrote 'Hayek's tract is Messianic not analytic'. Fischer went on to become vice Chair of the US Federal Reserve so perhaps his position is unsurprising.
6 Bulpitt's concept of statecraft bears some similarity to the concept of governmentality developed by Michel Foucault (2008). Foucault talked explicitly about neoliberal governmentality in his 1979 lectures at the Collège de France.
7 The idea that an effective monetarist policy could be primarily pursued by reducing borrowing, rather than rule-guided action, was dismissed by Friedman (Tomlinson, 2012, p. 75).
8 Hayek's pamphlet provided a stimulus to a subsequent body of work on free banking and private currencies (White, 2009; Dowd, 1989; Selgin, 1988).

Works cited

Bulpitt, J. 1986. 'The Discipline of the New Democracy: Mrs. Thatcher's Domestic State-craft', *Political Studies* 34, pp. 19–39.

Champion, R. 2013. 'Hayek Bartley and Popper: Justificationism and the Abuse of Reason' in Robert Leeson (Ed.), *Hayek: A Collaborative Biography, Part 1 Influences from to Bartley* (pp. 213–225). London: Palgrave Macmillan.

Clapham, J. 1944. *The Bank of England*. Cambridge: Cambridge University Press.

Dowd, K. 1989. *The State and the Monetary System*. New York: Phillip Allen.

Fisher, S. 1986. 'Friedman versus Hayek on Private Money: Review Essay', *Journal of Monetary Economics* 17:3, pp. 433–439.

Foucault, M. 2008. *The Birth of Biopolitics, Lectures at the College de France 1978–1979*. M. Senellart (Ed.). London: Routledge.

Friedman, M. and Schwartz, A. 1987. 'Has Government Any Role in Money?' in Michael D. Bordo and Milton Friedman (Eds.), *Money in Historical Perspective: Anna J Schwartz* (pp. 289-314). Chicago: University of Chicago Press.

Gamble, A. 1994. *The Free Economy and the Strong State*. London: Palgrave.

Hamowy, R. 1990. 'Cato's Letters, John Locke and the Republican Paradigm', *History of Political Thought* 11, pp. 273–94.

Hayek, F.A. 1960. *The Constitution of Liberty*. Chicago: University of Chicago Press.

Hayek, F.A. 1994. *Hayek on Hayek: An Autobiographical Dialogue*. Stephen Kresge and Leif Warner (Eds.). Chicago: University of Chicago Press.

Hayek, F.A. 1999g. 'Choice in Currency' [1976] in Stephen Kresge (Ed.), *Good Money Part Two: The Collected Works of F.A. Hayek, Vol. 6* (pp. 115–127). Chicago: University of Chicago Press.

Hayek, F.A. 1999h. 'The Denationalisation of Money' [1976] in Stephen Kresge (Ed.), *Good Money Part Two: The Collected Works of F.A. Hayek, Vol. 6* (pp. 128–229). Chicago: University of Chicago Press.

Hayek, F.A. 1999i. 'Towards a Free Market Monetary System' [1977] in Stephen Kresge (Ed.), *Good Money Part Two: The Collected Works of F.A. Hayek, Vol. 6* (pp. 230–237). Chicago: University of Chicago Press.

Hayek, F.A. 1999j. 'The Future Unit of Value' [1981] in Stephen Kresge (Ed.), *Good Money Part Two: The Collected Works of F.A. Hayek, Vol. 6* (pp. 238–252). Chicago: University of Chicago Press.

Howard, D.H. 1977. 'Review of Denationalisation of Money', *Journal of Monetary Economics* 8, pp. 483–485.

Howells, P. 2013. 'The U.S. Fed and the Bank of England, International', *Journal of Political Economy* 42:3, pp. 44–62.

Huckle, S. and White, M. 2016. 'Socialism and the Blockchain', *Future Internet* 8:49, pp. 1–15.

Klein, B. 1976. 'Competing Monies: A Comment', *Journal of Money, Credit, and Banking* 8:4, pp. 513–519.

Kukathas, C. 1989. *Hayek and Modern Liberalism*. Oxford: Oxford University Press.

Luther, W. 2013. 'Friedman Versus Hayek on Private Outside Monies: New Evidence for the Debate', *Economic Affairs* 33:1, pp. 127–135.

O'Driscoll, G.P. and Shenoy, S. 1974. 'Inflation, Recession, and Stagflation', *Economic Staff Paper Series* 181, pp. 1–37.

Popper, K. 1945. *The Open Society and Its Enemies, Vol. 1*. London: Routledge.

Selgin, G. 1988. *The Theory of Free Banking: Money Supply under Competitive Note Issue*. Lanham: Lexington Books.

Tomlinson, J. 2012. 'Thatcher, Monetarism and the Politics of Inflation' in Ben Jackson and Robert Saunders (Eds.), *Making Thatcher's Britain* (pp. 62–77). Cambridge: Cambridge University Press.

Weber, B. 2016. 'Bitcoin and the Legitimacy Crisis of Money', *Cambridge Journal of Economics* 40:1, pp. 17–41.

White, L. 1999. 'Why Didn't Hayek Favor Laissez Faire in Banking', *History of Political Economy* 31:4, pp. 754–769.

White, L. 2009. *Free Banking in Britain: Theory, Experience and Debate 1800–1845*. London: Institute of Economic Affairs.

Wood, J. 2005. *A History of Central Banking in Great Britain and the United States*. Cambridge: Cambridge University Press.

9 Liberal authoritarianism and market republicanism

In his major published works, Hayek gives little indication of how the threats to market freedom might be resisted and his intellectual emergency equipment implemented. However, over the 1970s, particularly in a series of letters to *The Times*, the method by which democracy might be limited and the pursuit of social justice terminated became clear. The new constitutional and legal framework required for true individualism to survive could not be introduced by the old order. A moment of exception, of transformative change, was necessary. A period of liberal authoritarianism, a regime that would decisively limit democracy and push back the forces of organised labour and the emancipatory movements of the 1960s and '70s would be required.

Dictatorship was originally a Roman republican institution. It was a form of emergency rule, placing unlimited power in the hands of an extraordinary magistracy, enabling them to counter an internal or external threat to the republic. In keeping with the classical turn his thought had taken, Hayek turned to this Roman ideal of dictatorship as offering a means of escaping the totalitarian outcome he associated with unlimited democracy. He sharply distinguished between authoritarianism and totalitarianism. The former could take a liberal form that preserved and even extended market freedom even as it eroded political rights. The latter involved the socialisation and direction of the economy and was intolerable from the perspective of his epistemic economics. Hayek's endorsement of a temporary period of dictatorship is, therefore, fully consonant with his market republicanism. However, the transformative function he hoped the liberal authoritarian would perform far exceeded that associated with the dictatorships of antiquity.

Isonomia, demokratia and demarchy

Hayek's studies in intellectual history saw him develop his analysis of the failings of contemporary democracy with reference to the classical world. He delineated a strict difference between the Greek concepts of *Isonomia*, the rule of law, and *Demokratia*, democracy. 'The Greeks', Hayek (1953a, pp. 518–519) wrote, 'fully understood that the two concepts, although related, did not mean the same thing'. He had always been clear that fundamental to the epistemic functioning of the market was a stable set of rules that served to guide and restrict action. Out of this came his insistence that liberalism was virtually synonymous with the rule of law. Hayek therefore privileged the legal framework over popular will with the result that he was able to dispense with democracy and still regard himself as a liberal. It was false individualism, he argued, that had embraced the 'doctrinaire' democracy associated with the ideals of the French revolution in the belief it was both possible and legitimate to shape society according to the wishes of the majority (Hayek, 1948a, pp. 29–32). In *The Constitution of Liberty,* he was quite clear that:

> The difference between the two ideals stands out most clearly if we name their opposites: for democracy it is authoritarian government; for liberalism it is totalitarianism. Neither of the two systems necessarily excludes the opposite of the other: a democracy may well wield totalitarian powers, and it is conceivable that an authoritarian government may act on liberal principles.
>
> (Hayek, 1960a, p. 103)[1]

Furthermore, Hayek viewed the rule of law and democracy not just as distinct phenomena but as being in tension. In ancient Greece, the chronologically later demand for democracy had, he argued, worked to undermine an older respect for the rule of law as 'democratic government soon proceeded to destroy that very equality before the law from which it derived its justification' (Hayek, 1953a, p. 518). This dynamic re-emerged in 20th century Europe when the age of unlimited mass democracy undermined the previous liberal order of the 19th century. Hayek's definition of true liberalism as a fundamentally market doctrine enabled him to endorse forms of authoritarian rule that would preserve *isonomia* and free market action via the removal of the political rights and liberties associated with *demokratia*.

This desire to disentangle liberalism from what he regarded as its democratic encumbrances is further evidence of Hayek's rejection of 19th century developments within the liberal movement. It also makes clear his distance from other 20th century classical liberals, such as Milton Friedman and Frank Knight, who emphasised a strong connection between free markets and modern democratic institutions.[2] It was Knight who took Hayek to task for seeking to break the connection, which was particularly prevalent during the years of the cold war, as the economically liberal states of the west positioned themselves as champions of democracy (Burgin, 2009). Coming from an American perspective that did not necessarily view liberalism as the product of a Whig inheritance, he placed far greater emphasis on democratic participation. He insisted 'that man is a social being, and freedom in society rests on agreement on forms and terms of association, i.e. free agreement on the laws, i.e. "government by discussion"'. Hayek's book, he felt 'is propaganda for "government by law," but against law "making"' (Knight, 1967, p. 787).

For Knight, Hayek's desire to distinguish liberalism from democracy was both anachronistic and gave no real sense of how law might in future be made and changed in a way that met the needs of the moment. Consequently, Hayek's liberal vision was both unrealistic and unacceptable. Instead, Knight argued that 'the broad crucial task of free society is to reach agreement by discussion of the kind of civilization it is to create for the future; hence it must agree on the meaning of progress' (Emmet, 2011, p. 67). For Knight, democracy is crucial to this process and must not be reduced to a procedural husk but should be regarded as constitutive of liberalism itself. If this resulted in measures that had a greater degree of social justice as their object, so be it. Knight (1942) felt that a large disparity in the distribution of wealth between groups of individuals could pose a threat to liberty. Whereas Hayek consistently opposed progressive taxation, Knight argued that 'such measures as progressive taxation and relief and the provision of public services, especially free education for the children of the poor' were necessary for the maintenance of a liberal order.[3] Tellingly, Knight (1967, p. 789) criticised Hayek for not recognising the importance of the democratic revolutions of the 19th century to the liberal tradition complaining that, 'Hayek does not mention the crucial events that led to or constituted the Liberal Revolution, establishing free society, that is, democracy in the broad meaning' and he pointedly criticised his 'pretentiously detailed history' for what should be 'clear to any attentive reader', that Hayek 'is scornful of politically organized freedom.'

By the period of his intellectual emergency equipment, Hayek had come to realise that his best efforts to change how people conceived of democracy had failed. That particular project had been bound up with the mission of *The Road to Serfdom* which had aimed to show that a true democracy was a limited democracy. As he lost hope in the possibility of a self-limiting democracy, he came to regard the very word as an obstacle to the realisation of his intellectual project. As a result, Hayek (1982d, p. 40) came to favour the term *demarchy* in order to 'describe the old ideal' of a representative government constrained within the republican form of a mixed constitution 'by a name that is not tainted by long abuse'. This term denoted a 'system of government in which the *demos* has no brute power (*kratos*) but is confined to ruling (*archein*) by "established standing laws promulgated and known to the people, and not by extemporary decrees"'. In apparent confirmation of Knight's critique, the term reveals the extent to which Hayek wished to erase the agency of the *demos*, confining it instead to established processes, which were themselves the product of a legal framework that had evolved to preserve existing property rights.

Endorsing dictatorship

If *demarchy* was the ideal outcome of Hayek's intellectual emergency equipment, he became increasingly convinced that a period of liberal authoritarianism would first be required to bring it about.[4] In his 1960 radio broadcast, 'New Nations and the Problem of Power', Hayek (1960b, p. 820) reflected on the relationship between authoritarian rule and economic liberalism in the context of decolonisation. The nation which commanded most of Hayek's attention, however, was Portugal, which can in no way be described as 'new', and he spoke approvingly of the Portuguese Prime Minister, António de Oliveira Salazar. When discussing his nascent idea for the separation of law-making and government Hayek opined that,

> one can conceive of a man like Salazar in Portugal, anxious to bring things into a situation which can last for a long time, adopting this sort of principle and transferring to a democratically elected assembly those limiting powers I am suggesting, and feeling much more reassured than if he had to restore the kind of system where the legislature had unlimited powers and could do what it pleased.
>
> (1960b, p. 820)

Aside from the fact that Hayek thought it was more important to reassure rather than resist an authoritarian such as Salazar, by 1960 it was strikingly apparent that the only situation that had lasted for a long time in Portugal was Salazar's own rule. (Oliviera Marques, 1972; Gallagher, 1979; Ramos Pinto, 2013). He had acted as the authoritarian Prime Minister of Portugal from 1932 and would continue to do so until 1968. Hayek's support for him is at first surprising. It is true that Salazar governed with a veneer of constitutional respectability following the implementation, by plebiscite, of a new constitution in 1933, but this is hardly an unusual move for a dictator. In reality, Salazar's rule was a period devoid of free or fair elections and of prevalent police repression. The 1930s had seen the regime ape the Italian fascist organisations of Italy and Germany with the Portuguese Legion and Portuguese Youth organisations, replete with fascist salutes and uniforms. Hayek had earlier denounced such groups as symptoms of serfdom but by 1960, apparently, he was more accepting. The constitution Salazar introduced was, moreover, avowedly corporatist, espousing ideas that were anathema to Hayek's market republicanism. Like Hayek, Salazar had been a professor of economics in the 1920s but unlike Hayek he was no believer in free trade. Even as he gave his broadcast on the BBC, a second *Plano de Fomento*, the Portuguese version of the Soviet Five Year Plans, was already underway.

As a champion of a conservative brand of Catholic social doctrine Salazar was decidedly not a liberal but wished instead to 'proscribe definitely liberalism'. However, Salazar's definition of liberalism was much like Schmitt's. What he disapproved of most of all was a parliamentary pluralism that led to 'partisan or social struggles' (Oliviera Marques, 1972, p. 183). Salazar had come to power six years after a 1926 coup, the result of dissatisfaction with the 'unlimited' but ineffectual democracy of the First Portuguese Republic. He had saved Portugal, in Schmitt's terms, from a 'crisis of parliamentary democracy' of the sort which Hayek warned 'new nations' might face in 1960, and which he subsequently insisted Britain faced in the 1970s. Hayek (1962) sent Salazar a copy of *The Constitution of Liberty* along with a note wishing him well 'in his endeavour to design a constitution which is proof against the abuses of democracy'. However, there was to be no new constitution under Salazar or under his successor

Marcelo Caetano. Three years earlier there had, however, been an amendment to the 1933 constitution that placed responsibility for the election of the president in the hands of a small body of electors rather than the people, whose free vote was already utterly compromised. Given his subsequent approval of the regime, Hayek could hardly have been opposed to this particular 'dethronement of politics'.

Salazar was not the only authoritarian figure to whom Hayek was sympathetic. In 1967, in a letter to *The Sunday Times*, he defended General Suharto's new regime which had been established that year in Indonesia following a coup. The new government should not be thought of as simply a military imposition, he argued, as its members were 'mostly not what we would regard as military men. They are in many instances men coming from other professions who in the fight for independence have risen in rank and remained in the army to ward off communism.' Hayek (1967n) also approved of a recent article in *The Sunday Times* which described appreciatively how the new regime was denationalising industries and welcoming foreign investment (Farrant and McPhail, 2014, p. 336).

If denationalisation and encouraging foreign investment were markers of an authoritarian liberalism of which Hayek could approve, six years later he would recognise them again in another military regime, this time in Chile. In September 1973, General Augusto Pinochet deposed the democratically elected government of Salvador Allende. Allende was a socialist who had been elected president in 1970 at the head of a popular unity government composed mainly of socialist and communist parties (Huneeus, 2007, p. 33). The radical programme of the unity government exposed long-standing divisions in the country. Inflation, as in most parts of the developed world, was high and rising. In this context the government sought first to make goods and money available to those from lower socio-economic groups. It proceeded to bring important industries under state control and the production of low-cost high-end consumer goods became a priority. Minimum wages were also increased across many industries to keep pace with inflation. All of this took place alongside a radical programme of land redistribution that had begun under Allende's predecessor, Eduardo Frei Montalva (Sigmund, 1977). These policies, combined with the continuing national and global economic crisis, stoked business and middle-class resentment resulting in a major strike in protest of government actions in March 1972. As a consequence, Allende invited members of the military into the government and the Commander in Chief of the army, General Prats, joined the cabinet. He, however, was forced to resign by anti-government elements within the military and was replaced by Pinochet. The details surrounding the eventual takeover by Pinochet and his military collaborators are complex and the full role of outside actors such as the US Central Intelligence Agency remains uncertain (Haslem, 2005). What is known is that the treatment of left-wing activists and trade unionists that followed the coup was brutal: thousands were murdered and many thousands more imprisoned, tortured and exiled.

For Hayek, events in Chile leading up to the coup had been further confirmation of the dangers of unlimited democracy and Allende's reforms had only proved the distinction between liberalism and democracy. He explicitly sought to link the political history of the continent as a whole with his own work in intellectual history and the binary between British and continental liberalism. The 'tradition in South America' he believed, was overly influenced by the rational constructivism of 'the French Revolution . . . a tradition that lies . . . in maximum government power'. Hayek continued that, 'South America has been overly influenced by the totalitarian type of ideologies.' Accordingly, Latin America 'sought to imitate the French democratic tradition, that of the French Revolution, which meant giving maximum powers to government' (Farrant et al., 2012, p. 533). For market republican liberty to survive, it would be necessary to enforce the anglophone political tradition.

Hayek made two trips to Pinochet's Chile, one in 1977 and another in 1981. His appraisal of the regime there has been a source of much controversy.[5] The conservative Chilean newspaper *El Mercurio* covered Hayek's November 1977 visit to the country during which he met with Pinochet. It reported that during a conversation with the general, Hayek,

> told reporters that he talked to Pinochet about the issue of limited democracy and representative government . . . He said that in his writings he showed that unlimited democracy does not work because it creates forces that in the end destroys democracy. He said that the head of state listened carefully and that he had asked him to provide him with the documents he had written on this issue.
>
> (Farrant and McPhail, 2014, p. 336)

Hayek had delivered a similar message in Argentina, the country he had visited before travelling to Chile. In an interview there, with the magazine *Somos*, he said 'generals had been forced to take power [in] Argentina, Bolivia, Brazil, Chile and Uruguay' in order to save the countries from the ravages of unlimited democracy. (Farrant and McPhail, 2014, p. 337). On his return to Europe, Hayek (1978k, 1978l) wrote two letters to *The Times* in which he continued to assert the greater danger of an illiberal democracy than of a supposedly liberal authoritarianism.

Charlotte Cubitt, Hayek's personal secretary from 1977 until his death in 1992, recalled in her memoirs that he 'took time off from his official commitments to walk around and see for himself whether people were cheerful and content. He told me that it was the sight of many sturdy and healthy children that had convinced him' that Chile was on the right track. She also revealed that Hayek did indeed find the documents Pinochet had asked for. Just as he had sent *The Constitution of Liberty* to Salazar, so Hayek sent a draft of his chapter 'A Model Constitution' to Pinochet two years prior to its publication (Cubitt, 2006, p. 19). One can only guess whether Pinochet took the time to read it, but according to Karin Fischer (2009), the constitution enacted in

September was named after Hayek's 1960 work, *The Constitution of Liberty*.[6] In fact, this title is missing from the official document but it was referred to as such in popular and official circles (Hudson, 1994). On his return from Chile, Hayek (1978m) published an essay in which he was sympathetic to the Chilean regime, '*Internationaler Rumford*', which can be translated roughly as 'International Calumny'. Fischer has argued that he openly defended Pinochet although the truth is that Hayek was careful not to go this far. Instead he sought to highlight what he regarded as the hypocrisy of the western press in its treatment of Chile compared to Communist regimes. Nonetheless, the editor of the *Frankfurter Allgemeine Zeitung*, Germany's leading free market newspaper, refused to print it as it was deemed too favourable to the dictator (Farrant et al., 2012, p. 515).

Nicholas Kaldor (1978), the Keynesian inspired economist and a fellow émigré from central Europe who had also been a former colleague of Hayek at the L.S.E., responded in *The Times* to Hayek's assessment,

> Chile is a dictatorship equipped with secret police, detention camps, etc. where strikes are ruled out and the organization of workers in trade unions is prohibited ... if we take Professor Hayek literally, a fascist dictatorship of some kind (along with monetarism) should be regarded as the necessary precondition ... of a 'free society.'

The repressive apparatus Kaldor described was not, to Hayek's mind, irreconcilable with liberalism. As long as market relations were respected, so long as the dominating power of the state was excluded from the market sphere, the polity remained essentially liberal. It was when it began to redistribute wealth and plan the economy, even within the bounds of law, that it became illiberal and unacceptable.[7]

Although Hayek was careful not to explicitly endorse the apparatus of a police state, he nonetheless defended the regime. He certainly regarded Pinochet as an 'honourable general.' When a Venezuelan interviewer asked in 1981 about the proliferation of 'totalitarian' regimes in South America, Hayek responded:

> Don't confuse totalitarianism with authoritarianism. I don't know of any totalitarian governments in Latin America. The only one was under Allende. Chile is now a great success. The world shall come to regard the recovery of Chile as one of the great economic miracles of our time.
>
> (Ebenstein, 2001, p. 300)

This attitude reveals the ordoliberal, rather than the Schmittian roots of his model of dictatorship. Hayek could not countenance, because of his epistemic economics and his market republican concept of liberty, the type of total state that Schmitt had outlined. The ordoliberal dictator, at least conceived as an ideal type, did not seek to intervene in or shepherd the economy in the manner of Schmitt's dictator, but was restrained enough to recognise the benefits of overseeing and maintaining a legal framework that would create the conditions for optimal competition.

Across his South American interviews Hayek recognised that any return to the rule of law, preferably structured around his Model Constitution depended on the 'good faith' of the dictator. This is remarkable for a man who had spent the earlier part of his career, most forcefully in *The Road to Serfdom*, warning of the dangers of dictatorship. Yet Hayek had earlier been concerned about a particular, socialistic type of dictatorship. When the dictator believed in the free market he was willing to reverse his position going so far as to insist that 'democracy needs "a good cleaning" by strong governments' (Farrant et al., 2012, p. 533).

In 1982, Hayek wrote to Margaret Thatcher with some advice. The letter is missing from both the Hayek and the Thatcher archives, but her reply is not. Although she agreed that Chile, 'offered many lessons' Thatcher (1982) continued,

> However I am sure you will agree that, in Britain with our democratic institutions and the need for a high degree of consent, some of the measures adopted in Chile are quite unacceptable. Our reform must be in line with our traditions and our Constitution. At times the process may seem painfully slow. But I am certain we shall achieve our reforms in our own way and in our own time. Then they will endure.[8]

What Hayek was advising is unclear. It has been suggested that he may have been recommending some form of severe anti-union legislation (Farrant and McPhail, 2017). He had, however, already written to her on this subject previously, even suggesting a referendum to gain public assent for such a measure, but his advice had been politely declined (Ebenstein, 2001, p. 292). Although anti-unionism certainly remained a prominent concern, given this, and all that he had recently written on the need for a radically different form of democracy, it is not unimaginable Hayek was suggesting that the government acquire emergency powers allowing it to reshape the British constitution in a much more fundamental way. It is probable that Hayek held out similar hopes for Thatcher to those he had harboured for Salazar and Pinochet. Just as he had sent them his work, so he sent the Model Constitution to her when it appeared in print in volume three of *Law, Legislation and Liberty* in 1979, the year of her first election victory (Ebenstein, 2001, p. 292).

To what extent Hayek felt Britain should follow Chile's lead remains, then, something of an open question. Based on his endorsement of authoritarianism over this period it seems reasonable to conclude that he viewed dictatorship as a legitimate vehicle for the implementation of his intellectual emergency equipment. On the basis of his position that this equipment would be imminently needed in Britain, it seems reasonable to conclude that he also believed a period of authoritarian rule would be necessary in his adopted country to bring it about. He had regarded dictatorship as necessary in places such as Chile because market freedom had been under threat. He certainly believed that same freedom was imperilled in Britain also. It seems unlikely, but by no means impossible, that Hayek would have been bold enough to suggest the full-scale implementation of his intellectual emergency equipment. Such a move would certainly have been legally and constitutionally inadmissible. Nonetheless, it is clear from Thatcher's letter of response that Hayek was indeed suggesting something extra constitutional. This perception is reinforced by his insistence that when communicating with Thatcher he did not give opinions on what was currently politically possible, but on what he believed was right and ought to be done (Ebenstein, 2001, p. 292).

Hayek had come to regard the doctrine of parliamentary sovereignty as constituting the most dangerous manifestation of unlimited democracy. It is therefore hardly 'lurid' (Farrant and McPhail, 2017, p. 270) to suppose the intention of any advice he offered would have been to shift the conduct of government in the direction of *demarchy*, This, after all, was his clearly stated preference for how government should function. Charlotte Cubitt (2006, p. 19) wrote that she thought Thatcher's rebuff must have been painful for Hayek, as he did not show her the letter for at least two weeks 'and even asked me whether he needed to reply to it. I said I thought not because I could not imagine what he could possibly say to her.'

Despite Thatcher being in power, Hayek did not feel entirely comfortable that the slide towards increasingly totalitarian government had been arrested. As late as 1981 he envisaged the possible need, owing to economic crisis, for a re-introduction of rationing of basic goods in Britain (Ebenstein, 2001, p. 280). It was not that he doubted Thatcher's good faith, but he was concerned that without a radical redrawing of the constitution, trade unions would again be able to use their influence to bring to power a left-wing government and the electorate would once more be seduced by the appeal of social justice. Yet there is an irony in his eventual readiness to endorse dictators and oligarchies and reject the existing parliamentary model. In the years after 1979, the Thatcher government was to use the power of unlimited democracy to bring down inflation, assault the trade unions, remove political oversight from large areas of the economy by means of privatization, and effectively terminate the pursuit of social justice as a core duty of government. It was thus able to achieve some of Hayek's more immediate political goals, precisely because it was unrestrained by his intellectual emergency equipment. Furthermore, as Thatcher had advised, the measures her government put in place have largely endured precisely because they were introduced according to the established constitution and have therefore not been regarded as illegal or illegitimate, even as they remain politically controversial.

Dictatorship and the oligarchic market republic

Hayek's distinction between liberty and democracy was also common in the long republican tradition. The Romans, with whom the conception of liberty as non-domination originated, were not democrats in any fundamental sense. The aspiration of the plebeians was not democracy, but protection from becoming *in potestate domini*, from falling into dependence upon the will of the powerful.[9] Daniel Kapust (2004, pp. 398–399) has noted that 'despite the fact that no one denies the Roman people to have been the sole source of legal authority in Rome at least in theory, it is difficult to argue that they were self-governing' and that 'it remains the case that attaining a position of political leadership was firmly linked to one's property qualifications, and the power of those with wealth was surely immense compared with that of the citizen in the lower census classes.' This attitude towards democracy was to carry down to the early modern and Whig authors on whom so much of Hayek's thinking about liberty rests and for whom, in Pettit's (1997, p. 28) words, the 'focus on avoiding interference rather than on achieving participation remains in place.' Indeed, the concept of democracy was generally equated with anarchy and social catastrophe. As Pettit (1997, p. 29) accepts, even James Harrington, one of the most radical of their number, who 'follows Machiavelli in regarding democratic controls as important for liberty . . . clearly sees people's liberty as consisting in something distinct from participation in government', and:

> Sometimes Harrington actively downplays popular democracy. 'The spirit of the people is no wise to be trusted with their liberty, but by stated laws or orders; so the trust is not in the spirit of the people, but in the frame of those orders.' The distrust evinced in this remark is echoed in contemporary republicans such as John Milton, who actively shuns 'the noise and shouting of a rude multitude' and, a little later, Algernon Sidney who says of 'pure democracy': 'I know of no such thing. And if it be in the world have nothing to say for it.'

It is this characteristic of the tradition upon which neo-republicanism draws that has been criticised by John McCormick (2003, pp. 616–617). For him, the republican focus on guarding against the *imperium* associated with the 'tyranny of the majority' has leant itself to 'aristocratic' and senatorial concerns that place too much emphasis on checks and balances. He argues that such are the traditional 'oligarchic tendencies of republicanism', that it 'can only reinforce what is worst about contemporary liberal democracy: the free hand that socioeconomic and political elites enjoy at the expense of the general populace'.[10] These tendencies are certainly evident in the work of Hayek's 'liberal' hero Cicero, for whom it was a good and proper thing that the superficial political equality of the citizens of Rome was conditioned and constrained by a mixed constitution in which power was actually concentrated among the upper orders, particularly within the Senate. This aspect of republican thinking again comes to the fore in Hayek's Model Constitution, where the senatorial role would be fulfilled by the *nomothetae*.[11]

It is necessary at this point to underline a distinction between normative neo-republican theory and historical accounts of republicanism. For the neo-republicans, democracy is an indispensable aspect of any modern political community. Pettit (2012) has countered claims that the neo-republican project associated with his work is too restrictive of popular sovereignty in his book *On The People's Terms*, where the emphasis is placed firmly on the importance of democratic participation. The ability to remove representatives from office is crucial, he argues, to ensuring that their actions will 'track' the interests of those whom they represent. It therefore reduces the scope of *imperium*. For others, such as McCormick, however, the focus on limiting majority power leaves neo-republicanism susceptible to the very elitism we see exhibited in Hayek's work. Whatever the case, it remains an inescapable historical truth that the majority of 'authors in the Roman and neo-Roman republican tradition . . . did not see it (freedom) as being tied definitionally to participation in a self-determining polity' and that 'while the republican tradition finds value and importance in democratic participation, it does not treat it as a bedrock value' (Pettit, 1997, p. 8).

It is not simply that republicanism has historically lacked a commitment to democracy; dictatorship, at least for a limited period, can also be considered a legitimate form of rule within the tradition. Dictatorship originally refers to a legally defined office of republican Rome, 'an extraordinary magistracy which, released from the constriction of collegiality, concentrates temporarily unprecedented powers in the hand of one individual with the mandate to save the *res publica*' (Arena, 2016, p. 16). Schmitt's (2013) early work, *Die Diktatur*, offered a history of western political thought that placed dictatorship at its core (Kelly, 2017). In it, he termed this classical republican form of dictatorship 'commissarial' as it involved an individual being commissioned by the existing institutions to restore order with a term set at six months. Hayek (1978l, p. 15) certainly couched his defence of liberal authoritarianism in classical terms and with reference to the long republican tradition. In one of his letters to *The Times* he asked whether it was not the case,

> that in some historical circumstances personal liberty may not have been better protected under an authoritarian than democratic government. This has occasionally been true since the beginning of democracy in ancient Athens, where the liberty of the subjects was undoubtedly safer under the '30 tyrants' than under the democracy which killed Socrates and sent dozens of its best men into exile by arbitrary decrees. In modern times there have of course been many instances of authoritarian governments under which personal liberty was safer than under democracies.

Furthermore, Hayek cited and mentioned approvingly that exemplar of early modern republican dictatorship, Oliver Cromwell, on a number of occasions (Hayek, 1960a, pp. 39, 428, 464, 530).

In keeping with the republican model of dictatorship, Hayek also insisted that liberal authoritarian dictatorship should not become permanent. 'As long-term institutions', he reflected,

I am totally against dictatorships. But a dictatorship may be a necessary system for a transitional period. At times it is necessary for a country to have, for a time, some form or other of dictatorial power. As you will understand, it is possible for a dictator to govern in a liberal way. And it is also possible for a democracy to govern with a total lack of liberalism. Personally, I prefer a liberal dictator to democratic government lacking in liberalism.

(Farrant et al., 2012, p. 521)

This sounds like an endorsement of commissarial dictatorship, with the liberal authoritarian embarking upon a restorative project that will limit democracy, break the power of the trade unions and re-establish the rule of liberty as non-domination in market relations. Yet we have seen that it was Hayek's great hope that liberal dictators would implement his intellectual emergency equipment, thus establishing an oligarchic market republic in which economic liberalism could thrive. Only then would they retire from public life in the manner of the Roman general and dictator Cincinnatus. This corresponds not to the classical commissarial model of the dictator but to what Schmitt termed the model of 'sovereign' dictatorship.[12]

As Schmitt (2006) wrote in *Political Theology*, 'sovereign is he who decides on the state of exception'. The sovereign dictator is one who identifies just such a moment and therefore exists both 'outside of and prior to the constitution itself' (Kelly, 2017, p. 142). They are not charged with upholding any particular extant order. Instead, this model of dictator should be understood as 'a potentially all-powerful sovereign who not only must rescue a constitutional order from a particular political crisis but also must charismatically deliver it from its own constitutional procedures' (McCormick, 1997, 163). Whereas commissarial dictatorship is essentially conservative, the 'sovereign' dictator is, therefore, a revolutionary actor who, in the name of the people, transforms the existing constitutional order. The key progenitor of this model for Schmitt is Rousseau, although the experience of the English Civil War and the role of Oliver Cromwell was also foundational. It was in revolutionary France that it began to displace the commissarial model with profound consequences for modern Europe. On reflection then, Hayek's endorsement of liberal authoritarianism is best understood as endorsement of this revolutionary sovereign dictatorship. Despite his self-identification as an 'old Whig', it is very difficult to regard this as being in any way Whiggish.[13]

Conclusion

For Hayek, the democratic principle contained within it a threat to the rule of law, as demonstrated by his distinction between *isonomia* and *demokratia*. When the rule of law was compromised, so was liberty and thus the epistemic functioning of the market and indeed of the broader economy. The supposed danger of unlimited democracy led to Hayek endorsing a series of liberal dictatorships over the course of his career. He regarded these authoritarians as being essentially the opposite of the decisionist totalitarians Schmitt had earlier described, because their mission was to preserve private property and extend the reach of the market into areas of the economy that had previously been socialised. By promoting the rule of the market, they became liberty's greatest champions in a moment of crisis. Whatever the abuses of such military regimes, unlike the social democratic state, they could not be accused of *imperium*. By the mid-1970s Hayek believed that such a crisis had come to Britain.

In his defence of dictatorship, Hayek drew on the long republican tradition. It is important to distinguish the historical iterations of republicanism from contemporary normative neo-republican theory within which democracy is essential and dictatorship anathema. Ultimately, despite Hayek's claims, his ideal dictator was not on a mission to restore an old order. We should not be surprised that the new settlement he hoped they would bring into being was that which he had sketched in his intellectual emergency equipment. The future society was to be the oligarchic market republic.

Notes

1 He cites Schmitt in support of this position.
2 Knight is often regarded as the father of the Chicago school of economics. Hayek and Knight had clashed earlier in the 1930s over what determines the rate of interest. This may in part explain the caustic tone of Knight's reflections on Hayek's work. See Cohen (2003).
3 Contrast with Hayek (1953b)
4 Invaluable work on Hayek's attitude towards dictatorship has been carried out by Andrew Farrant, Edward McPhail and Sebastian Berger and this section draws upon their analysis and translations of key texts.
5 For an entry point into the discussion see Robin (2013).
6 Although the direct influence of Hayek on Chile is perhaps debateable, the impact of another branch of the neoliberal family, the Chicago school of economics, is clear. Inspired by the writing of Milton Friedman and his colleagues a group of Chilean economists, who became known as 'The Chicago Boys', put in place many of the monetarist policies and associated measures he recommended. See Karin Fischer (2009).
7 Underscoring his distinction between political rights and individual liberty Hayek also insisted, 'nor have I heard any sensible person claim that in the principalities of Monaco or Lichtenstein, which I am told are not precisely democratic, personal liberty is smaller than anywhere else!' With liberty conceived of in exclusively market terms, the truly liberal authoritarian could never be considered a threat to it (Hayek, 1978l, p. 15).
8 It could reasonably be asked to what extent the Thatcher government did remain within the constitution and the rule of law, as Thatcher insisted it must. The conduct of the police during her time in office remains highly questionable. For example, at the time of writing there are calls for a public inquiry into the conduct of West Yorkshire police during the miner's strike of 1984–5 (Conn, 2016; Perraudin, 2019). There is also significant evidence of collusion between state forces and loyalist paramilitaries over the period of her premiership, that resulted in a number of political murders. Some regiments of the British army are also reputed to have held a 'shoot to kill' policy.
9 Even institutions of popular representation, such as the plebeian tribunes, developed out of this concern.

10 Rather than a senatorial constitutional architecture McCormick (2011) advocates an interpretation of the republican tradition that places political participation at its core rather than individual independence. Only in this way, he argues, will it then become possible to secure the type of independence that Pettit and Skinner want to see. In this McCromick is inspired by Machiavelli.

11 Remarkably, one could regard Cicero (1999) as the greater democrat as he maintained that all citizens should participate in the political process whereas Hayek was willing to restrict the franchise.

12 Farrant et al. (2012) have also described this as Hayek's 'transitional'.

13 He does, however, build the potential for a return to the commissarial model into his Model Constitution. According to his design, the Legislative Assembly would have the power to declare emergency powers which would then be exercised by the Governmental Assembly. The Legislative Assembly would then have the ability to terminate the emergency. The purpose was to avoid the potential for future unlimited dictatorship once the oligarchic market republic had been established.

Works cited

Arena, V. 2016. 'The Roman Republic of Jean Jacques Rousseau'. *History of Political Thought*, 37:1, pp. 8–31.

Bellamy, R. 1994. 'Dethroning Politics': Liberalism, Constitutionalism and Democracy in the Thought of F. A. Hayek', *Journal of Political Science* 24:4, pp. 419–441.

Beniston, J. 2006. 'Culture and Politics in Red Vienna', *Austrian Studies* 14, pp. 1–19.

Burgin, A. 2009. 'The Radical Conservatism of Frank H Knight', *Modern Intellectual History* 6:3, pp. 513–538.

Burgin, A. 2012. *The Great Persuasion: Reinventing Free Markets Since the Depression*. Cambridge, MA: Harvard University Press.

Cicero, M.T. 1999. 'On the Commonwealth' in J. Zetzel (Ed.), *On the Commonwealth and On the Laws* (pp. 1–103). Cambridge: Cambridge University Press.

Cohen, A. 2003. 'The Hayek/Knight Capital Controversy: The Irrelevance of Roundaboutness, or Purging Processes in Time?' *History of Political Economy* Fall 35:5, pp. 469–490.

Conn, D. 2016. 'Orgreave Inquiry Calls Grow After Damning Hillsborough Verdict for Police', *The Guardian*, 16 May.

Cubitt, C. 2006. *A Life of Friedrich August von Hayek*. Bedfordshire: Authors On Line.

Ebenstein, A. 2001. *Friedrich Hayek: A Biography*, New York: Palgrave, St Martin's Press.

Emmet, R. 2011. 'Discussion and the Evolution of Institutions in a Liberal Democracy: Frank Knight Joins the Debate' in Andrew Farrant (Ed.), *Hayek, Mill and the Liberal Tradition* (pp. 57–78). London: Routledge.

Farrant, A., McPhail, E. and Berger, S. 2012. 'Preventing the "Abuses" of Democracy: Hayek, the "Military Usurper", and Transitional Dictatorship in Chile', *American Journal of Economics and Sociology* 71:3, pp. 513–538.

Farrant, A. and McPhail, E. 2014. 'Can a Dictator Turn a Constitution into a Can-opener? F. A. Hayek and the Alchemy of Transitional Dictatorship in Chile', *Review of Political Economy* 26:3, pp. 331–348.

Farrant, A. and McPhail, E. 2017. 'Hayek Thatcher and the Muddle of the Middle' in Robert Leeson (Ed.), *Hayek: A Collaborative Biography, Part 9 The Divine Right of the 'Free' Market* (pp. 263–284). London: Palgrave MacMillan.

Fischer, K. 2009. 'The Influence of Neoliberals in Chile Before, During, and After Pinochet' in Philip Mirowski and Dieter Plehwe (Eds.), *The Road from Mont Pelerin: The Making of the Neoliberal Thought Collective* (pp. 305–346). Cambridge, MA: Harvard University Press.

Gallagher, T. 1979. 'Controlled Repression in Salazar's Portugal', *Journal of Contemporary History* 14:3, pp. 385–402.

Haslem, J. 2005. *The Nixon Administration and the Death of Allende's Chile: A Case of Assisted Suicide.* London: Verso.

Hayek, F.A. 1948a. 'Individualism: True and False' [1945] in Friedrich Hayek (Ed.), *Individualism and Economic Order* (pp. 1–33). Chicago: University of Chicago Press.

Hayek, F.A. 1953a. The Decline of the Rule of Law', *The Freeman*, 20 April, pp. 518–520.

Hayek, F.A. 1953b. 'The Case Against Progressive Income Taxes', *The Freeman*, 28 December, pp. 229–232.

Hayek, F.A. 1960a. *The Constitution of Liberty.* Chicago: University of Chicago Press.

Hayek, F.A. 1960b. 'New Nations and the Problem of Power', *The Listener*, November, pp. 819–821.

Hayek, F.A. 1962. Letter to António de Oliveira Salazar, 8 July Friedrich A. von Hayek papers, Box no. 49, Folder no. 29, Hoover Institution Archives.

Hayek, F.A. 1967n. 'The Generals', *The Sunday Times*, 5 November, p. 10.

Hayek, F.A. 1978k. 'The Dangers to Personal Liberty', *The Times*, 11 July, p. 15.

Hayek, F.A. 1978l. 'Freedom of Choice', *The Times*, 3 August, p. 15.

Hayek, F.A. 1978m 'Internationaler Rufmord', *Politische Studien* 1, pp. 44–45.

Hayek, F.A. 1982d. 'The Political Order of a Free People' [1979] in *Law, Legislation and Liberty: A New Statement of the Liberal Principles of Justice and Political Economy* [3 Volume edition]. London: Routledge Kegan Paul.

Hudson, R. 1994. *Chile: A Country Study.* Washington: Federal Research Division, Library of Congress.

Huneeus, C. 2007. *The Pinochet Regime.* London: Lynne Rienner.

Kaldor, N. 1978. 'Chicago Boys in Chile', *The Times*, 18 October, p. 17.

Kapust, D. 2004. 'Skinner Pettit and Livy: The Conflict of the Orders and the Ambiguity of Republican Liberty', *History of Political Thought* 15:3, pp. 377–401.

Kelly, D. 2017. 'Carl Schmitt's Political Theory of Dictatorship' in J. Meierhenrich and O. Simons (Eds.), *The Oxford Handbook of Carl Schmitt.* Oxford: Oxford University Press (online).

Knight, F. 1942. 'Science, Philosophy, and Social Procedure', *Ethics* 52:3, pp. 253–274.

Knight, F. 1967. 'Laissez Faire: Pro and Con', *Journal of Political Economy* 75:6, pp. 782–795.

McCormick, J. 1997. 'The Dilemmas of Dictatorship: Carl Schmitt and Constitutional Emergency Powers', *Canadian Journal of Law and Jurisprudence* 10:1, pp. 163–187.

McCormick, J. 2003. 'Machiavelli against Republicanism: On the Cambridge School's "Guicciardinian Moments"', *Political Theory* 31:5, pp. 616–617.

McCormick, J. 2011. *Machiavellian Democracy.* Cambridge: Cambridge University Press.

Oliveira Marques, A.H. 1972. *History of Portugal, Vol. 2: From Empire to Corporate State.* New York: Columbia University Press.

Perraudin, F. 2019. 'Battle of Orgreave: Home Office Rejects Independent Review', *The Guardian,* 4 March.

Pettit, P. 1997. *Republicanism: A Theory of freedom and Government.* Oxford: Oxford University Press.

Pettit, P. 2012. *On the People's Terms: A Republican Theory and Model of Democracy.* Cambridge: Cambridge University Press.

Pinto, P. 2013. *Lisbon Rising: Urban Social Movements in the Portuguese Revolution, 1974–75.* Manchester: Manchester University Press.

Robin, C. 2013. 'Hayek von Pinochet'. Accessed at http://coreyrobin.com/2012/07/08/hayek-von-pinochet/ also http://crookedtimber.org/2013/06/25/the-hayek-pinochet-connection-a-second-reply-to-my-critics/

Schmitt, C. 2006. *Political Theology: Four Chapters on the Concept of Sovereignty*. Chicago: University of Chicago Press.

Schmitt, C. 2013. *Dictatorship*. Cambridge: University of Cambridge Press.

Sigmund, P. 1977. *The Overthrow of Allende and the Politics of Chile 1964–1976*. Pittsburgh: University of Pittsburgh Press.

Thatcher, M. 1982. Letter to Friedrich August Hayek 17 Feb. Friedrich A. von Hayek papers, Box no. 101, Folder no. 26, Hoover Institution Archives.

Conclusion

I began this book with a reflection on the relationship between freedom and power. I hope the subsequent chapters have made it clear that I, like Hayek, regard the rule of arbitrary power as being not only at odds with individual liberty, but also as deeply injurious to the epistemic exchanges and collaboration upon which a successful economy is based. It should, however, also be apparent that, unlike him, I want to insist that we must consider the ways in which arbitrary private power, *dominium*, as well as arbitrary public power, *imperium*, undermines freedom and frustrates the fullest use of knowledge in society.

In truth, the form of arbitrary power that individuals encounter most intensely is *dominium*, and the site at which exposure to this arbitrary power occurs most regularly, indeed constantly in most cases, is the workplace. Lifting the limits Hayek places on his conception of liberty as non-domination, to integrate a fuller consideration of *dominium* as well as *imperium* into his theory, demands that we address this. Doing so inevitably draws us towards a very different form of political economy than the market republican formulation he settled on.

Hayek, Mises and others in the Austrian tradition, have demonstrated the centrality of both individual liberty and market processes to economic coordination and the determination of value. Planning and commands do indeed run counter to both freedom and epistemic efficiency. Yet this insight holds true not just at the macroeconomic level, but also at the level of the private firm. While it may not be possible, or even desirable, to institute or replicate market competition within the firm, we can at least prevent firms from functioning as islands of tyranny, locations where power is unchecked and largely unaccountable (Phillips and Rozworski, 2019). The question that those who care about individual liberty and value Hayek's epistemic insights must answer is: how do we do this?

We can make a start in our efforts to answer the question by turning again to the republican tradition which makes the control of power its core concern. Yet within the neo-republicanism of the last twenty years, engagement with issues of economic freedom have been tentative. Indeed, considerations of how matters of liberty and political economy converge have been rare. Neo-republicans have generally recognised the market as an important site of freedom to the extent that its functioning requires a degree of legal independence and its operation and outcomes stand as a bulwark against the historic, centralising tendency of states and their efforts to concentrate power. However, there has been little consideration of how the economy is structured and how the distribution of wealth and power produced by the functioning of the economy impacts individual liberty, or indeed how imbalances of power and the instances of arbitrary rule they result in can be countered by bringing about a new political and economic settlement. In general, the neo-republican literature has been comfortable with the existing nature of market and economic relations, seeking only to graft further legal and constitutional protection onto them (Pettit, 2007).

Beyond this, the prevailing response among neo-republican thinkers has been to advise that leaving open the possibility of exits from tyrannical workplaces will largely suffice to prevent individuals from becoming dominated by their employers (Taylor, 2017). This is a position with which, as we have seen, Hayek agreed. From a genuinely republican perspective, however, this can hardly be satisfactory. For comparison, a historic republican or neo-republican would not say that the inhabitant of a nation under tyrannical rule can be considered free because they are afforded the option to leave. Instead, they would insist that only a regime based upon a conception of liberty as non-domination can render the individual free. The same logic must apply to the workplace, particularly when considered from the epistemic perspective Hayek provides us with.

I have then argued that if we are to take Hayek's epistemic insights seriously, something more radical is required. In seeking to understand how we can establish a regime of liberty across the broader economy, there are other elements of republican thinking, and other moments within the republican tradition to which we can turn. Many of the great republican struggles of the 19th century sought not only to achieve universal access to electoral politics, but also to reintegrate a concern for *dominium* into republican thinking. In this, certain groups such as the radical left Chartists in Britain, labour republicans in the United States, and the social revolutionaries who constituted a force across 19th century Europe, insisted that liberty conceived as non-domination demanded not just freedom to trade in the market, but freedom in the productive process, in the workplace. If, therefore, we wish to take some historical direction regarding the manner in which we may counter *dominium*, we should look not merely at the largely aristocratic iterations of republicanism associated with the early modern period, the very same sources which Hayek himself found so amenable to his own intellectual project, but cross the threshold of the 19th century, and engage with its more radical and demotic renderings of the republican tradition. Valuable work has already begun to this end (Gourevitch, 2015; Clare Roberts, 2017; Leipold, forthcoming) While the issues we face in the 21st century are often radically different to those of the 19th, the neo-republicans have already demonstrated the value of drawing on a study of the past, and applying the insights gained, to considerations of contemporary politics. Given that 19th century republicanism, in its new industrial context, was more firmly concerned with economic matters its potential to inform the political economy of the 21st is significant. Furthermore, in the field of normative political theory there are also new attempts to apply liberty conceived as non-domination to the non-market economic relations that shape most people's lived experience (Gourevitch, 2013; Muldoon, 2019; O'Shea, forthcoming).

I have already outlined how the application of republican thinking to the workplace can lead to an identification of the conditions required to check arbitrary rule in a manner that will encourage creativity, collaboration and a better use of knowledge. In closing, however, it is worth repeating the conditions I believe necessary. First, relationships in the firm must be based on rules not commands; second, those who work in a private firm must have a stake in its ownership; third, a system of workplace democracy to hold those in positions of power to account must prevail. It is my belief that the combination of republican liberty – conceived to its full and proper extent – with Hayek's epistemic economics provides us with a powerful, potentially transformative, framework for thinking about future radical and emancipatory forms of political economy.

Works cited

Clare Roberts, W. 2017. *Marx's Inferno: The Political Theory of Capital.* Princeton, NJ: Princeton University Press.

Gourevitch, A. 2013. 'Labor Republicanism and the Transformation of Work', *Political Theory* 41:4, pp. 591–617.

Gourevitch, A. 2015. *From Slavery to the Cooperative Commonwealth: Labor and Republican Liberty in the Nineteenth Century.* Cambridge: Cambridge University Press.

Leipold, B. Forthcoming. 'Chains and Invisible Threads: Liberty and Domination in Marx's Account of Wage-Slavery' in Annelien de Dijn and Hannah Dawson (Eds.), *Rethinking Liberty before Liberalism.* Cambridge: Cambridge University Press.

Muldoon, J. 2019. 'A Socialist Republican Theory of Freedom and Government', *European Journal of Political Theory* (advance online).

O'Shea, T. Forthcoming. 'Socialist Republicanism', *Political Theory.*

Pettit, P. 2007. A Republican Right to Basic Income? *Basic Income Studies* 2:2, pp. 1–8.

Phillips, L. and Rozworski, M. 2019. 'The People's Republic of Walmart' in *How the World's Biggest Corporations are Laying the Foundation for Socialism.* London: Verso.

Taylor, R. 2017. *Exit Left Markets and Mobility in Republican Thought.* Oxford: Oxford University Press.

Index

'Abuse of Reason' (Hayek) 51
'Age of Tyrannies, The' (Halévy) 51
Allende, Salvador 156
American Institutionalists 17
ancient Greece 65, 146–147
Anderson, Perry 85
'Appeal from the New Whigs to the Old,
    An' (Burke) 64
Arendt, Hannah 65
Asquith, Herbert Henry 76
Attlee, Clement 46
Austria 16
Austrian Institute for Business Cycle
    Research 19
Austrian School 17
authoritarianism 7, 10, 148
Autobiography (Mill) 52–53

Bagehot, Walter 54, 138
balanced budgets 20–21
Banker, The (magazine) 96
Bartley, William Warren 12, 51, 138
Bastiat, Claude-Frédéric 17
BBC Third Programme 118, 122
Behrend, Hilde 103
Bellamy, Richard 126
Belloc, Hillaire 40
Bentham, Jeremy 51
Berlin, Isaiah 69–71
Bevir, Mark 54
Bitcoin 141–143
blockchain technology 141–143
Bodin, Jean 135
Boettke, Peter 128
Böhm, Franz 91
Bretton Woods agreement 103
Britain 11–12
British liberalism 47–54
Brutzkus, Boris 33
Buckle, Henry 53
Bulpitt, Jim 139

Burczak, Theodore 126
Burke, Edmund 64
Burrow, John 54
business cycle 20, 23, 26
Business Cycles (Mitchell) 18
Butterfield, Herbert 64–65

Caetano, Marcelo 150
Caldwell, Bruce 12, 18, 36, 52
Capitalism and the Historians (Hayek) 64
catallaxy 49
Catchings, Waddill 19
Cato's Letters (Trenchard and Gordon) 133
central bank policy 20, 132
central banks 131–132, 137
Centre for Policy Studies 110
Champion, Rafe 138
Charles I, King of England 63
Chicago School 108
Chile 150–154
'Choice in Currency' (Hayek) 133
Churchill, Winston 20, 46
Cicero, Marcus Tullius 2, 62, 155
Cincinnatus 157
Coase, Ronald 41, 46
coercion 69
Cole, G.D.H. 32
Collectivist Economic Planning (Hayek) 33
commercial republicans 66–67
commissarial dictatorship 157
common ownership 32
communism 33
Comte, Auguste 50, 52–54
Condorcet, Nicolas de 50
Considérant, Victor 50
Constant, Benjamin 61, 62, 65, 71
constitutional court 126–128
Constitutional Theory (Schmitt) 87
Constitution of Liberty, The (Hayek) 62, 68,
    71–72, 87, 106, 110–111, 118, 131, 135,
    147, 149, 151–152

'Counter Revolution of Science' (Hayek) 51
Country Whigs 64
Court Whigs 64
Crisis of Parliamentary Democracy,
    The (Schmitt) 88
Cristi, Renato 85
'critical rationalism' 138
Cromwell, Oliver 10, 156, 157
cryptocurrencies 10, 140–144
Cubitt, Charlotte 151, 154

Dagger, Richard 73
Dalberg-Acton, John Emerich Edward 64
d'Alembert, Jean-Baptiste le Rond 50
Das Kapital (Marx) 54
'Decline of The Rule of Law, The'
    (Hayek) 62
deflation 8, 107–110
demarchy 148, 154
demokratia (democracy) 146–148, 157–158
'Denationalisation of Money, The' (Hayek)
    116, 134, 144
Descartes, René 50
Dicey, Albert Venn 75
Dicey, A.V. 40
dictatorship: dangers of 96–98;
    endorsement of 10, 148–154; liberty
    and 76; model of 91, 93, 146, 156–158;
    oligarchic market republic and 154–158
Diktatur, Die (Schmitt) 156
discretionary monetary policy 19
discursive change 48
domination 74
dominium 5–6, 13, 74–78, 111, 140, 144
Dyestuffs Act of 1920 33

Ebenstein, Alan 12
Economica (journal) 23, 51
'Economic Calculation in the Socialist
    Commonwealth' (Mises) 33
'Economic Conditions of Interstate
    Federalism, The' (Hayek) 117
Economic Consequences of the Peace
    (Keynes) 25
economic freedom 2–4, 39, 42, 46, 62–64,
    68–69, 74, 85–86, 92, 120, 140, 162
economic planning 4, 32–33, 36–43,
    46–47, 50, 62–63, 87–88, 162
economics: development of 31–32; schools
    of 17–18
'Economics and Knowledge' (Hayek) 2, 36
Elizabeth I, Queen of England 62, 66
Enfantin, Prosper 50

English Civil War 62, 157
epistemic economics 2–4, 36–38, 69
equilibrium 15, 22, 25, 36–38, 42, 54, 74
Eucken, Walter 7, 91, 105

Fabian Society 32
'false' liberalism 5, 53–56
Fatal Conceit, The (Hayek) 12
Ferguson, Adam 48
First World War 7, 15, 19–20, 31, 33, 55, 84
Fischer, Karin 151–152
Fisher, Anthony 110
Foster, William Trufant 19
Foucault, Michel 12
Fourier, Joseph 54
Fox, Charles James 64
Frankfurter Allgemeine Zeitung (newspaper)
    152
Freeden, Michael 11, 47
freedom: economic freedom 2–4, 42, 46,
    62–64, 68–69, 74, 85–86, 92, 120, 140,
    162; economic planning vs 39–41; as
    non-domination 70, 73, 75; as non-
    interference 70
'Freedom and the Economic System'
    (Hayek) 39, 55, 94
Freeman, The (magazine) 62
French Revolution 50, 64, 111, 122, 147, 151
Friedman, Milton 9, 106, 137–139, 147
full employment 102–107
'Future Unit of Value, The' (Hayek) 137

Gamble, Andrew 13, 94, 103, 126
gender franchise 126
General Agreement on Tariffs and Trade
    (GATT) 103
*General Theory of Employment Interest and
    Money, The* (Keynes) 19, 24
Geneva Gold and Monetary Conference 133
German Historical School 17
gold standard 20–22, 26
Gordon, Thomas 6, 66, 67, 133
Governmental Assembly 122–124
Gray, John 127
Green, T.H. 39, 54, 55
Grundsätze (Menger) 16
Guardian of the Constitution, The (Kelsen and
    Schmitt) 87

Hailsham, Q.H. (Lord) 96
Halévy, Élie 51
Hamowy, Donald 123
Harberler, Gottfried 108

Harrington, James 95
Harrington, Thomas 6
Hayek, Friedrich, works of: 'Abuse of
    Reason' 51; 'any Englishman, For' 62;
    Capitalism and the Historians 64; 'Choice
    in Currency' 133; *Collectivist Economic
    Planning* 33; *Constitution of Liberty, The*
    62, 68, 71–72, 87, 106, 110–111, 118,
    131–133, 135, 147, 149, 151–152;
    'Counter Revolution of Science, The' 51;
    'Decline of The Rule of Law, The'
    62; 'Denationalisation of Money, The'
    116, 134, 144; 'Economic Conditions
    of Interstate Federalism, The' 117;
    'Economics and Knowledge' 2, 36;
    Fatal Conceit, The 12; 'Freedom and the
    Economic System' 39, 55, 94; 'Future
    Unit of Value, The' 137; '*Internationaler
    Rumford* ' ['International Calumny'] 152;
    'Intertemporal Price Equilibrium and
    Movements in the Value of Money',
    Hayek 18–19; *Law, Legislation and
    Liberty* 9, 87, 104, 121, 126, 153; 'Model
    Constitution, A' 121, 151; 'New Nations
    and the Problem of Power' 118, 148;
    'Paradox of Saving, The' 19; 'Pretence
    of Knowledge, The' 108; *Prices and
    Production* 19, 24; *Profits, Interest and
    Investment* 24; *Pure Theory of Capital, The*
    24; *Road to Serfdom, The* 40, 46, 48, 56, 84,
    86, 89–90, 93–95, 97–98, 105, 128, 148,
    153; *Tiger by the Tail, A* 107; 'Trend of
    Economic Thinking, The' 31–32; 'What
    is "Social"?-What Does it Mean?' 105
Heath, Edward 96, 108
Henderson, Hubert 19
Hewart, Gordon 40
Hindenburg, Paul von 89
Hitler, Adolf 7, 40, 89–90
Hobbes, Thomas 5
Hobhouse, L.T. 52, 55
Hobson, J.A. 55
Howson, Susan 23
Hume, David 6, 17–18, 21, 31, 48, 51, 66,
    122, 127, 139
Hungary 16

'Idea of a Perfect Commonwealth, The'
    (Hume) 122
illiberal democracy 151
imperium 5, 9, 13, 74, 83, 95, 111, 127, 129,
    140, 144, 155
individualism 48–50

individual liberty 2, 4, 6, 26, 31, 38, 40–41,
    55, 65, 67, 70, 74, 78, 111–112,
    133, 162
Industrial Relations Act of 1971 96
inflation 8, 102–103, 111, 113, 135
Institute for Economic Affairs 110
interference 69
'*Internationaler Rumford*' ['International
    Calumny'] (Hayek) 152
International Monetary Fund (IMF) 103
'Intertemporal Price Equilibrium and
    Movements in the Value of Money'
    (Hayek) 18–19
'invisible hand, the' 17–18
isonomia (the rule of law) 146–147, 157–158

Jay, Peter 96
Jefferson, Thomas 6
Jenks, Jeremiah 16–18
Jevons, William Stanley 17
Jones, Hugh Stuart 51
Joseph, Keith 110

Kaldor, Nicholas 152
Kalyvas, Andreas 73
Kant, Immanuel 127
Kapust, Daniel 155
Katznelson, Ira 73
Kaukathas, Chandran 137
Kelsen, Hans 87
Keynes, John Maynard 19–20, 23–26,
    47–48, 56, 94, 107, 137, 139
Khan, Richard 23
Klein, Benjamin 140
Knight, Frank 147–148
knowledge 36–38, 41–42, 69, 77
Kukathas, C. 138
Kun, Béla 16

Labriola, Arturo 53
Lagrange, Joseph-Louis 50
laissez-faire 33, 46, 56, 88, 91, 93, 105
Lange, Oskar 31
Laski, Harold 52
Law, Legislation and Liberty (Hayek) 9, 87,
    104, 121, 126, 153
Lecky, William Edward Hartpole 53
Legislative Assembly 122–124, 127
Lenin, Vladimir 33
Lerner, Abba 31
liberal authoritarianism 10, 151, 156
liberalism: British/continental binary
    47–51; 'false' liberalism 5, 53–56; losing

its way 40; market freedom and 11, 47–49, 53, 56; New Liberalism and 39, 53, 55; nineteenth-century 4–5, 41, 65, 147–148; parliamentary democracy and 90–98; as politico-cultural phenomenon 85–87; Roman 62; 'true' liberalism 1–2, 5, 53–56, 61–62, 63, 147

Liberalismus (Mises) 52

liberals 1–2

liberty: concept of 68–73; individual liberty 2, 4, 6, 26, 31, 38, 40–41, 55, 65, 67, 70, 74, 78, 111–112, 133, 162; limits of 73–78; neo-Roman concept 69–72; as non-domination 5–6, 11, 77–78, 95, 111, 123, 128, 132; origins of 72; in Roman Law 2, 68–69

Livy 62

Lloyd George, David 19, 32

Locke, John 48

Logic of Scientific Discovery, The (Popper) 37

London School of Economics (L.S.E) 19, 20, 23–25, 31, 39, 42, 152

Lopez, Edward 128

Macaulay, Thomas Babington 64

MacMillan, Harold 32

Maitland, Frederic William 64

Mandeville, Bernard 18, 48

Marcuse, Herbert 12

market freedom: of entrepreneurial minority 126; individual liberty and 41; liberalism and 11, 56; liberty and 67–71, 78; as non-domination 90; order required for 120; 'rediscovery' of 63, 92, 120; threats to 7, 43, 47–49, 74, 76, 83, 86, 102–103, 121, 124–125, 127–128, 131, 134–135, 140, 146, 154

market republicanism 9, 110–113

Marshall Society 23

Marxism 54

Marx, Karl 63

McCormick, John 155–156

'Meet the Press' (television news/interview program) 108

Menger, Carl 16–18

Mercurio, El (newspaper) 151

Methodenbuch (Menger) 16

Middle Way, The (MacMillan) 32

Miksch, Leonard 91–92

Mill, James 51

Mill, John Stuart 51–53, 65

Mises, Ludwig von 16, 19, 31, 33–34, 42, 52, 121, 162

Mitchell, Wesley Clair 17–18, 52

Model Constitution: constitutional arrangements 121–129, 155; constitutional court 126–128; development of 116–118, 139; dictatorship and 153; Governmental Assembly 122–124; Legislative Assembly 122–124, 127; monetary policies and 136; of oligarchy 124–128; origins of 9, 118–120, 131

'Model Constitution, A' (Hayek) 121, 151

Monday Club 23

Monetarism 139–140

monetary policy 107–111

money: cryptocurrencies 10, 140–144; denationalisation of 9, 131–140

Montesquieu 50, 66

Müller Armack, Alfred 91–92

Myrdal, Gunnar 107

Nakomoto, Satoshi 140

Nation, The (magazine) 46

Nazism 40

neo-classical economics 54–55

Neurath, Otto 31, 33

New Despotism, The (Hewart) 40

New Liberalism 39, 53, 55, 76

new morality 104–107

'New Nations and the Problem of Power' (Hayek) 118, 148

New Republic (magazine) 46

Nietzsche, Friedrich 11

Nobel Memorial Prize 36, 107

nomothetae 155

non-domination 5–6, 11, 68–75, 77–78, 90, 95, 111, 123, 128, 132

non-interference 5, 70

Nozick, Robert 94

Oceana (Harrington) 95

O'Driscoll, Gerald 24

oligarchy 124–128

Open Society and Its Enemies, The (Popper) 139

Ordo (journal) 91

ordoliberal school 7, 90–93, 105

Orwell, George 40

'Paradox of Saving, The' (Hayek) 19

parliamentary democracy 90–98

parliamentary sovereignty 7–8, 9, 83, 95, 98, 118, 121, 154

People's Terms, On The (Pettit) 156

Pettit, Philip 66, 71–73, 74, 127, 155–156
Piketty, Thomas 90
Pinochet, Augusto 150–151, 153
plebiscitary democracy 89
pluralism 85
Pocock, John 65
Polanyi, Michael 49
political economy 88
political freedoms 124
Political Theology (Schmitt) 157
Polybius 83
Popper, Karl 37, 138–139
Portugal, 149–150
Powell, Enoch 109–110
'Pretence of Knowledge, The' (Hayek) 108
prices 38, 42
Prices and Production (Hayek) 19, 24
Profits, Interest and Investment (Hayek) 24
property franchise 126
Ptak, Ralph 92
public spending, 19–21
Pure Theory of Capital (Hayek) 24

rationalism 51–53
republicanism 63–66
Republicanism (Pettit) 66, 74
Road to Serfdom, The (Hayek) 40, 46, 48, 56,
   84, 86, 89–90, 93–95, 97–98, 105, 128,
   148, 153
Robbins, Lionel 19, 23, 33, 39, 42, 47
Robertson, Denis 23
Romans 10, 135, 154–155
Roosevelt, Franklin Delano 90
Röpke, Wilhelm 91–92, 108
Rosanvallon, Pierre 50
Rothbard, Murray 94
rule of law 62, 65, 68, 70, 123, 127, 147, 153
rules 4, 37–38, 42, 49, 70, 74, 77–78, 83, 91,
   95, 112, 120, 122–123, 127, 139, 147, 164
Rüstow, Alexander 91–92

Saint-Simon, Henri de 50, 52–54
Salazar, António de Oliveira 149, 153
'Saving and Spending' (Keynes) 23
Schmitt, Carl 7, 9–10, 84–92, 97, 118, 149
Schmoller, Gustav 17
Schumpeter, Joseph 17, 35, 97
Schwarz, Anna 138
Second World War 5, 20, 39, 47, 76, 105, 112
self-limiting democracy 90–95, 148
Servile State, The (Belloc) 40
Shenoy, Sudha 107
Sidney, Algernon 75

Skinner, Quentin 66–67, 71
Smith, Adam 6, 17, 24, 31, 48, 51, 66, 136
socialism 40, 47, 51, 52–53, 90
Socialism (Mises) 16
socialist calculation debates, 3, 31–43
social justice: conception of 125; full
   employment and 102–107; inflation
   and 8, 102–103, 111, 113; market
   republicanism and 110–113; new
   morality and 104–107; unlimited
   democracy and 8
Socrates 156
Somos (magazine) 151
Soviet Union 32, 40
Spectator, The (newspaper) 96
Spencer, Herbert 53
Sraffa, Piero 24
static equilibrium 3
Streek, W. 117
'Strong State and a Healthy Economy, A'
   (Schmitt) 87, 92
Suharto 150
Sunday Times, The (newspaper) 150
Sunstein, Cass 73
System of Logic, A (Mill) 53
System of Positive Policy (Comte) 52

Tacitus 62
Tawney, R.H. 32
Taylor, Harriet 52
Taylor, Robert 76
Thatcher, Margaret 9, 110, 153–154
Theory of Moral Sentiments, The (Smith) 18
Thucydides 127
Tiger by the Tail, A (Hayek) 107
Times, The (newspaper) 96, 146, 151,
   152, 156
Tocqueville, Alexis de 40, 50
Tomlinson, Jim 107
Tooze, Adam 90
totalitarianism 7
Trades Disputes Act of 1906 75–76
trade unions 105–107
Treatise on Money, A (Keynes) 19, 23
Trenchard, John 6, 66, 67, 133
'Trend of Economic Thinking, The'
   (Hayek) 31–32
'true individualism' 48, 63, 71
'true' liberalism 1–2, 5, 53–56, 61–62, 63, 147
Tucker, Josiah 48
un-freedom 5–6
unlimited democracy: arbitrary power and
   95–97; dangers of 87–90, 125–126, 147;

decline of 7–8; parliamentary democracy and 90–98; role of central bank 131–132; social justice and 8; as threat to market freedom 83, 86, 90, 92, 124–125, 129; total state and 84–90; ungovernability of 95–97

Vanberg, Victor 105
Veblen, Thorstein 17

Wealth of Nations, The (Smith) 24, 136
Webb, Beatrice 32, 34
Webb, Sidney 32, 34, 52

Weber, B. 141
Weber, Max 33, 88
'What is "Social"?-What Does it Mean?' (Hayek) 105
Whiggism 54
Whigs 2, 48, 54, 64–65, 75, 79, 147, 157
White, Lawrence 132
Wicksell, Knut 23
Wieser, Friedrich von 16
Wilson, Harold 96
Winch, Donald 54
Wlassak, Moriz 16
World Bank 103

Printed in the United States
by Baker & Taylor Publisher Services